Amakomiti

Wildcat: Workers' Movements and Global Capitalism

Series Editors:
Immanuel Ness (City University of New York)
Peter Cole (Western Illinois University)
Raquel Varela (Instituto de História Contemporânea (IHC)
of Universidade Nova de Lisboa, Lisbon New University)
Tim Pringle (SOAS, University of London)

Also available:

Amakomiti

Grassroots Democracy in
South African Shack Settlements

Trevor Ngwane

First published 2021 by Pluto Press
345 Archway Road, London N6 5AA

www.plutobooks.com

Copyright © Trevor Ngwane 2021

The right of Trevor Ngwane to be identified as the author of this work has been
asserted in accordance with the Copyright, Designs and Patents Act 1988.

British Library Cataloguing in Publication Data
A catalogue record for this book is available from the British Library

ISBN   978 0 7453 4199 6   Hardback
ISBN   978 0 7453 4200 9   Paperback
ISBN   978 1 7868 0765 6   PDF eBook
ISBN   978 1 7868 0767 0   Kindle eBook
ISBN   978 1 7868 0766 3   EPUB eBook

This book is printed on paper suitable for recycling and made from fully managed
and sustained forest sources. Logging, pulping and manufacturing processes are
expected to conform to the environmental standards of the country of origin.

Typeset by Stanford DTP Services, Northampton, England

Simultaneously printed in the United Kingdom and United States of America

Contents

Figures and Tables

Photos

Abbreviations and Acronyms

ACO	Alexandra Civic Organisation
ADP	African Democratic Party
AMCU	Associated Mining and Construction Union
AMPLATS	Anglo American Platinum
ANC	African National Congress
APF	Anti-Privatisation Forum
BEC	Branch Executive Committee (ANC)
CDF	Community Development Forum
COSATU	Congress of South African Trade Unions
CPF	Community Policing Forum
CPSA	Communist Party of South Africa
DA	Democratic Alliance
DVRA	Duncan Village Residents Association
EPWP	Expanded Public Works Programme
LPM	Landless People's Movement
MACODEFO	Makause Community Development Forum
NUM	National Union of Mineworkers
NUMSA	National Union of Metalworkers of South Africa
OKM	Operation Khanyisa Movement
PAC	Pan Africanist Congress
PPE	personal protection equipment
RDP	Reconstruction and Development Programme
RSA	Republic of South Africa
SAAWU	South African Allied Workers Union
SACP	South African Communist Party
SAFTU	South African Federation of Trade Unions
SANCO	South African National Civic Organisation
TCC	Thembelihle Crisis Committee
UDF	United Democratic Front
UDM	United Democratic Movement

Series Preface

Workers' movements are a common and recurring feature in contemporary capitalism. The same militancy that inspired the mass labour movements of the twentieth century continues to define worker struggles that proliferate throughout the world today.

For more than a century, labour unions have mobilised to represent the political-economic interests of workers by uncovering the abuses of capitalism, establishing wage standards, improving oppressive working conditions, and bargaining with employers and the state. Since the 1970s, organised labour has declined in size and influence as the global power and influence of capital has expanded dramatically. The world over, existing unions are in a condition of fracture and turbulence in response to neoliberalism, financialisation, and the reappearance of rapacious forms of imperialism. New and modernised unions are adapting to conditions and creating class-conscious workers' movement rooted in militancy and solidarity. Ironically, while the power of organised labour contracts, working-class militancy and resistance persists and is growing in the Global South.

Wildcat publishes ambitious and innovative works on the history and political economy of workers' movements and is a forum for debate on pivotal movements and labour struggles. The series applies a broad definition of the labour movement to include workers in and out of unions, and seeks works that examine proletarianisation and class formation; mass production; gender, affective and reproductive labour; imperialism and workers; syndicalism and independent unions, and labour and Leftist social and political movements.

Preface

It is hot and dry in Graaff-Reinet, the Great Karoo, at midday. I see a man sitting under a tree as I drive up the dusty and unpaved road into Vrygrond shack settlement. It is the second settlement I am visiting since I arrived in this town in the Eastern Cape. The petrol guy gave me directions after filling the tank of the white University of Johannesburg sedan with its ridiculous woodpeckers emblazoned on the two front doors and the institution's name written in Afrikaans. Who cares? Certainly not the man I have decided to approach, he does not look up until I stop the car right next to him.

'*Yebo, baba!*' I greet him, bending towards the passenger side front window which frames his face, allowing for eye contact.

'*Molo, tata,*' he responds unenthusiastically in isiXhosa, a language very similar to my isiZulu, calling me 'father' in return. The response prompts me to cut the engine, get out of the car and walk over to him. I stand not far from the car, allowing a safe distance between us. It is long before COVID, but still I have long learnt never to encroach on people's space.

'How are you today?' I ask. He tries to hide it, but my researcher's instinct signals a curiosity. He is sizing me up. I am used to the momentary distance that I suspect will pass. You see, I am a social researcher, and I go around begging, cajoling, seducing even, strangers to talk to me.

'*Mina baba ngiphuma le eGoli, eyunivesithi.*' ('I come from Johannesburg, from the university.') I move aside so that he can see the logo, and I gesture towards it. Maybe because he had already seen it, he is unimpressed. He is a middle-aged man, more or less my age, and this can make things easy or difficult. We have a lot in common, but also a lot to fight about. The distance between the urban and the rural can be as wide as the Sundays River in full flow on whose banks the town lies. This is a town of contrasts typified by the fact it was here that apartheid's first prime minister, D.F. Malan, practised his trade as a preacher and it was the birthplace of one of the country's greatest freedom fighters, Robert Mangaliso Sobukwe.

'*Ngingalitholaphi ikomiti lalendawo?*' ('Where can I find this place's committee?') I sketchily explain that my job is to interview people and write reports and books, that's what people do in universities.

'I can show you the committee. Did you come all the way from Johannesburg to this place? How do you know this place? Living here is terrible; there are no jobs. And it can be hot.' This is a good start; I might even interview him. He must first show me the committee. Even better, he must take me to it.

He did.

From December 2012 to March 2013, I spent a good time driving around from province to province, town to town, looking for shack settlements and people to interview. I visited four provinces: Gauteng, North West, KwaZulu-Natal and Eastern Cape. I did not have a map of the settlements, I just drove from town to town, and when I saw some shacks, I went there. If I did not see any, I would ask around: 'Oh, you mean *amagali*?[1] Drive straight, you will see a gravel road, turn left there.'

I would just drive up and ask whoever was willing to talk to me or looked like they would know, 'Where can I find *ikomiti* of this place?' They would, without fail, direct me to a man or woman who was a member of the local committee. But especially in smaller settlements, they would not say the person is a member of the committee, they would refer to the person as the committee ('He is *ikomiti*'). Indeed, in some instances, the person would be *the* committee. Finding *ikomiti* was no problem because everyone knew where he or she lived, and if they were not there at their abode, someone knew where they had gone to.

In 45 out of 46 settlements I visited as part of my research tour, there operated one or more committees. I found people willing to explain to me how the committee in that particular place worked. This book is about the committees I came across: *amakomiti* in isiZulu, *dikomiti* in Sesotho. (*Ikomiti* is singular, *amakomiti* is plural.)

It was fascinating to find that in every settlement there are these community structures that residents expect to take care of the community's collective business. When introduced to various committee members, they would be ordinary people, some young, some old, men, women, employed, unemployed, literate, illiterate, sober, drunk, etc. Some operated one- or two-person committees that hardly held meetings but would still find a way of fulfilling their duties, some had elaborate protocols with office bearers and portfolios, two or more meeting days each week, relations with other local committees, joint structures, etc. In any shape or form, in all the settlements there were *amakomiti*.

The existence of *amakomiti* challenges our view of shack settlements. In the South African literature, 'informal settlements' are often viewed as reflective of the challenges faced by a state committed to providing decent housing for all. The less generous see them as representing a failure of the government of national liberation in this respect. A closely related literature sees shack settlements as arenas of struggle where the poorly housed are left with no choice but to challenge and fight against living in intolerable conditions. Richard Pithouse captures this characterisation well in his phrase 'the left in the slum'.[2] This approach focuses on the agency of the shack dwellers rather than on (state) structures, policies and housing projects. A focus on *amakomiti* raises questions about what happens when there is a lull in the struggle, when there is no government housing project in the offing: what are the constituents of daily public life, associational activity and ordinary democratic process in the shacks?

Doing research into *amakomiti* was a pleasure and a privilege. I conducted the study as part of a PhD research project. With funding from the state and a supportive research institute, I had enough time and money to spend three months driving around, sleeping over in bed and breakfasts, visiting shack settlements, interviewing people, finding out more about these grassroots organisations. I enjoyed it, and I must confess that at no time did it feel like onerous work. Perhaps it is because I have done a fair amount of research in my life, so I knew what to do. Or the fact that I found the subject matter fascinating. Probably it was because I enjoy talking to people, I have respect for workers.

Who built the seven gates of Thebes?
The books are filled with names of kings.
Was it the kings who hauled the craggy blocks of stone?[3]

Here was a form of organisation that scholars of democratic theory paid little attention to, I was thinking while trying to figure out which topic to choose for my research project. It is perhaps true that a book, essay or poem sometimes seems to choose the writer rather than the other way round, because as soon as this thought crossed my mind, I knew that this was what I was going to do. I was going to learn everything about *amakomiti*.

This book is about what I learnt. I should emphasise that self-organisation in the informal settlements of South Africa and of the world is not new; it is not a 'discovery'. Certainly, those who live in the shacks long knew about it because they did it. Researchers have written about it. During the height of the anti-apartheid struggle in the 1980s, we saw the emergence of grassroots forms of community self-organisation, namely township civics which were constituted by area, block and street committees. *Amakomiti* are part of this tradition, except that while civics have declined, *amakomiti* are still going strong.

Colin Barker was concerned that those who study social movements tend to adopt a reformist perspective.[4] He points to historical forms of self-organisation such as soviets, factory committees and neighbourhood councils that have emerged during periods of revolutionary upheaval in Russia, Italy and Portugal respectively. These structures were part of a project for the revolutionary transformation of society. Today, commentators tend to view social movements as pressure groups designed to win some reforms and to keep governments on their toes. The description of their protests as coming in 'waves' and 'cycles' is suggestive.

Those who have studied *amakomiti* have largely done so without assessing their potential role in transformative politics in the spirit of Colin Barker. They correctly depict *amakomiti* as forms of self-organisation necessitated by the challenging conditions shack dwellers live in. Most shack dwellers establish their settlements against the will of the state, with the authorities sometimes actively discouraging the construction of homes. This leaves the shack dwellers no choice but to organise for themselves, in the face of state neglect or hostility, the provision of basic services such as water and sanitation in their new homes. Committees are set up to do this.

Karl Marx's Third Thesis on Feuerbach refers to human activity as 'self-change'.[5] The shack dwellers, in the process of establishing and providing for their new communities, change not only their circumstances, but also themselves. They learn to see themselves differently, becoming people who organise basic services for their communities, people who improvise a form of self-government in their areas, who take their destiny into their own collective hands. Certainly, they change from victims to fighters, from homeless and landless to people taking over land and creating homes for themselves. There is something profound about this.

The Paris Commune did not last long before the national guard of the Third French Republic massacred the communards. But it lived long enough for Marx to glean from their audacious experiment at self-rule a model for a future workers' state, one run by the toilers, and not those who live off their toil.

The global economic crisis has arguably led to a crisis of democracy as perceptions that governments serve the rich and powerful rather than the masses abound. People take to the streets against modern states seen as more responsive to the needs of big corporations rather than of ordinary people.[6] The dream of a society where the economy and the state are run and controlled by the people themselves, to the equal benefit of all, was seriously set back and tarnished by the distortion and defeat of the socialist experiment in the Soviet Union and other countries. We have to search for signs and instances of democratic practice that can inspire and inform political practice as we try to retrieve and realise that dream.

Can we learn anything from *amakomiti* as a grassroots form of democratic practice during this era of crisis in democratic governance? Can we learn something about how to build sustainable human settlements for all from the practice of the shack dwellers? I ask the reader to keep these questions in mind, because some parts of the book provide detailed information about the nature and operation of *amakomiti*, and you may begin to wonder why. We might find ideas that can contribute to the quest for human emancipation in the most unlikely places.

Decolonisation theory warns against Eurocentrism and looks to the Global South for answers. I say we must also look at the lower end of the class structure. Those without adequate shelter may be the ones who truly appreciate the urgent necessity for houses for all. The victims of liberal democracy may be leaders in creating alternative democratic forms. The shack dwellers' collective self-management structures point to the existence of a form of 'democracy on the margins' which is distinct from the dominant democratic state form.

The potential of *amakomiti* as seeds of future democratic systems is hard to see or advocate because shack dwellers occupy the lower end of the class structure. Some analysts categorise them as the 'underclass', others as the 'lumpenproleriat'.[7] Since Marx proposed the working class as the revolutionary subject, shack dwellers do not play this role. I disagree with this class analysis. In the book, I argue that shack dwellers constitute a section of the working class.

Neoliberal restructuring has led to a rise in precarious employment. Outsourcing and contracting out have seen many workers lose job security and good pay with benefits. Some labour analysts spend their time contrasting and opposing secure, 'well-paid', permanent workers versus insecure, casual and underpaid workers. The key task is to find out where the majority of workers are in the twenty-first century: for example, the service sector employs a lot more workers today than manufacturing or mining. We need to find out the conditions of their work, the challenges they face, their struggles. Where do they live? It will not be a surprise to discover that a significant proportion of them live in informal or substandard accommodation.

Shack dwellers and their committees deserve a place in the ranks of the working-class movement. The struggle in the workplace finds its counterpart in the struggle in living spaces. Living in terrible conditions is a class issue that should concern all workers whether they live in brick houses, apartments or villas. The broader movement for social change, locally, nationally and internationally, should be a home for shack dwellers and their *amakomiti*. Knowledge about life in the shack settlements is useful in engaging with this suggestion and the strategic questions it raises.

I must make clear that what I saw of *amakomiti* is not heaven on earth. I saw the good and the bad, the progressive and the reactionary. They can be the voice of the people in a settlement, or they can serve sectional interests, including external players like the state. Their political terrain can be as shaky and dangerous as the physical ground upon which many settlements stand, namely dolomitic, below the flood line, near waste dumps and always the threat of eviction. The African National Congress uses its control of the government to tame, control and dominate *amakomiti* because it fears the anger of the shack dwellers. It also has the power to build houses and provide services.

I coined the term 'democracy on the margins' to underline the contested terrain and oppressive conditions under which this experiment in democratic grassroots self-governance occurs. At the end of Chapter 7, I quote Antonio Gramsci, who spoke of the 'organic capacity of the working class'. It is a reference to the indomitable fighting spirit and creativity of the working class that many do not see, but now and again flaunts itself. We saw it in the Spirit of Marikana.[8] This gives me hope that *amakomiti* will remain important in the struggle for houses for all and be part of the broader movement for universal human emancipation.

Preface

My gratitude in writing this book goes to Immanuel 'Manny' Ness, who has gone out of his way to encourage me to write it. To Luke Sinwell, who inspired me with his and Siphiwe Mbatha's book on Marikana and the workers' committees behind the Lonmin strike. To Ashwin Desai, whose books inspire. To Patrick Bond, comrade and co-author. To Sam Ashman, my close friend. To my comrades in the Socialist Group, Soweto Electricity Crisis Committee, Thembelihle Crisis Committee, South African Federation of Trade Unions, National Union of Metalworkers' of South Africa and the United Front. To my University of Johannesburg Department of Sociology colleagues, and our leader Pragna Rugunanan for her encouragement and support. To my favourite students, Terri Maggott and Nicole Levine van Staden. To my children, Lindiwe, Lehlohonolo, Thato, Bongani, and their mom, Miranda Malele. To my grandchildren, Tshiamo and Tumelo. To my mom, Zanele Ngwane, and my brother and sister, Sandile and Duduzile. To David Shulman at Pluto Press and the team. And to the shack dwellers, township residents and members of *amakomiti*.

Amandla awethu!

1

Introduction: Disrupting Private Land Ownership?

If the success of a land invasion is the entrenchment of a new land occupation, Marikana was certainly successful.[1]

Fundis Mhlongo is an interesting character who enjoys respect and support as the leader of his community. He is the one-man committee of Ekupholeni, a very small shack settlement located in Durban, a populous South African city on the Indian Ocean coast. Tonight he has agreed for me to accompany him to a community meeting that will take place in Bottlebrush, a nearby shack settlement that is much bigger and older than Ekupholeni. Both settlements are located at the edges of Chatsworth, a sprawling suburb where only 'Indians' were supposed to live under apartheid laws. Like everything else in South African shantytowns, there is a story and a history in the relationship between the two settlements. However, for now, let us go to the meeting with Mhlongo and see what happens.

The crowd turns out to be excitable. Not a big crowd, mind you, about 40 or so people standing under cover of darkness next to a brick structure in the midst of Bottlebrush shacks. A murmur of approval lowers the tension at the sight of Mhlongo joining the meeting – it is the tension of an arrow awaiting release. He has a calming effect on people and is obviously an old hand at handling high-stakes community meetings. The meeting has only one agenda item, namely hatching a plan to invade a piece of land that lies on the eastern border of the Bottlebrush settlement.

'Only you can help us, Njomane!' pleads one man, using Mhlongo's clan name, a sign of respect and, if you like, flattery.

An agitated youth cannot wait to take action and does not really understand why they had to call on Mhlongo. 'We must just go there now and put up our shacks,' he harangues the crowd.

Mhlongo is in his element and relishes the discussion; his interventions are well timed and articulated, and despite divergent views concerning the when and how of the land invasion, his suggestions enjoy unanimous support. He patiently makes the meeting go over the reasons for the planned action, perhaps also for my benefit because I am the researcher who has been interviewing and shadowing him for about a week now. Ethnography is my thing. In any case, going over the reasons proves to be a good tactic because it reminds the people of what unites them – overcrowding, high rents, harsh landlords – making it easier to agree on the tactics of the land invasion. By the end of the meeting, Mhlongo is the one chairing and summing up the decisions taken. The invasion will take place early in the morning of the following day despite some people not having gathered enough material to stake their land claim. You need some planks, nails and corrugated iron in order to set up a structure that marks out your stand. Not to worry, Mhlongo advises, the police are going to come anyway and pull down the structures and confiscate the material, it is better to use less rather than more of your building material, plastics will do just fine. The meeting ends on a high note. Mhlongo announces that he will not personally lead the invasion. When we leave the meeting, people are busy discussing what to do the next morning and leaders who will be at the forefront of the invasion emerge organically.

The next morning, the invasion happens as planned and without Mhlongo. I arrive a couple of hours after it has started. I can see the occupied land while standing on the downward slope on the eastern border of the shack settlement; the land is on a hill a couple of kilometres across the valley. Flimsy-looking structures made up of planks, corrugated iron, plastics and sacks dot the hill, wavering in the wind. As I move closer, I can make out stones, wires and wooden pegs on the ground; these serve as improvised markers of the 'stands' parcelled out by the invaders. Some people have scraped the ground, removing grass and making the earth flatter to map the *stoep* of their dream homes.[2] I am busy taking in the scene, taking pictures, fascinated by what I see, when, lo and behold, disaster strikes. The police are here! In the form of the eThekwini Municipality Anti-Land Invasion Unit.

A longish moment of silence ends when uniformed black-clad men descend from their cars and trucks, then proceed to swiftly and ferociously attack the structures that are people's future homes. Not so many people are there to be indignant at what is happening because not all the land invaders are around, many having left the area after putting up their structures; maybe they went to work or did not wish to face the music, or were observing proceedings from Bottlebrush across the valley, it was hard to say. The anti-invasion invaders, some armed, some wearing welding gloves, not finding any resistance to speak of, systematically and efficiently dismantled the planks and plastics. Within half an hour or so, they had collected most of the material and had it in a pile on the ground. The man in charge, wearing the eThekwini Municipality Metro Police uniform, issued the incendiary order and a plume of smoke went up to the blue sky, and that was that.

Mhlongo appeared from nowhere and began talking to the small group of stony-faced would-be land occupiers. His calmness suggested that he had seen it all before, and he probably had. Placating them, he shared his idea of organising a march to the city hall soon to protest the burning of building material and to demand houses for the people. He also spoke to the officials who were hanging around. The top official seemed to know him. It could be that burning the material was signalling a harder line by the municipality against land invasions. Afterwards, dejected like soldiers from a battle that did not go too well, and with Mhlongo in front, we walked back to Bottle-brush and Ekupholeni, both settlements born of land invasions. The action had failed; a Che Guevara aphorism came to mind: 'battles [are] won or lost – but fought'.[3]

Indeed, perhaps it was not all for nothing, because when I visited Bottlebrush again three years later, the hill across the valley was covered with shacks. Still around, Mhlongo told me that pressure had made the municipality relent a couple of years after this invasion and many other failed attempts. The City Council had allowed people to build a hundred shacks in a site-and-service scheme, and as Mhlongo put it, 'Shacks are mushrooms, they multiply before dawn. There are 6,000 now.'[4] Mhlongo had also in the meantime seen his star rise as a community leader, but more about this later.

ARE LAND INVASIONS SPONTANEOUS OR PLANNED?

Some academics wonder aloud whether land invasions are spontaneous or organised affairs; in this respect, a distinction is sometimes made between rapid invasions and slow 'encroachments'.[5] Underlying the debate, of course, is the age-old disagreement about the role of spontaneity and organisation in the struggle for human emancipation (by the masses). Well, the Bottlebrush land invaders are people who found living in overcrowded and overpriced shacks increasingly intolerable; they decided enough is enough and took matters into their own hands. They organised a meeting and invited a leader from a nearby settlement to advise them and give them support. Mhlongo had lived in Bottlebrush until a couple of years before the invasion. He had left Bottlebrush to establish a new settlement at Ekupholeni, which means 'a place of bliss', because of irreconcilable differences with the local African National Congress (ANC) branch executive committee, the undisputed local power structure in Bottlebrush, of which he had been a member. This committee had gone bad and been sucked into the semi-corrupt and highly exploitative shack landlordism that thrived in the settlement. For the committee, overcrowding was not a problem, but a potential source of profit as rents soared in the area and they, as the sole local power, thrived by milking and aiding the exploitative reign of the shacklords. The land invasion indicated that Mhlongo still had support in Bottlebrush, but he told me that he had not wanted to lead the invasion because he had to be cautious with his former committee. His political stratagem seems to have paid off from his point of view because a couple of years later, he was elected chairperson of the ANC branch committee whose jurisdiction covers Bottlebrush, Ekupholeni and adjacent parts of Chatsworth. The ANC even nominated him as its candidate for ward councillor in the 2011 local government elections, but lost the ward to the Democratic Alliance (DA). From these observations and machinations, we can see elements of both spontaneity and organisation in the aborted land invasion.

There is a high rate of community protests in South Africa.[6] The country arguably also has a notably high rate of land invasions and land occupations. My research suggests that a substantial proportion of informal settlements are established through invasions.[7] The occupation of land can be through newsmaking land grabs, usually involving a large number of people doing so at the same time, or through less dramatic and slower land encroachments where a few shacks gradually increase in number until hundreds or even thousands live in the area.[8] According to government statistics, about 7 million people live in shacks in South Africa, some in backyard shacks erected behind 'brick' houses in built-up working class townships, and others living in 'stand-alone' shack settlements.[9] It is the latter category of shacks that are established through land occupations, although, as we will see in the story of Duncan Village in Chapter 4, there have been instances where backyard shacks have been erected *en masse* through self-organisation and against the wishes of the (apartheid) state.[10] Given the reluctance of the apartheid state to provide adequate housing for the black working class in 'white' South African cities, people suffered from housing shortages, as not everyone could live in the deplorable single-sex compounds and hostels. Self-organisation and large doses of spontaneity have been crucial in the not so easy feat of housing millions of people in the face of state failure to do so.

In the literature, the academic debate that opposes spontaneity to organisation is related to broader conversations about the role of political organisation and the party in the struggles of the masses on the one hand, and the desirability of bottom-up rather than top-down leadership of social movements on the other. The argument against organisation as such does not hold much water because *amakomiti* do exist, and apparently in most shack settlements, as this book attests. Also, in the general literature on social movements, this position is unsustainable for all sides, although we do find echoes of it among those preferring 'horizontal' and 'loose' forms of organisation as opposed to 'hierarchical' and 'tight' organisation, for example the Occupy Movement.[11] My research findings on *amakomiti* will hopefully shed some light on these questions. Furthermore, some writers have suggested that shack dwellers only engage in 'those strategies and associations that respond directly to their immediate concerns' rather than any grand designs for broader or fundamental social change.[12] This is a position against ideology and organised politics, seen as emanating from 'intellectual elites', that appears to limit and diminish *a priori* the political agency of shack dwellers by discounting the existence of organic intellectuals. Empirical findings go a long way in clarifying such questions, although the rub often lies in the researcher's interpretation of the data.

A study by Rayner Teo of a land invasion and establishment of a shack settlement in Philippi, Cape Town, the city where the Indian and Atlantic Oceans meet, illustrates the usefulness of evidence-based debate while bringing out the subtle influence of ideology and perspective.[13] The study provides a detailed picture of the establishment of the 'Marikana' settlement in this city, from which one can draw out the general pattern and strategy of invading and occupying a piece of land for residential purposes in the country. It also sheds some light on the question of spontaneity and organisation. In his analysis, Teo distinguishes and maps the trajectory between the process of invading the land and a subsequent period of 'consolidation' of the settlement.[14] His main finding and argument is that although there was undeniable evidence of organisation and planning, the occupation of land was largely spontaneous. He bases this on the fact that only about a hundred people would participate in planning meetings, but when the invasion happened, thousands turned up. These thousands did not access their knowledge of the invasion through organised channels, but rather – and he regards this as his important empirical discovery and conceptual contribution – through 'the passive network'.[15] The latter concept is borrowed from Bayat,[16] and it excludes organised 'activist networks' as sources of information for the invaders, but points to 'atomised individuals' acting collectively because of 'common, overlapping identities and recognising a common interest between each other'.[17] Bayat has argued that the poor 'seem to be uninterested in any particular form of ideology and politics',[18] and in his later work conceptualises their social movements as 'non-movements', defined as 'the collective action of dispersed and unorganised actors'.[19]

The Marikana residents elected a 'task team' to organise defence against eviction by the Cape Town municipality during the invasion process.[20] The team had to take on more tasks, including sorting out 'town scheme' problems – 'the people they just builded [*sic*] shacks in front of others, [so] then we start to strategise, saying, we must have some committees'.[21] Later, they elected a committee with a broader mandate of exercising 'grassroots governance' during the consolidation phase of the newly established settlement. Teo distinguishes between the 'functional' purpose of the task team and the more generic 'grassroots governance' role of the later committee.[22] The latter's duties included crime prevention and liaison with external bodies such as the City Council. Teo emphasises the disjuncture or discontinuity between the committees formed during the invasion and those formed during the consolidation phase. While noting similarities and some liaison with local committees or civics operating in Cape Town's working-class townships, he emphasises the peculiarity of the Marikana committees born of the specific conditions associated with the establishment and mode of life in the shack settlement. Nevertheless, he concludes, that *amakomiti* in the shacks and 'street committees' in the townships share a common history and culture.[23]

The research I present in this book corroborates this general outline in the development of *amakomiti* in the informal settlement. My book com-

6

plements and benefits from Teo's close-up portrait of a single case. In my research, I visited dozens of informal settlements and reported findings from 46 settlements, including in-depth investigation of four case studies. I find Teo's distinction between the land invasion and consolidation phases of the settlement illuminating. I also find his argument for conceptualising shack committees as 'grassroots governance structures' persuasive.[24] As to be expected, a bigger sample adds more colour to the picture he paints. For example, I found that in some settlements there were indeed notable changes in the character and personnel of different committees existing at different periods in the development of a particular settlement. In the case of Nkaneng, a shack settlement in Rustenburg's platinum belt, to which I devote a chapter, the leader of the invasion left after the establishment of a competing committee. The new committee was itself later violently dissolved by the community in a kind of shack *coup d'état*. In other cases, the original leader might thrive beyond the invasion into the consolidation phase and beyond, as was the case with Jeff of Jeffsville, and Boyana of KwaBoyana, discussed in the next section. There are a variety of experiences, approaches and intrigues to self-organisation in the informal settlements. For every committee that emerges or disappears, there is always a story and a history. I find this fascinating and inspiring; this is what led me to conduct the research presented in this book.

SHACK SETTLEMENT LEADERS AND *AMAKOMITI*

Comrade Jeff of Jeffsville is proof that in some instances, leaders of the invasion continue serving in the grassroots governance structures of shack communities beyond the process of establishing the settlement. I visited him in his home in Jeffsville, located in Pretoria, the capital city of South Africa. He told me how he had led the successful occupation of land that gave birth to the shack settlement named after him. The ingredients of victory were researching and surveying the land earmarked for invasion, liaising with surrounding township community structures for support, and tenaciously warding off repeated eviction attempts by the Pretoria municipality. He is the chairperson of the people's committee in the thriving settlement. The committee maintains ties with civics, movements and political organisations in Pretoria and beyond. The notion of solidarity and a perceived commonality of the struggles of all working-class communities came through strongly in what he said in the course of the interview.

Baba Boyana, leader of the KwaBoyana ('at Boyana's') shack community near Vryheid in the KwaZulu-Natal midlands, earned recognition by having the place named after him because of being among the first in the settlement established through gradual encroachment rather than dramatic invasion.[25] He negotiated with the farmer who owned the place, winning security of tenure for the people. Like Jeff, he is part of the local *ikomiti* and has been since those early days. I have not met a humbler and gentler soul in my life.

Strong leaders have often caught the attention of commentators to the detriment of a balanced characterisation of leadership and organisation in the shack settlements. Part of the problem is the apartheid government's stigmatisation of shack settlements as 'squatter camps' that had to be eradicated like a *boer* fighting vermin on his fields. Political violence during the apartheid era also gave some shack settlements a bad name, especially the notorious 'warlords' who ruled over these areas. Who can forget the brutality of the Crossroads leader, Johnson Ngxobongwana, whose reign of terror in this Cape Town shack settlement during the 1980s left many dead.[26] His feared militia, the Witdoeke, became part of the apartheid strategy of black-on-black violence aimed at crushing opposition in black areas. Peace-loving leaders like Jeff of Jeffsville and Boyana of KwaBoyana, because of the respect and recognition they enjoy in their communities, could easily be mistaken for undemocratic big men lording it over their settlements. In any case, a focus on leaders very likely diverts attention away from community self-organisation and the *amakomiti*. This book sets out to explore and present a more nuanced picture of leadership in the settlements through its focus on self-organised grassroots governance structures.

The most famous leader of shack dwellers in South African history is undoubtedly Mr James Sofasonke Mpanza, known as the 'father of Soweto'.[27] Famous for riding his horse around Orlando 'native location', today part of Soweto, the biggest working-class township in South Africa, he made a name for himself by his local political antics and irreverent attitude towards the white state. Like Malcolm X, who began as a petty criminal, Mpanza had a rather shady background, once sentenced to death for murder. He made history in 1944 when he led a large group of people 'across the River Jordan', establishing a big shack settlement near Orlando, earning himself the name *Magebhula* ('grabber' of municipal land).[28] He was responding to the cries of the people who were suffering because of the foot-dragging of the white state in building houses for the black working class in Johannesburg. The massive 'squatter camp', named Sofasonke Village, lasted for 16 years; it spearheaded a broader squatter movement in the city and forced the government to embark on housebuilding projects for the urban proletariat, thus changing the face of the city. In the history books, the larger-than-life Mpanza drew all the attention, but less known are the committees that ran the settlement.[29] *Amakomiti* go back a long way in the history of the shack settlements of South Africa.

The 'charisma' and 'controversy' associated with big 'squatter leaders' like Mpanza sometimes hide the organising skills, political acumen and ideological underpinnings involved in leading shack dwellers. (More about Mpanza's talents in this regard in Chapter 2.) Besides, researchers who are sympathetic with and correctly focused on the grassroots may, as I have noted with Bayat, deny the ideological underpinnings of the struggles of the 'poor', including James Scott's well-meaning but debatable 'weapons of the weak' conception.[30] By so doing, they may miss the class content, transformative and prefigurative aspects inherent in subaltern struggles and organisations. The bane of social movement theory, Colin Barker laments, is its denial of the revolutionary potential of grassroots self-organisation because of its preoccupation with 'cycles of protest' and 'waves' without consideration of the possibility that movement organisations can 'nurture and expound the ideas of transcending "militant petitioning" in favour of "taking over"'.[31]

Simphiwe Zwane of Thembelihle, a settlement in Lenasia, in the south of Johannesburg, cut her teeth in the struggle during a difficult time in the life of the settlement when it fought against relocation and forced removals initiated by the post-apartheid democratic government, a threat it never faced from the apartheid regime. She became a member of the Thembelihle Crisis Committee (TCC), the organisation that was made by leading the victorious struggle against the relocation. Courage, determination and ideological clarity delivered the community's victory against the bulldozers. Since then, Zwane and her comrades have built a social movement organisation that has made a name for itself leading protests and, rarely for *amakomiti*, explicitly espousing socialism as its ideological compass in the struggle of shack dwellers. Its progressive role during the 2008 and 2011 xenophobia violence against migrants was recognised by the state; the TCC was awarded the 'Mkhaya Migrants Award: Most Integrated Community' in South Africa.[32]

TCC militants organised against the attacks, actively defending vulnerable migrants, including searching for and returning looted property.

For five years, Zwane served as an independent councillor in the Johannesburg City Council, representing her constituency in a joint electoral platform with the Soweto Electricity Crisis Committee.[33] The TCC enjoys strong community support in Thembelihle, and we shall see more of it in Chapter 6, where I suggest that this committee has been able to contest hegemony in its area through a 'combination of concrete victories, the development of a culture of solidarity, and the development of a political analysis'.[34] In the TCC, we can perhaps see glimpses of the true potential of shack settlement self-organisation and the importance of this constituency in the struggle to eradicate all forms of exploitation and oppression.

SHANTYTOWNS AND THE PRIVATE OWNERSHIP OF LAND

... ground rent in turn presupposes landed property, the ownership of particular bits of the globe by certain individuals ....[35]

It is possible to approach the plight of people living in inadequate shelters with sympathy, but without going to the root of the problem. Some shack committees such as the TCC see their struggle as having a goal beyond getting a house, important as this is in the lives of shack dwellers. I remember attending a meeting in Thembelihle and an old comrade, Baba Makama, now late, standing up and emphasising that 'All I want is a brick house, then I will have peace.' In what amounted to a mini-tirade, he also mentioned that he had been in South Africa for more than two decades. He originally came from Mozambique. Later, in a light conversation with some committee members outside the meeting, someone recollected Makama's passionate outburst. Everyone was laughing because the militants knew that this was certainly not 'the position'. I cannot remember now whether anyone had tried to 'correct' or 'clarify' during the meeting; it does not seem to matter now.

'*Eish*, comrade, the masses! We must be patient,' said Siphiwe, then chairperson of the committee, with a broad grin. Makama was not really 'the masses', because even though he did not hold any formal position on the elected committee, he was a very much loved and respected veteran member of the TCC, always there and at the forefront. His opinion on many issues was important to the leadership. I even think that it was comrades like him who affirmed the younger or more ideologically inclined comrades, making their work seem real and worth their while. The joke was that no one expected him to speak like that, although comrades were collectively forced to self-introspect because what he was reminding them of was that, as someone said, 'The road is still long, comrades.' The source of the problem for TCC leaders is capitalism, a system of exploitation. For many of them, this position is ingrained in their thinking and everyday activism.

Land invasions and occupations are arguably direct attacks on the private ownership of land. Even if you are Comrade Makama and all you want is a house, the action of taking over land is a violation of property ownership laws. The reality, though, is that respecting the law will leave you sleeping out in the open veld. Often shack settlements are established on land located nearer transport nodes, bulk infrastructure and, most importantly, job opportunities. Good location derives from 'historically and socio-spatially produced conditions' that puts it 'in a distinctive (advantageous or disadvantageous) position vis-à-vis other places'.[36] Desperation turns the land-hungry into scavengers, and often they target dangerously located terrain for occupation, including land below the flood line, on dolomitic ground, etc. Such land lies unused, and the calculation is that the owners will not protest too much. Many settlements, such as some that I have already mentioned here, Bottlebrush, Ekupholeni, Thembelihle and Jeffsville, are located in areas adjacent to suburbs designated 'Indian' by the apartheid Group Areas Act. Perhaps it is easier to target these areas than invade a white suburb; this underlines the importance of (apartheid) history and geography in these matters.

Putting race aside, despite its deep implication in class antagonisms, the entire sordid business derives broadly from the centrality of land as means of production in a capitalist economy. Landowners may demand the removal of a shack settlement because of profit-generating plans for the land in question; this raises the issue of the underlying conflict between land use for productive versus reproductive purposes. Shacks can be regarded a threat by 'host' surrounding areas because of a fear that proximity will reduce property values. On the other hand, such threats, including the threat of crime, may be weighed against the convenience of having a source of cheap labour close by.

Do land invasions seriously challenge, or at least disrupt, the private ownership of land? There might be a contradiction here. Shack settlements are established through flouting the capitalist principle of private ownership, but no sooner is this done than the land is parcelled out into 'stands' for individual ownership. This ostensibly reinstates the capitalist relation to land. The appropriation of land effected collectively results in private ownership. Indeed, people dream about their own space, yard and house even during the planning phases of invasions. It can be argued that 'land ownership serves a decidedly ideological function as it helps to legitimise the commodification and private ownership of everything as the bases of and for social organisation'.[37] This is because the 'ownership of land ... is one of the pillars of a system of generalised commodification and private ownership of means of production and reproduction'.[38] Land ownership breeds the capitalist spirit. Perhaps Comrade Makama is being realistic: the TCC leadership might dream of a socialist future, but in practice, life in the shack settlements is an affirmation, and even reinforcement, of the capitalist system.

There is a silence in the literature about this conundrum that probably hides a divergence in ideology. I clearly remember some social movement debates in the early 2000s, during what I think we can regard as the golden age of the 'new' social movements in post-apartheid South Africa, where some comrades were arguing that shack dwellers and anti-eviction activists were not concerned with political-ideological questions, but rather with 'bread and butter issues'. Some holders of this position explicitly denounced 'politics' as a distraction and hindrance, while a more sophisticated position advocated a 'living politics', supposedly less abstract and ideological. Underlying these perspectives was the characterisation of subalterns as 'non-ideological' and an inclination by the ideologues to discuss 'big questions' in the absence of the masses ('We are wasting their time').

The aim of my 2009 research in Bottlebrush was to investigate the causes of the violent xenophobia outbreak in 2008. This was part of a large project funded by Atlantic Philanthrophies. My findings suggested that an important aspect of the conflict between 'locals and foreigners' was rent. Migrants from Malawi, Mozambique, Zimbabwe and other African countries were being bled dry by greedy and ruthless shacklords. The ANC committee in charge had assumed the role of an 'extra-economic configuration' regulating the uses of land in the area. It did so in favour of the local shacklords while probably also personally benefiting from the arrangement. Denigration of the migrants became part of the ideological stratagem to keep them oppressed and vulnerable to exploitation and abuse. The migrants told me how they had to suffer the same fate at work, with both employers and fellow South African-born workers taking advantage of them. Capitalist exploitation and the capital–labour, landlord–tenant relation were not abstract ideological issues in Bottlebrush for the migrants, they were part of their everyday life of vulnerability, exploitation and abuse. This was their daily 'bread and butter'.

AMAKOMITI AT THE CLASS CROSSROADS

An important and illuminating idea in Karl Marx's analysis of capitalism is the concept of 'contradiction'. He wrote that the capitalist system is full of contradictions, identifying the capital–labour relation as perhaps the most consequential one. Land invaders becoming landowners might be an aspect of the contradictions generated by the capitalist system. Certainly, Marx pointed to the contradiction of collective work organisation and private ownership of the means of production. There are tendencies towards collectivist 'socialisation', and contrary ones towards individualist 'atomisation'. The chief conflict between capital and labour is the contradiction between production for profit and production to satisfy human needs. It is therefore a contradiction that in order to have shelter over their heads, shack dwellers must break the law.

The capitalist state is always there to enforce the law of private ownership. The law is not the law in the air, but on the ground at the point of implementation. The state takes various steps to enforce the law of private property, including physically stopping land invasions using the police and the 'Red Ants' (private security specializing in evictions). When forced to back down in the face of a land occupation, the state will 'regularise' the informal settlement concerned. As a form of bringing the shack dwellers back within the fold of legality, this concession comes with demands on *amakomiti* to co-operate and uphold the law inside the settlement. The standard demand is: 'You must stop allowing more people to come into the settlement.' The state will install basic services such as communal water taps and sometimes 'chemical' or 'VIP' toilets. The implicit or explicit understanding, from the point of view of state officials, is not rights, but *quod pro quo*.

The leader of the Nhlalakahle committee, in Pietermaritzburg, told me how, after a very long struggle, the government threw in the towel and agreed to leave the shack settlement alone.[39] Communal taps were installed

13

and an 'audit' was done to establish the number of shacks, with the understanding that no more shacks should be built. The leader explained: 'We no longer allow people unless they are very desperate, especially if it is a woman with children.' Some researchers have characterised leadership committees in the shack settlements as 'balancing bureaucratic and democratic logics'.[40] They expend bureaucratic and administrative efforts to secure 'order and development' in co-operation with local government officials while engaged in 'internal mediation and democratic procedures to keep conflicts at bay' among the people.[41]

Marx spent almost all his life exposing the limitations of the liberal faith in the operation of the capitalist market. He pointed to the emancipatory possibilities that existed in capitalist society, such as general economic well-being, labour-saving technologies, individual development, privacy and freedoms. However, the class basis of the system excluded most of humanity from enjoying the benefits. The solution was collective action against the minority capitalist class and its system in order to overthrow the system. That was the only way all of humanity could benefit from what humanity has achieved under the capitalist system.

Land invaders carry out daring deeds to get for themselves what many take for granted: a decent home. Their committees are part of the mechanisms they use to achieve this. They instinctively keep them operating and alive even after consolidation and 'proclamation' of their settlements because they know that strength lies in organising collectively and acting in unity. Things are not simple, let alone easy, in the settlements. *Amakomiti* operate in the context of various factors, pressures and constraints. Their biggest constraint is the law of profit that pushes their needs to the bottom of the societal to-do list. At different times, they may or may not see it that way. Often they have to accept that they do not have the resources nor the power to do what they believe is good for themselves and their communities. Nevertheless, the existence of *amakomiti* points to a profound recognition of the need of shack dwellers to control their destiny, to protect and sustain their agency, to have a hand in the construction of their future – to make the judgement and take a side when the time comes to resolve the contradictions.

AMAKOMITI AND 'DEMOCRACY ON THE MARGINS'

Post-apartheid society is reaping the dragon's teeth sown by apartheid because the stigma surrounding shack settlements has not disappeared from the popular imagination, including the elite. Communities living in the settlements are sometimes treated like unwanted stepchildren in the family. During mega-events hosting international guests, shack settlements may become 'eyesores' and shameful steps taken to 'hide' them from view.[42] Officials sometimes use hostile language such as 'eradicating' shack settlements that contains violent undertones suggesting a failure to come to terms with the realities of uneven development in capitalist urbanisation. Shacks are not the problem! The problem is a system that is failing to provide adequate shelter for all.

Some observers downplay the role of shack residents in the struggle of the oppressed and exploited because of their ignorance of the distinctive conditions in the informal settlements or because of political prejudice or theoretical imprecision. Mike Davis locates shack dwellers outside the working class and argues that they are a hybrid social stratum capable of 'myriad acts of resistance', but incapable of leading movements of struggle because they are a 'chaotic plurality' of 'charismatic churches and prophetic cults to ethnic militias, street gangs, neoliberal NGOs and revolutionary social movements.'[43] Some commentators have looked at class struggle in Africa and taken a different view, noting that shack dwellers are in fact quite active in struggles led by social movements.[44] As Alex Callinicos has observed, contrary to Davis's negative assessment: 'Sub-Saharan Africa … is host to many great slum settlements – but is also the site of a series of major mass strikes.'[45]

Where we locate shack dwellers in the social structure has important consequences for the political assessment of the role of shack dwellers and their movements in struggle. Like Davis, Richard Pithouse locates them outside the working class in political analysis even as he affirms their activism.[46] However, in so doing, he bends the stick too much to the other side, emphasising the importance of shack dwellers' movements, bordering on uncritical exaltation. He underlines the distinctive character of political activism in the shantytowns, drawing lines between it and that of the broader working-class movement, including township-based community struggles. Are shack dwellers a section of the working class, or do they form a separate stratum with distinct characteristics and interests? I answer this question in the course of presenting my research findings in the following chapters.

The National Union of Metalworkers of South Africa (NUMSA) moment came to South Africa when the 300,000-plus-strong metalworkers' union left the African National Congress-South African Communist Party-Congress of South African Trade Unions Alliance, signalling a serious reconfiguration of South African class politics. Everyone on the left was excited when in its special congress NUMSA resolved to form a united front to bring together labour and community struggles, and a workers' party to lead the struggle for socialism. The struggles of shack dwellers were indirectly addressed in a sentence in a resolution where it is noted that:

> Although there are protests everywhere and every day in the country, the Alliance is not an instrument in the hands of these struggling masses nor does it provide leadership to these struggles which is largely leaderless struggles [*sic*]. The reality is that there is a political vacuum and the working class is on its own.[47]

Shack dwellers are very active in the 'leaderless' protests noted here, raising the question of to what extent *amakomiti* are recognised by the union as constituting a leadership in the shack settlements. This book seeks to provide accurate information about this constituency that can inform strategic analysis and united political action for left forces in the unions and movements as part of the further development of the NUMSA movement.

Amakomiti exist in nearly all South African informal settlements, and in this book I explore the different types of committees, their role, history, politics, etc. In addition to this empirical-analytical goal, I also raise theoretical and political-strategic questions about the committees. I explore to what extent *amakomiti* can be understood in relation to other working-class forms of self-organisation such as the soviets that arose in Russia, which historically were the basis for a workers' state. I refuse to lock *amakomiti* and shack dwellers' movements in small-time roles in the theatre of struggle as some analyses arguably do. They are not sidekicks to the proletariat in the revolution nor a constituency beset by its own special and more burdensome problems separate from everyone else. Nor should we limit the significance of their struggle within national borders. Theoretically locating them in the broader canvass of working-class struggle may draw attention to aspects hitherto unnoticed and perhaps help realise potentialities yet undeveloped. Broad alliances of struggle require knowledge of the character, needs and strengths of allies.

There is general discontent with the promises and failures of bourgeois democracy in many parts of the world. The search for alternative democratic forms should look and learn from historical instances of 'bottom-up' experiments in popular forms of democracy such as the Paris Commune, the soviets, factory councils in Italy, the *shuras* (workplace and neighbourhood councils) during the revolution in Iran, the street committees and civics in South African townships, etc. The time has come to look at experiences in the Global South. Are there aspects of democratic practice of the shack committees, including successes and failures, that, if studied and understood, could be useful in crafting new and improved democratic arrangements in South Africa and other countries? Where are the advocates of decolonisation looking in their search for indigenous inspiration in the struggle to rid politics and culture of Eurocentrism? It seems to me that among the areas we should look at are places and practices hitherto neglected, unappreciated and marginalised.

Before going into the research field, I coined the concept of 'democracy on the margins'. This refers to the development and practice of local democratic practices and cultures by 'neglected' communities that have little apparent power to influence mainstream political developments because of their disadvantaged political and economic insertion into unequal power relations in society. The dominant liberal-democratic state form disadvantages and even marginalises the working class and the poor from key decisions that shape society. Grassroots governance structures such as *amakomiti* play a multitude of roles in this context: sometimes directly challenging the dominant form, other times negotiating with it, and sometimes turned into its handmaiden. I view the operation of popular committees in the shacks of South Africa as an aspect of a democratic practice and ethos that operates in many places but is not yet properly understood nor theorised.

CHAPTER OUTLINE

In this introductory chapter, I have tried to present some theoretical issues using a light touch in order to encourage people who are not necessarily academics or specialists on the subject to read the book. Chapter 2 provides a history of *amakomiti* in South Africa, and Chapter 3 is an overview of how and where *amakomiti* exist and operate. This requires providing a profile of the conditions in the various settlements, hence there are many tables in this chapter. Chapters 4, 5 and 6 present findings from the three case studies: Nkaneng (Rustenburg), Duncan Village (East London) and Thembelihle (Johannesburg). Chapter 7 notes the significance of the key findings for our understanding of *amakomiti* and the political implications.

METHODOLOGY

My research methodology borrows from Burawoy's 'extended case method', which is based on a reflexive model of science whereby the empirical component of the study is both theoretically informed and is aimed at contributing to theory construction.[48] It seemed to me that the questions I wanted the research to help answer required an ethnographic approach that allowed in-depth investigation of a particular case, getting under its skin, as it were, in order to understand the historical, ideological and social bases of meanings and practices. At the same time, I also wanted to find out the extent, the breadth and width, of the operation of *amakomiti*, suspecting that different circumstances, and personnel, might influence their character. The study uses interviews, observation, participant observation and documentary analysis. The research design consists of two major components.

The first component was an overview study that involved an excursion visiting 46 informal settlements whose aim was to establish the state of self-organisation in the settlements. I visited informal settlements in each of four provinces: Gauteng, North West, KwaZulu-Natal and Eastern Cape.

The second component of the fieldwork involved the selection of four case studies which allowed me to conduct an in-depth investigation of the operation of committees in each of these four areas. The cases were located in the four provinces that were covered during the overview component of the study. In my analysis and presentation of findings, I have focused my attention on the 46 settlements, although in practice I visited more than this number, and have written chapters on only three of the four case studies for the sake of manageability and due to time and space constraints. The findings from the fourth case, the Nhlalakahle settlement located in Pietermaritzburg, KwaZulu-Natal province, are incorporated into the overall report presented in the book. It is important to declare my close association with the Thembelihle community and the TCC over the past 20 years while wearing 'many caps', including as fellow activist and as researcher. I have been in jail more than once with some TCC leaders after being arrested by the ANC-run state for demanding the provision of basic services for the residents in Thembelihle and Soweto. Rather than compromise my study, I think this experience has served to enrich it and provide greater insight into the issues I raise here.

2

'The People Cannot Live in the Air': History of the Squatter Movement in South Africa

Theorists of working-class self-organisation have observed that grassroots decision-making structures tend to proliferate during periods of heightened struggle and revolution, for example the Russian soviets, Italian factory councils and Iranian *shuras* (workplace and neighbourhood councils).[1] In South Africa, black working-class communities formed grassroots community organisations such as the township civics and street committees on a mass scale during periods of upsurge in the struggle against apartheid. In the post-apartheid era, these community structures have declined significantly in terms of their reach, operation and dynamism, presumably because of the lull in struggle. On the other hand, a*makomiti*, as my research indicates, appear to continue to thrive in the post-apartheid era.

In this chapter, I look into salient aspects of the history of the squatter movement in South Africa in the mid-twentieth century and during the 1980s resurgence of opposition to apartheid in order to reflect on what form and character *amakomiti* take during upswings in the struggle. This will help clarify the twin roles of the *amakomiti* as organs of struggle and as grassroots self-governance structures. It will also allow us to assess the argument that in addition to *amakomiti* existing to carry out functional duties, they also exist because of a culture or tradition that has developed around them and is presumably being passed on from generation to generation.

In looking at earlier forms of grassroots organisation in South Africa's shantytowns, it is important to locate the discussion in the context of the political economy of the country because this provides the conditions and factors that shape these areas and the life situation of the inhabitants. If we go back in history far enough, we find that migrant labour was a key feature of the form proletarianisation and urbanisation took in South Africa. The black working class came into existence with the movement of people from peasant economies in the rural areas to the mines and factories in the cities. The shortage of housing for black workers is a key factor in the emergence of shack settlements then and now. Here, I want to approach the history of migrant labour and the movement of workers from country to town by focusing on Mpondoland (located in the Transkei bantustan during apartheid, and today in the Eastern Cape province) because it is from this area, among others, that migrant labour was historically sourced, and indeed continues to be today. More importantly, in Mpondoland we find earlier rural forms of community organisation whose legacy and features still exist in the *amakomiti* of Nkaneng, the shack settlement in Rustenburg where many workers from this area live.

From Mpondoland, the chapter moves to the story of the squatter movement in Johannesburg in the 1940s. The focus here will be on the committee system built by James Sofasonke Mpanza in the settlement he built which later became part of Soweto. The shack settlement Sofasonke Village was born of a struggle for proper housing by black workers in Johannesburg. The chapter then leaps to a discussion of the role of shack dwellers and their movements during the 1980s, a period of upsurge in struggle, exploring shack self-organisation and its relationship to the broader movement of struggle, especially in the townships. This aspect of the discussion is very brief here because the case study on Duncan Village in Chapter 4 explores some of these issues in detail and in a specific context. However, I do briefly discuss shack self-organisation in Alexandra in the 1980s, a most tumultuous time in the history of this township. The key point from this chapter is perhaps that past struggles, strategies and historical forms of organisation have influenced to a greater or lesser extent present-day forms of struggle and organisation in the shack settlements today.

IINKUNDLA ZAMAMPONDO, MIGRANT LABOUR AND PROLETARIANISATION[2]

It was early in the nineteenth century, and amaMpondo were busy herding their cattle and tending their fields when the penetration of merchant capital from its launching pad in the Cape of Good Hope rudely and irreversibly disrupted their lives. The first indigenes to feel the early winds of what was to become the hurricane of conquest, dispossession and colonialism were the Khoi and the San (the 'Hottentots' and the 'Bushmen'). The former were pastoralists who had lived in the area since the fifth century, while the latter, hunters and gatherers, lived in the southern tip of Africa for millennia. Both groups had a very rough time under the settlers. The interaction between the Khoi and the white settlers was marked by violence as the latter fenced the land on which the indigenous people reared their Nguni herds. The San were hunted like animals by the newcomers and were forced to move north. The Khoi's relatively stable and prosperous nomadic way of life was shattered by the arrival of the settlers.[3] The new colonial order subjugated and integrated them as labourers, lovers, and later as soldiers.

In 1820, about 4,000 British immigrants settled further east, on the doorstep of amaXhosa, amaMfengu, amaMpondo and other peoples living there.[4] Empire sent the white settlers as reinforcements in the light of the perceived threat of the African societies ruled by kings, chiefs, clan leaders and powerful household heads, and whose mode of production we can describe as tributary.[5] Behind the empire were the dynamics of merchant capitalism and its rapid transformation back home into manufacture and then industrial capitalism. The political history of class struggle in South Africa that began with the decimation of the Khoi and San way of life now found permanent definition and shape in the contradictory and tumultuous interaction, from the point of view of political economy, of the capitalist and tributary modes of production.[6] Earlier forms of capitalist relations in these parts of the world were characteristically commercial and agricultural, but with the discovery of gold and diamonds, the ground was laid for the development and dominance of the capitalist mode of production proper with all its laws of motion operative within the confines of a colonial and peripheral economy. But as Mamdani has argued, the colonists could not ride in willy-nilly and take over these independent African societies, they had to fight and find other ways and means of subjugating them, they had to use force and consent, brutality and guile.[7]

The social, economic and political organisation of the Eastern Cape African societies was based on the homestead that was the basic and main unit of production and consumption. A cluster of homesteads could find unity and governance in the person of a chief or prominent clan leader whose rule was premised on exacting tribute from homestead heads in the form of goods and services, mainly cattle and labour service. William Beinart's study of the amaMpondo of Phondoland provides us with a detailed picture of their way of life at the turn of the twentieth century.[8] The chiefs or headmen, including homestead heads with large households, regularly held councils, generally known as *iinkundla*, in which the affairs of the homestead, clan, community, chieftaincy or kingdom were discussed. *Inkundla* (singular; plural *iinkundla*) literally refers to an open space or 'courtyard' with a strong connotation of processes taking place therein being transparent and occurring before the eyes of everyone.[9] The appropriate patriarch and leader chaired *iinkundla* sessions, and this typically involved a lot of listening by him and then his having the prerogative of closing the discussion with a ruling (a chairing style, *psst*, preferred by Nelson Mandela in more modern settings). The *inkundla* also had a dispute resolution function, adjudicating between warring parties; it also acted as a court that had the powers to try and, if necessary, punish offenders, usually in the form of fines.

Anthropologists suggest that in pre-colonial times, the king or chief was often compelled to be extremely responsive to the various interests and wishes of his 'subjects', and in fact, in many instances he would be elevated to his position by his peers.[10] Also, as Mahmood Mamdani has argued, 'in 19th century Africa ... kin groups contested with and balanced the claims of state authority'.[11] The colonial state interfered by giving chiefs more powers over the people, powers backed by its might, thus introducing a despotism that had in some instances not previously existed.[12]

Harold Wolpe seminally theorised the preservation of indigenous institutions such as the chieftaincy, communal land ownership and a 'free' peasantry within the 'articulation of modes of production' paradigm.[13] His 'cheap labour power thesis' explained the native reserves from the perspective of capital: they served to reduce the cost of labour reproduction by keeping wages down. Stephen Friedman has given an incisive and comprehensive account of the criticisms levelled against Wolpe's theorisation, in particular by African(ist) scholars such as Mafeje, Magubane and others.[14]

Beinart worked within the articulation model, but his research findings led him to question amaMpondo's loss of agency implied by this paradigm.[15] He provides evidence to suggest that the pattern of labour migration in Phondoland at the turn of the nineteenth century was not simply the result of colonial state policy or the related interests of mining and/or agricultural capital. Rather, the form of labour migrancy was partly a specific response by amaMpondo to their deteriorating economic circumstances wrought by natural disasters and the encroachment of the colonial state and capitalist relations. The chiefs were struggling to maintain their economic and political power with colonial pressures often pitting them against their own people. Nevertheless, according to Beinart, the commoners supported the chiefs, and chieftaincy as an institution, because they stood for and supported communal land ownership, thus guaranteeing everyone land for living and grazing.[16] Besieged by colonial conquest and capitalist relations, the Mpondo strategy was to adjust and adapt on better terms rather than escape the capitalist juggernaut. In a kind of war of position, they sought incorporation into capital's circuits from a position of relative strength with a semblance of economic security.[17] Migrancy linked to the cattle advance system illustrates this.

A system of payment preferred by household heads for sons that went to work in the gold mines was cattle advance, whereby a beast was handed over by the labour tout, usually a white trader, before the migrant worker left for the mines. This ensured that the migrant contributed directly to the maintenance and growth of the domestic herds. It also ensured that the sons did not spend their money in the city. This suggests active engagement with rather than passive surrender to the power of capital. In other words, amaMpondo were neither 'modernists' nor 'traditionalists', as some dual economy analysts imagine, they were pragmatists, attempting to negotiate their way around real constraints emanating from 'both worlds'. This analytical approach recovers the migrant workers' agency, including that of their peasant communities. As V.L. Allen has pointed out, mineworkers shape their own history despite the odds being heavily stacked against them in the mines.[18] The migration of *iinkundla* characteristics into *amakomiti* formed by Mpondo miners in Rustenburg illustrates this.

THE SQUATTER MOVEMENT IN THE 1940S

We can see traces of the organisational forms of the 1940s squatters' movement in *amakomiti* of today. This movement took over land, establishing 'squatter camps' despite strong opposition from the white state because, as one ANC minister put it much later, 'the people cannot live in the air'.[19] In Cape Town, for example, the squatter camps established in the 1940s and 1950s met the fate of many others in other parts of the country: demolition and the herding of the people into black townships and bantustans by the apartheid government that came to power in 1948.[20] However, further influx into the urban areas followed in the late 1960s due to economic expansion, which at first was tolerated by the state, and then followed by another spate of demolitions with the recession; in Cape Town, the affected settlements were Modderdam, Unibel and Werkgenot.[21] Crossroads, which later became the site of major struggles, was established as a transit camp in 1975 in the course of these demolitions and forced removals.[22] Umkhumbane (Cato Manor), the largest shack settlement in Durban, noted for its vibrant cultural and political life, was demolished in the early 1960s after protracted struggle.[23]

In this section, I will focus mainly on the Sofasonke movement in Soweto, Johannesburg, as a case study of internal camp processes related to committee organisation, without completely neglecting the development of similar movements in other urban centres of South Africa. The movement at its height in the second half of the 1940s involved 'between 63,000 and 92,500 Africans [who] settled in squatter camps in and around Johannesburg'.[24] It commanded the attention of the state, oppositional political organisations and ordinary workers; the United Party government drove it back, and the apartheid 'hard men' finally routed it when they took power in 1948. It nevertheless achieved its goal of forcing the state to build houses for the black working class, albeit on the cheap. It was an inspiration for the mass resistance to racial and class domination that coalesced and began to challenge 'racial capitalism' in the 1950s. As Martin Legassick observes: 'This was a decade of organisation and struggle – of mass demonstrations, boycotts, defiance, strikes and near-uprisings – against poverty wages, the pass laws, price and fare rises, Bantu Education, "Bantu Authorities", "cattle-culling", police repression, and all the other burdens.'[25]

The focus of the squatter movement was 'houses for all', its epicenter was Orlando township,[26] and its undisputed leader was James Sofasonke Mpanza, the founder of the Sofasonke Party.[27] The movement was born on Saturday 25 March 1944, when Mpanza exhorted hundreds of Orlando sub-tenants and other poorly housed workers to follow him and cross the River Jordan, set up a camp of improvised shelters on an open veld across a small stream next to the township, and thereby defy the state.[28] This audacious act caught everyone by surprise, in particular the Labour Party-controlled Johannesburg City Council, and thus was born Shantytown, or Sofasonke Village.[29] Baruch Hirson notes: 'Several men emerged in 1944–45 as shantytown leaders, but it was James Sofasonke Mpanza who initiated, inspired, and planned the greatest shantytown of all.'[30]

From Shantytown, the movement spread to various parts of Johannesburg, including Pimville, Alexandra, Sharpeville, Albertynsville and Zuurbekom.[31] Everywhere, the modus operandi was the same: organise a group of people in need of houses, identify a piece of land, erect shelters, and demand that the state builds houses or else the camp stays put.[32] In a few instances, the squatters occupied half-completed council-built houses *en masse*.[33] Mpanza's leadership and focus seem to have centred on his constituency in Orlando, and he inspired rather than led the broader movement.[34] He was an outspoken, charismatic, shrewd, brave and fiercely independent political organiser and fighter who influenced and embodied the spirit of the squatter movement at its strongest moments.[35] The dimensions of this spirit, I would argue, are autonomy, independence, irreverence, popular democracy, mass mobilisation, direct action and challenging the authorities and the system of private property they defend. Mpanza's intervention in the politics of housing in Johannesburg, and to an extent in the politics of black opposition to white rule, was to match words and appeals to reason with mass mobilisation and action. The militancy of the ANC Youth League that saw the ANC turn to the masses and lead the defiance campaigns of the 1950s was preceded by:

> thousands of men, women, and children who set up their shacks on the veld, in the face of a hostile Council and government, and withstood all attempts at removing them, who had carved out the land. Mpanza, in leading these people, put himself at the head of the biggest social and political upheaval of the war years.[36]

The ANC and CPSA (Communist Party of South Africa) were not impressed.[37] The ANC's problem was that it did not envisage any independent action by the masses, and for the CPSA the problem was political method, whereby it found it hard to relate its theory of revolution to grassroots dynamics.[38] For the ADP (African Democratic Party), in addition to other political problems, its leaders such as 'Paul Mosaka and Self Mampuru were committee men, not activists ... their dark suits and ties marked them as strangers in the midst of hessian shacks and cardboard shelters'.[39] These political parties increasingly found themselves losing the battle to 'the short term, rather immediate, localised and personal nature of Mpanza's politics. Also his ability to exploit popular sentiments.'[40] Lopez[41] explains the ideological character of 'squatting' by reference to the following quotation from Foucault:

> These are 'immediate' struggles for two reasons. In such struggles people criticise instances of power which are the closest to them, those which exercise their action on individuals. They do not look for the 'chief enemy' but for the immediate enemy. Nor do they expect to find a solution to their problem at a future date (that is, liberations, revolutions, end of class struggle).[42]

Hence: 'Unconcerned about long term goals or national party programmes, Mpanza was less constrained in the means he was prepared to use to achieve his ends', including the use of strong-arm tactics, self-promotion, and flexibility in tactics and allies.[43] Nevertheless, primarily 'Mpanza was able to sway his audience. He spoke their language, the language of those who hungered for houses .... He was looked upon with reverence as the man who fought for and spoke on behalf of the underdog.'[44] Furthermore:

> It was Mpanza's brilliance as an organiser, his deeply rooted empathy with the ordinary people, specifically the working class and his ability to translate this into action .... [H]is daring at placing himself at risk in a struggle for working class goals which has kept him alive in the minds of working people today ... the Mpanza who organised the squatters, against the threat of the Council – the Mpanza who gave them houses, the Father of Soweto.[45]

The power of Mpanza and the squatter movement stemmed from self-organisation and mass action. All the land invasions or squats of the 1940s had a leadership, but the people were expected to be actively involved in the process, including erecting their shelters, paying money to the organisation, braving the harsh conditions and defending the camp against attacks by the authorities. Organising an invasion and running a camp required many meetings, with the leaders consulting with and guiding the constituency. Mpanza himself, although he was severely criticised for his lapses in this respect, 'never failed in all his civic activities to obtain a mandate from the residents … he said a leader should always get a close connection with the people. He said a good leader must be a follower of the people.'[46] It is thus possible to speak of a form of popular democracy that operated in the squatter camps. In contrast, the state offer of democracy was voting for a racially based Advisory Board system whose recommendations it largely ignored.[47] Women were expressly excluded from voting, and in any case, without a husband, 'widowed, deserted, young unmarried, or newly arrived women faced ejection from the township if discovered', whereas 'in the shantytown they enjoyed a new freedom', and as a result, 'women were among the group's most devoted members'.[48]

Segregationist and apartheid planners disliked women because they preferred cheap male black labour coming into the mines and farms to work, not to set up families. The arrival of women represented the latter, and there was undisguised hostility to women, amounting to official misogyny.[49] But this did not stop them coming to the towns; their frosty reception by the authorities put them at the forefront of squatter movements. Women could not access housing, and squatting was a solution to their problem. Patriarchy and racism deemed single women undesirable to the extent that when a husband died, apartheid officials would force the widow to choose a new man through lots using men's hats in order to secure her marital house.[50] The involvement and leadership of women in the squatter movement are notable in many other areas, including the beer wars in Cato Manor in 1959 that were part of a struggle against the demolition of uMkhumbane in Durban.[51]

The Council and the government were mostly driven by a fear, real or exaggerated, that: 'Whenever Natives have been allowed to develop a township without being under municipal control, the result has been disastrous.'[52] But 'Mpanza was maintaining order in the camp', and special people were assigned to combat crime, enforce the camp's laws and carry out communal duties.[53] As a rule, the associations and committees running the various squatter camps took care of affairs: 'Their leaders controlled site allocation and provided amenities, had their own "strong-arm" corps, meted out justice in courts, levied fines and floggings, and controlled entry to the camp.'[54] Mpanza went further: 'The fuel depot was being run as a co-operative store by this stage selling coal and wood at less than 20 percent of Orlando prices.'[55] Entry into the camps was controlled, and traders' vehicles paid a levy to the 'office' for the privilege of coming into the camp to do business.[56] In most camps, 'followers paid a weekly toll …. All monies were in the hands of the leaders, to be used at their discretion.'[57] The money was used to pay the camp workers, including the crime-fighters, and in the case of Mpanza, to also fund the various legal cases he initiated or had to defend against the state. Money also went to cleaning the camp, funding trips carried out in the name of the camp, and related expenses. Self-governance was a key aspect of the camps.

'Municipal control over the Orlando township ... is practically nil', and the squatter leaders 'had arrogated to themselves "all state and governmental functions in Tobruk and Alexandra camps"'.[58] These were arguably seedlings of 'dual power' emerging in the camps, with the committees and their leaders taking over powers normally exercised by the municipality.

The aspect of 'self-management' might have posed the greatest threat to the government, because not only was it the fruition of a struggle against and in defiance of the state, but it also disproved the theory that 'natives' could do nothing by themselves and needed the paternalistic hand of the white state. In the words of the Minister of Health: 'the squatter movement should be controlled by the authorities instead of being left to spontaneous, sporadic eruptions, or worse still, to organisation and control by unlawful elements'.[59] The main concern 'was one of control. The actual responsibility of providing housing was secondary', as is evident in the words of the Secretary of the Department of Native Affairs: 'The most pressing need of the Native community is adequate housing. Only by the provision of adequate shelter in properly planned native townships can full control over urban natives be regained.'[60] This explains why the Council often viewed the action of squatters 'as a trial of strength rather than emanating from legitimate grievances. Hence the call for force.'[61]

Martin Legassick has argued that the main constraint on the South African state during the era of the squatter movement and beyond had been the necessity of controlling the working class, in particular containing the struggles of black workers in order to maintain the cheap labour system.[62] The peculiar uneven development of the capitalist economy made the suppression of wages the key factor in maintaining profit levels, as other cost factors were beyond the control of the mine owners.[63] Although the South African economy grew rapidly between 1947 and 1954, the heyday of Mpanza and the squatter movement, African living standards declined.[64] It is in the city that 'contradictions in the capitalist mode of production therefore play themselves out most forcefully', because cities are 'the spatial forms that most emphatically support the production and circulation of capital'.[65] From this point of view, there were real constraints on the capitalist state in South Africa adopting a liberal reformist approach to labour, and only the struggles of the workers themselves could force concessions out of capital. As a result, when the party of apartheid took power in 1948: 'The task confronting the NP [National Party] government was to reinforce the cheap labour system – against a movement of the oppressed working class that had suffered defeats, but was still rising.'[66]

Peter Alexander, in a study of labour militancy during the war years, provides a clue to the political economy of the emergence of the squatter movement:

> the character of capitalist development in the 1940s had implications for urbanisation. It encouraged a massive growth in the total number of Africans who were living in the cities at any one time, whilst simultaneously ensuring that many, if not most, such people were not settled urban dwellers.[67]

The state was constrained both politically and economically when it came to the provision of housing to African workers. On the one hand was the Stallard Commission: 'The Native should only be allowed to enter into the urban areas ... when he is willing to enter and minister to the needs of the White man, and should depart therefrom when he ceases so to minister.'[68] This represented a desire to halt, slow down or control the process of urbanisation and proletarianisation from the point of view of racialist capital and the state – a Sisyphean task, as the case of the 3,000 squatters at Orlando West in September 1946 proved. Many came from the Pimville tanks, where they had been housed by the state 'temporarily' for 41 years, and more importantly, most were employed in Johannesburg; there were thus no legal grounds for the Council to tell them, as was its habit, 'to go back to where they came from'.[69] 'Secondary industry, wanting to take advantage of a more mobile labour force, exercised considerable influence on the central government' and contradicted the Council's Stallardist stance.[70]

The squatter movement was a working-class urban movement, it involved 'struggles in which the working class [were fighting] in establishing themselves as a community'.[71] It was a movement mostly of sub-tenants, what today are called 'backyarders', and other 'houseless' people.[72] However, this was a working class still in the making, with many people fresh from the rural areas and still struggling to find a toehold in the city and establish themselves either permanently or as migrant workers. The migration into Johannesburg is estimated to have swelled the black population by 69 per cent in the 1940s,[73] and significantly, the proportion of females migrating increased.[74] The futile and harsh efforts of various state structures to halt or otherwise control and re-direct this exodus created a lot of hardship for workers and provoked movements of resistance such as the squatter movement. Understanding the dynamics of the social movement, its political character, the nature of leadership and its organisational forms is no easy task. As Patrick Bond notes:

> It is not always feasible to specify the construction of social movement identity in urban settings, where conjunctural features are legion, but where overt market processes have torn asunder land relations, rural ties, indigenous culture, and many forms of pre-existing authority and social control.[75]

Key concepts in mainstream social movement theory are not adequate to the task, namely political opportunity structure, resource mobilisation, framing and related aspects. The main difficulty is the tendency of these theories to overlook or underplay class contradictions in society.

In his critique of Piven and Cloward's[76] theory of 'poor people's movements', French notes the use of 'vacuous concepts like "poor people"', and laments the theory's lack of a 'materialist concept of power nor a theoretical commitment to historical specificity'.[77] We need, instead, studies that 'show in a more integrated way the actual playing out of the specific historical forces in a specific context'.[78] A promising line of inquiry is provided by approaching the squatters as workers who needed adequate shelter in the urban areas where they worked or sought work. Alexander's research into labour militancy during the war years takes on new light when we widen our lens because it suggests that the increase in struggle at the workplace was occurring in tandem with heightened struggle in workers' living spaces.[79] Alexander provides data to show that 'the level of strike action was far greater than officially admitted'.[80] In other words, there was a general increase in working-class militancy, including in working-class residential areas, which suggests the emergence and development of a working-class movement during this period.[81] This provides a broader context for understanding the squatter movement.

From the account here, the squatter movement was arguably a working-class movement that arose out of the contradictions of the capitalist process, in particular its uneven and combined development, which, in deed if not words, attacked capitalist private property, albeit mostly in the form of state land. It developed 'unique' alternative forms of self-organisation and political practice that would stretch the conceptual categories of social movement theory to its limits. Whereas Mpanza organised the squatters into a political party, the Sofasonke Party,[82] for Castells, 'autonomy means, basically, a neat separation of activists from institutionalised actors like political parties and unions'.[83] This definition fits the manner in which contemporary South Africa's most important movement of shack dwellers, Abahlali baseMjondolo, projects itself (and is understood by its analysts), but differs from Mpanza's political practice, which was complex and multi-pronged.[84]

Stadler has argued that the 1940s squatter movement tended to be 'always inward-looking', did not develop wider support and longer-term political objectives, and did not expand its repertoire of tactics beyond land invasions and setting up camps.[85] Part of developing longer-term political objectives would have included linking up with other organisations such as the ANC, ANC Youth League and South African Cultural Observatory, organisations that refused to give their support to the movement.[86] Stadler argues that the authorities developed a response to the tactic of land invasion and the setting up of squatter camps by providing alternative accommodation, thereby leading to the cessation of the camps and the political challenge they represented.[87] These criticisms are valid. However, they partly reflect the development of a movement in the absence of support from the broader workers' movement. With hindsight, it is apparent that available strength from the workers' movement was left unused. Opportunities for building a formidable movement against the racist and exploitative oppressor went to waste. For example, at the time, the authorities' hands were full dealing with the war and maintaining the wartime industry, worker combativity was on the increase in workplaces and living spaces, the petty bourgeoisie in the ANC Youth League was radicalising, and in Africa the politics of national liberation were on the rise.[88] Failure to build the squatter movement to its highest level of militancy and politics was a lost opportunity from the perspective of the workers' movement and the struggle for national liberation.[89]

SHACK DWELLERS AND THE UNITED DEMOCRATIC FRONT IN THE 1980S AND 1990S

Shack residents played a significant role in the anti-apartheid movement, with shack settlements often the terrain upon which vicious battles and key struggles were waged that ultimately led to the demise of apartheid.[90] Some writers have questioned this assessment, observing that, in fact, the poorest of the poor tended to distance themselves from the township-based heightened political activism of the 1980s. They argue that in some instances, the distance between shack settlement and township politics was so great that it opened the door for the abuse of informal settlements as springboards to launch pro-apartheid violence against the anti-apartheid movement.[91] Underlying the opposing assessments are the assumptions made about shack dwellers.

This question is a complex one. This is because not only were experiences not uniform across all areas, but many settlements were themselves in the process of formation or were undergoing profound changes as a result of the apartheid state's relaxation of influx control laws in a context of heightened struggle, widening divisions in society and generalised social turmoil. The first assertion is premised on the theoretical postulation that those with little to lose, such as shack dwellers, have a lot to gain if they involve themselves in struggle. The second assertion argues the opposite, stating that those with little tend to cling hard to it and do not want to risk the little they have, and hence distance themselves from political activism. Furthermore, the first position tends to see shack dwellers as part of the working class, while the second position emphasises the distinction between the employed and unemployed, between the formally housed working class and the informally housed 'underclass'.

I am going to consider different experiences related to this debate with reference to the United Democratic Front (UDF), an organisation born in 1983 to unite and give focus to numerous local and sectoral struggles that were the hallmark of this period of heightened opposition to and mass action against apartheid.[92] Many community organisations operating in the townships and settlements were UDF affiliates or looked to it for leadership.

The UDF played a major role in the final push against the apartheid system. It also facilitated the emergence of the ANC as a dominant player in the anti-apartheid opposition forces.[93] The significance of the UDF lies in the appreciation of the important role played by the myriad of local organisations that were its affiliates in the struggle against the apartheid state. Township civics, street and block committees operated at the local level, including the organisation and coordination of campaigns involving millions of ordinary South Africans in the anti-apartheid struggle.[94] What role did shack dwellers and their organisations play in the UDF?

The UDF's political approach based itself on its claim that it represents 'the people' as a whole.[95] It embraced all sectors of society, except the apartheid regime and its (official) supporters, as its constituency; and this included shack dwellers. The question posed in the literature is: 'Which voice, which class and which social groups within the class were dominant in the UDF?' Officially, the UDF embraced the idea of 'working-class leadership', but it has been argued that in practice, it tended to be dominated by middle-class leaders and was thus directed by 'populist' rather than working-class politics.[96] This debate was actually a bitter controversy in the 1980s, dividing the trade unions at the time into so-called 'workerist' and 'populist' camps, including violence between UDF and Black Consciousness-oriented organisations. The fearful accusation was that the UDF and the ANC would 'sell out' the people once in power.

Van Kessel has argued that the UDF did indeed neglect the interests of the poorest of the poor in a process involving 'inclusion and exclusion' in the creation of a new nation.[97] Her case studies conducted in Sekhukhune, Kagiso and Cape Town reveal that in the 1980s, hostel and informal settlement dwellers did not seek affiliation with the UDF and that shack dwellers' vulnerability, given their tenuous foothold in the urban areas, discouraged them from participation in 'confrontational' politics with the state.[98] Indeed, with the dawn of the 'new South Africa', fissures in the people's camp became apparent, especially at the local level where 'the marginalised and the outsiders in the new South Africa [became] most clearly visible: farmworkers, migrants, rural communities, squatters, immigrants, and sections of the youth, now dubbed "the lost generation"'.[99]

There was the growth of 'gigantic new squatter camps ... around the main cities' in the build-up to and aftermath of liberation, which Van Kessel attributes to tensions between township landlords and backyarders as the former increased rent in the context of housing shortages, overcrowding and rapid urbanisation.[100] She concludes, based on the outcomes of the struggle, that the UDF was guilty of subsuming, and even neglecting, the interests of 'the marginalised' in the course of the anti-apartheid struggle.[101]

To complement Van Kessel's *ex post facto* analysis, it is necessary to consider studies of the actual process of organisation and mobilisation in the informal settlements during the era of the UDF, such as in Alexandra township, where shack dwellers lived side by side with formally housed township folk.

Justine Lucas's ethnographic study of civic structures in Alexandra during the early 1990s gives us a clue of how shack dwellers would participate in different ways in the township organizational project because of diverse structural and political factors.[102] She found a marked difference between the mode of participation of shack dwellers who lived in the township's yards, consisting of about ten formal structures and ten shacks, and those who lived in freestanding shack settlements that filled the empty spaces inside and around the township. She argues that where there was no landlord relationship in a yard; the tenants tended to create and maintain a well-functioning yard committee that served to address the practical problems of the inhabitants and provide an enabling social environment for healthy social relations. The Alexandra Civic Organisation (ACO) provided the political guidelines for setting up such committees and used them to take forward its township-wide campaigns. The ACO admitted that it had not done so well organising in the standalone shack areas because of not putting in enough effort. Its organisational model also did not work well in the shack areas because their unit was the yard. There was also the problem of bad and opportunistic leadership, whereby a 'political entrepreneur' organised one shack settlement employing patronage and autocratic leadership, giving rise to a 'politics [that] was a combination of resistance, quasi-traditional leadership and intimidatory practices, a pattern that largely conforms to the stereotype associated with informal settlements'.[103] Despite all the problems, Lucas observes that: 'These yard committees are an inspiring example of self-organisation and participatory democracy in the face of poor leadership and harsh material conditions.'[104]

In civic organisation, there are underlying factors that go beyond the quality of organisational leadership and political strategy. Lucas notes that there appeared to be more social coherence, collectivism, co-operation and solidarity in the well-organised yards as a result of kinship and other social ties, while people living in the freestanding shacks had very little social connection and interaction with each other in the past and present. She concludes that 'civic organisation [is] a complex phenomenon, with internal contradictions and frequent transformations generated by, and embedded in, social dynamics', and that while leadership and organisation are important, 'a broader understanding of civics can only be addressed if one also undertakes to examine these underlying social dynamics'.[105]

Lucas's conclusion points to the need to contextualise the debate about the propensity or otherwise of shack dwellers to participate in struggle. It is necessary to view political phenomena with a wider lens, taking into account many surface factors and underlying dynamics such as those identified by Lucas, and indeed by Van Kessel.[106] The latter, for example, underlines the vulnerability felt by 'illegal dwellers', leading many to shun visible, confrontational politics of civics and youth organisations.[107] She also points to 'a general atmosphere of rising militancy throughout the country and of escalating state repression'.[108] The latter included apartheid sponsorship of 'black on black' violence in the townships and shack settlements.[109] The Inkatha versus UDF bloodbath in KwaZulu-Natal gave birth to many new shack settlements as people sought refuge from the violence: for example, the Nhlalakahle settlement in Pietermaritzburg began this way.[110] Refugees from the political violence formed the first *amakomiti* of Nhlalakahle. It is possible that the focus on the political violence and the machismo concomitant with it has served to downplay the role of women in the shack dwellers' movements.

The agency and leadership of women in the squatter movements of the 1970s and 1980s was highlighted in the struggle for Crossroads, whereby the Crossroads Women's Committee was formed by fighting against apartheid evictions that received international publicity and solidarity.[111] These powerful women led the struggle behind the vision of winning "'a place for people without a place", meeting basic human needs for social reproduction'.[112] In the new South Africa, there emerged the Women's Power Group in Crossroads that, in the spirit of South Africa's community protests, fought for services and quality houses, staging a four-month-long sit-in at the council offices from 21 January 1998. Its fate, according to Benson, underlines 'how this 1998 women-only, collective, public, political grassroots protest was, for the most part, not seen by local residents as part of an ongoing history of women mobilising in Crossroads'.[113] The process by which the sit-in was defeated and denounced by the authorities shows how women's struggles were largely demobilised and depoliticised during the transition to democracy in South Africa. Moreover, though 'women have asserted agency in the politics of informal settlements ... for the most part, these experiences have been incorporated into or written out of official histories'.[114]

3

Amakomiti are Everywhere

Our bodies itch every day because of the insects. If it is raining everything is wet – blankets and floors. If it is hot the mosquitoes and flies are always there. There is no holiday in the shacks.[1]

Self-organisation in the world's slums, shacks and favelas has attracted the attention of scholars and developed a modest body of literature.[2] However, my research reveals the large scale of the operation of committees: 45 out of 46 settlements I visited had committees in operation. Interestingly, there exists more than one committee in each settlement; in some instances, as many as six committees operate side by side. The categories or types of committees in operation were: people's committees, ward committees, ANC committees, headman committees, community policing forums (CPFs), community development forums (CDFs) and ad hoc protest committees. In many instances, shack dwellers form 'task teams', usually on a temporary basis to carry out specific functions, often in response to a major problem in the area.

It is important to note at the outset the distinction I make between committees formed autonomously by communities, which I call 'people's committees', and those formed at the behest of the state or some outside body such as a non-governmental organisation. For example, ward committees, are statutory committees that operate in all local government wards in South Africa, and shack constituencies will participate in them. However, we must always recognise the agency of the shack no matter what type of committee we are talking about because their inhabitants have to actively organise their participation in them and, for example, either dictate or negotiate the terms of such participation. In almost all cases, they have to nominate or elect representatives to be part of committees.

The questions I seek to answer in this chapter are the following: What is the character of the popular committees found in the informal settlements?

What are their roles and functions? What is their history and tradition? Of what significance are they in the struggle to meet the needs of shack dwellers? What role do they play in organising protest? Where are they located in the interface between democracy and development? In addition, the discussions in the previous chapters raised a number of questions, some related to the theorisation of *amakomiti* – for example, the question of their role as grassroots governance structures and as organs of struggle, and their relationship to township movements and organisations including civics and street committees. More generally: are shack dwellers' committees expressions of a form of 'democracy on the margins' that people create for themselves? And if so, how do these forms intersect with the dominant liberal democratic form of the post-apartheid state?

This chapter, because it is very much an attempt at a faithful report of empirical findings, will not answer some of the broader questions, but will hopefully provide a factual context and some clues. The case studies in the following chapters will help answer the broader questions, although interpretation of the case study findings benefits in turn from location in this chapter's wider-lens survey of other informal settlements.

Photo 3.1 Office of the Makause Community Development Forum in Makause, Germiston. (Photograph by author)

PROFILE OF THE SETTLEMENTS

It is important to give the reader a picture of the kind of settlements I visited. I will provide only the most essential information on the profile of the informal settlements due to space constraints. My priority in this book is to use as much space as possible focusing on the self-organisation processes in the settlements rather than on physical, social and economic conditions, although these are quite important as they provide the context for the formation of committees. However, the reports on the three case studies in the next three chapters provide more detail and may give the reader more insight into conditions in those particular settlements.

In the course of the overview study, I visited a total of 46 settlements in four provinces: Gauteng (10 settlements), North West (10), KwaZulu-Natal (10) and Eastern Cape (16). I had to stay longer in the Eastern Cape due to the longer distances involved in driving through this vast province, so this allowed me to visit more settlements.

Photo 3.2   A shack threatening to keel over in Bebelele, Duncan Village, East London. (Photograph by author)

The settlements visited ranged from small to very large. The smallest would consist of a small cluster of about 20 shacks or less, and the biggest about 8,000 shacks or more. Most shack settlements visited were of small to medium size: that is, they had between 100 and 500 shacks.

Most settlements, as we can see in Table 3.1, were established in 1990–1994.

Table 3.1 Periods of establishment of the informal settlements

Period established	No. of settlements	% Where N = 46
1985–1989	6	13
1990–1994	12	26
1995–1999	2	4
2000–2004	4	9
2005–2009	2	4
2010–2013	3	7
Unknown	17	37
Total	46	100

Source: Compiled by the author based on field research.

The last years of apartheid saw the relaxation of influx controls allowing greater movement of people and perhaps less diligence in eradicating settlements by the state.[3] Incoming residents were erecting about a thousand shacks a month in Alexandra during this period, according to the Alexandra Action Committee's estimate.[4] The establishment of shack settlements continues unabated in the post-apartheid society. The 1990–1994 peak coincided with the unbanning of political organisations, the release of political prisoners and the year of independence. The prospect of black majority rule may have emboldened people to defy apartheid laws, take over land and erect their shacks. Table 3.2 indicates that land invasion was the main method used in the establishment of the settlements.

Let me explain the terms used in Table 3.2: 'land invasion' and 'silent encroachment' are self-explanatory, and I have discussed them in Chapter 1. 'Rent/negotiation' is when people usually already living on the land approach the owner to make a formal arrangement to allow them to continue living there. 'Government relocation' refers to instances where the authorities relocate people, often 'temporarily', into a 'camp' consisting of informal building materials. 'Village in-migration' occurs in rural towns where a

Table 3.2   How the informal settlements were established

Method of establishment	No. of settlements	% Where N = 46
Land invasion	20	44
Rent/negotiation	4	9
Silent encroachment	6	13
Government relocation	7	15
Village in-migration	2	4
Unknown	7	15
Total	46	100

Source: Compiled by the author based on field research.

village gradually begins to look like a shack settlement as people moving closer to town erect shacks in an area hitherto consisting of village-type structures (brick and cement, wattle and daub, etc.). In some informal settlements, there were unclear or contradictory versions of how the place was first established, hence the category 'unknown'.

NAMING THE SETTLEMENTS

Shack settlement naming is related to the history, political life and culture of the places, which, like people, have an identity in the popular imagination. A name turns a space into a place.[5] Here I will only discuss names of the informal settlements I visited.[6] Other researchers have noted patterns and themes in the naming of informal settlements that are somewhat similar to South Africa. In Iran, for example: 'The squatters usually called their communities by the terms that described the mode of their construction. Thus *Muftabad* meant the community built free of charge; *Zoorabad*, by force; *Halabiabad*, those made of containers; and *Hasirabad*, of bamboo leaves.'[7]

A number of informal settlements have names that refer to their 'mode of construction'. There is *Vrygrond*, which means free ground (in Afrikaans). A most common name for informal settlements in South Africa is *Nkaneng* or *Nkanini*, which means 'by force' or '[constructed] through defiance' (SeSotho/Xhosa). Another common name is *Baipei*, which means 'those who put themselves there': that is, without official sanction (SeSotho). *Siyahlala* means 'we are staying here' (Zulu). *Zenzele* and *Itireleng* mean (in isiZulu and SeSotho respectively) 'do it yourself' or 'self-help'. All these

Photo 3.3   A shack below the floodline and too close to a stream in Princess, Roodepoort. (Photograph by author)

names arguably underline the agency involved in establishing an informal settlement and some of them point to the spirit of defiance or taking matters into your own hands.

Some names describe the conditions of life in that settlement, and often refer to the early days: for example, *Dunusa*, which is rude and means 'showing your bums', and may refer to a time when there were no toilets and people exposed themselves without dignity. There is also *Vez'unyawo*, which means 'showing your foot (feet)', which might refer to the days when the shelters were so small people's feet stuck out when they slept. Other names describe the geographic area where the settlements are found, such as *eSiteshini*, '[near] at the [railway] station', and *SASKO*, referring to the bakery company next to the informal settlement. *Bleskop* refers to a mineshaft next to the informal settlement concerned. Some settlements are named after political figures, mostly ANC national leaders, such as *Mandela Park*, *Mandelaville*, *Mandela View*, *Nomzamo Park* (Winnie Mandela's Xhosa name), *Ramaphosa*, *Duma Nokwe*, *Chris Hani*, *Tamboville* and *Elias Motsoaledi*.

Others are named after the founder of the settlement, who could be a prominent political figure, like *Mshenguville*, referring to Ephraim "Mshengu" Tshabalala (his clan name), who was a Sofasonke Party leader, or a local leader, such as *Jeffsville*, which is named after Comrade Jeff, the leader of the land invasion.

Photo 3.4 The Jeffsville community office, Pretoria, named after Comrade Jeff, who led the land invasion. (Photograph by author)

Some settlement names express the vision and hopes of the inhabitants: for example, *Nhlalakahle*, 'a place where we [can] live well' (without political violence from Inkatha attacks). There is *Khayelitsha*, 'the new home', and *Sibantubonke*, which means 'we are all people', a reference to the settlement welcoming everyone who needed a place they could call home. Other names have unique origins and meanings, such as *Yizo Yizo*, which refers to a popular television programme featuring youth and crime, *Beirut*, referring to the violence that once characterised the area, and *Gomorrah*, referring to what people perceived as the immoral behaviour once endemic in that settlement. The transition to a democratic order has seen a change of naming patterns and themes. New settlements are today unlikely to be named after

ANC leaders, probably because the novelty of freedom and the lionisation of the leadership are not so widespread. Today, the ANC leaders are more likely to be in charge of a state that is intolerant of land invasions. *Marikana* has become a popular name for new settlements established through land invasions or occupation of government houses. The name refers to the *Marikana* massacre, where 34 striking miners were shot dead by the state police, and symbolises defiance.[8]

A settlement will often start off without a name or recognised/given name, and then later adopt a name. Some names, such as *Dunusa*, may be changed later because they are felt to be too rude, and a 'better' name is then chosen and used. Sometimes it is only when the state recognises a settlement that the community is prompted to find a suitable name. It will be apparent from this discussion that names do indeed give us a clue as to how the settlement is viewed by its inhabitants and by others at a certain point in its history. They also symbolise the process of turning space into a place.[9]

INFRASTRUCTURE AND SERVICES IN THE SETTLEMENTS

The physical infrastructure in the settlements visited was poor, as Table 3.3 indicates. Almost all the 'houses' were shacks made up of mostly corrugated iron, although in some settlements, such as Nhlalakahle, Pietermaritzburg, it was wattle and daub. However, one or two people will build a brick house among the shacks. In Barcelona, Lamontville township, Durban, this was not allowed by the shack dwellers because they wanted to look poor and 'similar' in the eyes of the state.[10] The majority of settlements did not have (official) electricity (70 per cent). However, some settlements organised self-connections to the grid: for example, Duncan Village in East London, and Makause in Germiston. The larger settlements tended to have self-connections, although the organisation, extent and quality of the connections differed.

Most settlements had access to one or more communal water taps (65 per cent), but I noticed that they could be quite far from some households, and in one instance some residents complained that they had to lug their water up a very steep hill.[11] Where there were no toilets (39 per cent), people either individually dug long-drop toilets or used the bush. A VIP toilet is a 'Ventilated Improved Pit Latrine', sometimes provided by the state, that 'has been fitted or built with a vent pipe and a fly screen' to reduce the smell.[12]

Table 3.3   State of basic services in the informal settlements

Service	No. of settlements	% Where N = 46
No electricity	32	70
No toilets	18	39
No water	5	11
Communal tap	30	65
Electricity	6	13
Communal toilet	5	11
Bucket toilet	5	11
Toilet (VIP)	3	7

Source: Compiled by the author based on field research.

I don't think that the self-organisation of the informal settlements can be understood apart from the fact that people live in such poor conditions. However, the nature of organisation does not directly reflect the level of development (or underdevelopment) of a particular settlement. Other factors mediate the relationship between the objective need and the form that agency takes in response to the felt needs. For example, some settlements will not connect themselves to the grid because of internal and external political dynamics, while others will. The importance of agency will be apparent in the following presentation covering the different categories of committees found and how they operate.

CATEGORIES OF POPULAR COMMITTEES

Table 3.4 lists the committees found and their frequencies. The narrative that follows brings out the richness, diversity and complexities in their operation. I have provided descriptions and definitions of each of the different categories of committees. However, it will be apparent that the same category of committee does not always operate the same way in different contexts. In some instances, a particular category of committee will change the way it operates in the same informal settlement over time. Also, diverse categories of committees will exist and cease to exist in the course of the particular history of a community. For example, a people's committee might lead the initial land invasion that establishes the settlement, then later a ward committee might be set up because the settlement has won recognition by the state. In this regard, it can be argued that the operation of a committee or set of committees is peculiar, and even unique, to the particular settlement in which it is found. However, for the sake of analysis, it is necessary to identify some discernible similarities and differences in order to have a general picture or pattern of self-organisation in the informal settlements of South Africa.

Table 3.4 Categories of committees found in the settlements

	No. of settlements	% Where N = 46
Settlements with PC (with/without other committees)	35	76
Settlements with WC	21	45
Settlements with ANC	8	17
Settlements with CPF	5	11
Settlements with CDF	4	9
Settlements with HC	3	7
Settlements with PC and WC	9	20
Settlements with WC and HC	3	7
Settlements with PC and ANC	2	4
Settlements with WC and CPF	1	2
Settlements with WC and CDF	1	2
Settlements with PC, WC, ANC	2	4
Settlements with WC, CPF, ANC	1	2
Settlements with PC, WC, ANC, CPF	1	2
Settlements with PC, WC, CPF, CDF, ANC	1	2
No committee	1	2
Settlements with PC only (no other committees exist)	16	35
Settlements with WC only	3	7
Settlements with ANC BEC only	1	2

Key: PC = people's committee, WC = ward committee, CPF = community policing forum, CDF = community development forum, ANC = ANC committee, HC = headman committee.
Source: Compiled by the author based on field research.

The first group of committees in Table 3.4 refers to the existence of a particular category of committee irrespective of whether it exists alone or with other committees. The other groups refer to the existence of combinations of committees. The last group of committees refers to instances where a category of committee exists alone. For example, the people's committee is found in 35 settlements, it exists alone in 16 settlements, it co-exists with a ward committee in 9 settlements, and it co-exists with a ward committee and an ANC committee in 2 settlements, etc. If we state this information in terms of percentages, it will be apparent that the most frequently found committee is the people's committee. With respect to the headman committees, it is important to note that they only operate in rural areas governed by traditional leaders. This means that they are under-represented in my sample, in so far as I visited more areas not governed by traditional authorities. However, I believe that this table does give the reader an approximate overview of the occurrence of different categories of committees in the 46 settlements visited. Let us look at each category of committees found in turn.

People's Committees

Communities form people's committees independently of the state with the mandate of representing the interests of the community as a whole. They are more or less similar in structure and functioning to the township civic organisations of the 1980s.[13] People's committees in shack settlements may share the form and names of the township structures, such as 'civic', 'area committee' and 'street committee'. Both township and shack settlement people's committees share a history going back, according to Colin Bundy, as far as the vigilance associations and *iliso lomzi* ('the eye of the community') structures formed by late nineteenth-century African communities in the Eastern Cape.[14] In my research, people's committees were the most prevalent category of committee found in operation in 35 out of 46 settlements visited (76 per cent). In 16 settlements (35 per cent), the people's committee was the only functioning committee. From this point of view, people's committees are the 'true' or quintessential *amakomiti*.

The main functions of a people's committee are to organise the establishment of the settlement and to improve living conditions. After a land invasion, a people's committee is the structure that organises the provision of or access to basic services such as water, sanitation, energy, schooling, healthcare and crime prevention. My research suggests that during these very early days of the existence of a settlement, communities will hold numerous, even daily, meetings or assemblies in order to collectively address provision of these basics. Committees become necessary for co-ordination.

The level of organisation and the tasks needing to be carried out will differ according to the perceived needs of each settlement. For example, early in the establishment of the settlement, negotiations with the state might deliver communal taps. However, later on, some settlements organise the installation of water taps in people's yards that connect to the communal taps; some dig out long-drop toilets in organised fashion, and still others connect themselves to the electricity grid. Taking these additional steps depends not only on the conditions, but also on the ingenuity, drive and vision of each community and its leadership.

Table 3.5 lists the duties of people's committees as mentioned by informants in the course of the interviews. The table gives an idea of the duties people associate with the people's committee. It is a tally of informants mentioning a specific duty when asked what the functions of the committee are. People might mention more than one duty.

Table 3.5   Duties of people's committees

Duty	No. of times mentioned in the interviews
Development	10
Allocate stands	9
Solve disputes (people's court)	9
Crime prevention (marshals) and safety	8
Liaison with councillor	5
Services	4
Housing	4
Allocate project jobs	3
Lead land invasion	3
Solve problems of residents	3
Attend municipal meetings	2
Negotiations with municipality	2
Organise resistance to eviction	2
Future of settlement	2
Attend to court case	1
Organise protests	1
Do [control] everything	1

Source: Compiled by the author based on field research.

The level of organisation and structure of people's committees vary from simple and sparse to complex and elaborate. Sometimes what passes for a people's committee might be one person or a handful of people operating loosely without any clearly defined division of labour and attending to certain civic matters with varying degrees of rigour and vigour. Committee and public meetings might be held sporadically according to need, and office bearers might serve (long) unspecified terms in the absence of annual general meetings. In other settlements, people's committees are well-developed and formalised bodies consisting of chairpersons, secretaries, organisers etc., and may be at the apex of a system of block and street committees that report to an executive centre. There might be a constitution, a set of guiding policies, well-kept minutes of meetings, a dues collection system, and in some instances the committee might make common cause with an external structure such as Abahlali baseMjondolo. An annual general meeting and a battery of regular meetings are held, including with other committees such as the CPF and ward committee and/or the councillor. The level of organisation will differ between these two poles of simple and complex, intermittent and sustained; a particular committee might exhibit varying levels of organisation in its life cycle.

People's committees may be the original form of committee, because their existence is often traceable to the birth of a settlement, while other categories

Photo 3.5   People's committee leader at home in Vrygrond informal settlement, Graaff-Reinet. (Photograph by author)

of committees are only formed later. This emerges from individual histories of settlements, and is suggested by the fact that 18 of the settlements visited were established before the legislative birth of the ward committees, the second most prevalent committee (see Table 3.1). Ward committees only started operating in the year 2000.[15]

Photo 3.6   People's committee leader at home, Duma Nokwe, in Mdantsane township, East London. (Photograph by author)

The ethos of the people's committees appears similar to that of the township civic movement, whose ideological foundations were 'to build non-hierarchical, participatory forums where everyone was included in decision-making processes'.[16] The people's committee was said to be answerable to the community and was expected to cater for the needs of everyone equally and fairly, for example when allocating stands and when resolving disputes between residents. Informants acknowledged the possible occurrence of self-serving agendas among committee members, but everyone disapproved of this. I give these self-serving agendas some consideration in the in-depth accounts contained in the three case studies.

Photo 3.7   People's committee leader at home, KwaS'gebenga-Khayelitsha, in Ngcambedlana Farm, Mthatha. (Photograph by author)

Ward Committees

Ward committees are statutory bodies created by legislative edict that spells out their composition and function.[17] They were found in 25 settlements visited (45 per cent), tending to co-exist with people's committees, and enjoying sole existence in only three settlements (7 per cent). State policy on ward committees has evolved over time, but the basic idea is that they are forums through which citizens participate in matters of governance at local state level.[18] They are advisory in nature and have 'no original powers and duties', with their functioning governed by the municipal councils concerned.[19] The evolution of government policy has been towards the standardisation of the operation of ward committees, with the government publishing a set of detailed guidelines in 2005.[20] In 2012, the Independent Electoral Commission conducted the ward committee elections where ten members were to be elected to serve for five years, filling the following portfolios: environment and infrastructure, housing, health and social welfare (two portfolios), transport, development planning, community development (two portfolios) and public safety. This approach is called the 'sectoral electoral model', as opposed to the 'geographic model' in the legislation guidelines.[21] Committee members receive a R500 monthly stipend that some municipalities 'top up' to R1,000.[22] The purpose is to cover 'out of pocket expenses', according to the legislative guidelines, which state that 'No remuneration is to be paid to ward committee members.'[23] Committee members receive training. The ward councillor, an elected local public representative, chairs the monthly ward committee meetings. The legislation empowers ward committees to call public meetings chaired by the ward councillor.[24]

There is diversity in how ward committees operate and in their influence. Ward demarcation determines the extent of informal settlement representation. If the ward boundaries coincide with those of the settlement, the latter can enjoy full and sole representation on the committee. But in the majority of cases there is no such fit, and informal settlements will have one or two representatives on the ward committee, and sometimes none. Where committee representation and influence is weak, the people's committee often holds sway, including carrying out the function of liaison with the state. Some ward committees have access to facilities provided by the municipality, such as an office to carry out their duties.[25] Some ward representatives spend time visiting the sick and families in dire straits, help to organise government welfare grants to those in need, help rebuild collapsing shacks, etc.[26] However, researchers into the functioning of ward committees found that '[one] of the more discouraging findings that emerges out of the case studies is how little direct influence ward committees appear to have on council decision-making'.[27]

ANC Committees

ANC committees operate and have influence in some informal settlements. They operated in eight of the settlements visited, mostly co-existing with other popular committees, and in only one case were they the sole committee. Other political parties existed, but were relatively weak. The ANC's presence is pervasive because it has branches in every ward, but some informants complained that it does not service informal settlement constituencies adequately.[28] In townships and/or shack settlements where the ANC is dominant, it appeared to lead the other committees and acts as a hegemonic 'committee of committees', coordinating and supervising everyone, such as in Bhambayi in Inanda, Zenzele in Randfontein and Duncan Village in East London.

Photo 3.8   Members of the civic, ward and ANC committees in Zenzele, Randfontein. (Photograph by author)

A majority of people interviewed critically supported the ANC in government. It enjoys support because it led the national liberation movement. They put their hope in it to build them houses. It is nonetheless criticised by many shack dwellers for being slow in housing provision and failing to provide basic services adequately. However, there is awareness of its potential power to bring development, and influencing it towards this end is an important political project in the informal settlements. ANC leaders often go to informal settlements seeking electoral support for party or government positions – as do other political parties. Failure to deliver on the promises in the course of canvassing support creates resentment, and some informal settlements respond by threatening to withhold their vote, as in the 'No house, no land, no vote!' campaign.[29] Insult is added to injury because there is a feeling that the ANC politically exploits informal settlements' great need for socioeconomic improvement.[30] Dissatisfaction and even hostility to the ANC are rising in some settlements, as the following quotation suggests:

> The ANC lost the ward to the DA [Democratic Alliance] because it is not working. We have been here 25 years with the ANC promising to fix things all these years. People are now saying it is better to go back to Inkatha [Freedom Party]. As leaders we distribute ANC pamphlets but people don't want to see it anymore. Also, we say we are ANC but when we go to the ballot box we don't do what we say [we surreptitiously don't vote ANC].[31]

Community Police Forums

CPFs are statutory bodies that involve communities in crime fighting. They existed in only five settlements (11 per cent), despite the big problem of crime in the country. Informal settlement dwellers tend to be suspicious of the police. In several settlements visited there were no CPF structures despite attempts by the local committees to set them up. Some residents did

Photo 3.9   Leader of the people's committee in Nhlalakahle, Pietermaritzburg, at home. (Photograph by author)

not want police brought into their area 'to arrest us'.[32] This might be because of a desire for freedom and autonomous living away from the prying eyes and heavy hand of the state. In some settlements, the CPF has taken over the functions of the people's courts and community patrols that used to resolve disputes and keep the peace in some working-class areas during the anti-apartheid struggle. CPFs tend to exist in informal settlements where the hegemony of the ANC is well established, the settlement enjoys state recognition, and there is hope of development in the near future.

The CPF consists of a handful of community members that attend joint meetings with the police where crime prevention strategies are discussed. The CPF members interviewed saw their role as supporting the police in fighting crime. Their value lay in their intimate knowledge of their area and the people therein. They reduce the burden on the police and the justice system by, for example, resolving minor disputes.[33] An aspect of crime prevention that is peculiar to informal settlements begins with the stereotype that they are labyrinths of criminality where fugitives from the law are impossible to track down. Residents in built-up areas sometimes

Photo 3.10 Leader of the Malinda Forest CPF, East London, at home. (Photograph by author)

demand the removal of shacks complaining about falling property values and criminality. It is to ward off these allegations that people's committees are sometimes compelled to take measures against criminal activity.[34] Given the high levels of crime, in the absence of a CPF it is the people's committees that carry out patrolling functions and solve local disputes. Informants rank crime prevention and community safety third on the list of the duties of people's committees. The first one is 'development', followed by the allocation of stands (see Table 3.5).

A CPF provides direct access to the police in cases of crime and emergencies such as fires and floods. But sometimes the police are not as co-operative as they should be. They may not provide CPF members with the necessary equipment to carry out their functions, such as identification bibs, torches and the like. The absence of high mast lights, failure to cut long grass and the scarcity of other measures that would make it easier to fight crime frustrate CPF members.[35] Some members have a broad developmental approach and want the youth kept busy by providing recreation facilities, and the provision of counselling services to romantic couples in order to prevent domestic discord.[36] There is a vision of alternatives that goes beyond incarceration and a punitive approach to crime fighting. Meanwhile, the South African Police Service has removed the 'community' in CPF, replacing it with the new 'Sector Policing' programme which is emblematic of a backward slide away from the original progressive vision that informed the formation of these structures.[37] This lost element is arguably an aspect of 'democracy on the margins' that the CPF, as an invited space, had a problem accommodating and is in the process of discarding.

Community Development Forums

Residents establish community development forums to manage and monitor local development projects: the brand-new democratic state originally encouraged communities to form them. They existed in five settlements out of 46, raising the question of why they were so few in areas so much in need of development. Autonomously formed CDFs existed in H39 in Newcastle, in Itireleng in Pretoria and in Makause in Germiston. In the latter case, the then residents' organisation renamed itself the Makause Community Development Forum after a decision was taken to focus on development alternatives for the area.[38] These three CDFs had difficult relationships with their ward councillors, ward committees and the ANC. The opposite was the case in Bhambayi at Inanda, and Duncan Village in East London, where the CDFs were referred to as 'development committees' and worked closely with the ANC, ward committee, people's committees and the councillor. During the era of the Reconstruction and Development Programme (RDP), CDFs existed in many working-class areas. The ANC encouraged their formation in order to realise the goal of 'people-driven and people-centred' development.[39] A couple of years after independence, the RDP office was closed down as the ANC government adopted the Growth, Employment and Redistribution Programme (GEAR), which advocated a capital-driven, trickle-down development model.[40] The CDFs collapsed with the abandonment of the vision. However, some communities have re-established these structures, and the local state may find them useful, but in other cases, such as in Makause in Germiston, their relationship with the state is frosty.

Photo 3.11   Leader of the Makause Community Development Forum, General Moyo. (Photograph by author)

Headman Committees

In South African rural areas, in particular in former bantustans and 'black reserves', government authority is shared between elected public representatives and hereditary traditional authorities. The Communal Land Act of 2000 gives power over communal land to traditional councils, while the Traditional Leadership and Governance Framework Amendment Act of 2003 establishes a governance partnership between traditional councils and local municipalities.[41] The chiefs control land while councillors control municipal budgets in these areas, estimated to comprise about 40 per cent of the population.[42] Headmen or women sit on the 30-member king's or chief's traditional council, with 40 per cent elected and the rest appointed by the chief. This creates a hybrid system of elected and appointed headmen and headman committee members on the one hand, and elected ward committees on the other.

The growth of peri-urban areas represents 'the societal zone where the centrifugal forces of the city collide with the implosion of the countryside'.[43] In South Africa, parts of this 'urban edge' fall under the jurisdiction of traditional authorities; when people move into the urban areas, they erect shacks that make villages located on the outskirts of rural towns to look like informal settlements. The headman allocates stands to the newcomers, handles civil cases, engages in conflict resolution, and acts as the link between the community and the chief or king. He or she does this working with the headman committee. The pressing issues in the traditional areas visited were service delivery and development. Traditional authorities look to municipalities for this, and it provides the basis for co-operation and conflict between the respective institutions of traditional authority and those of liberal democracy.[44] The role of headman committees is neglected by the literature on traditional authorities.

Ad Hoc Protest Committees

Residents will form an ad hoc committee called a 'task team', 'concerned residents committee' or 'crisis committee' to address a burning issue or intolerable pressure felt by the community.[45] These are extraordinary measures, and suggest a failure of the existing committees and official channels to resolve the issue concerned. We can regard these structures as protest committees because protest action usually follows their formation. Many settlements visited had protested or nearly did so at least once. Existing popular committees tend to lead peaceful protests, whereas protests led by improvised protest leadership tend to be disruptive.

In South Africa, informal settlements are at the forefront of the burgeoning protest movement.[46] My research tour of settlements revealed that land invasions and housing occupations are widespread. In Vryburg, the operative popular committees were pushed aside as sections of the community invaded an adjoining RDP housing project.[47] A generational dynamic was involved, as the elderly leader lamented:

> People put me to be the leader because I fought [during the invasion that established the informal settlement]. But today the youth are not paying attention to my committee, they are moving into the RDP houses by force, occupying the new houses. Then they hire out their old shacks. There is no truth anymore.[48]

Researchers have noted the prominent role of the youth in protests.[49] A young committee member reported that he and other youth had led most protests in their village.[50] Many land invaders were young adults under pressure to set up their own homesteads away from their overcrowded parents' homes in Ikageleng township.[51] In a group discussion consisting of youth and adults, the youth insisted that protest action was necessary to register their unhappiness with a ward councillor who did nothing for their area.[52] The youth appear to have the time, the energy and feel the pressure to take action in order to improve their lives.

Sometimes existing popular committees will lead protests, other times they will be unwilling to do so, or they will stand aside and watch, especially if the protests are disruptive. Various stipulations in the legislation, guidelines, constitutions and codes of conduct of ward committees expressly prohibit ward committee members from participating in protest activity while simultaneously affording them little power *vis-à-vis* officialdom.[53] There were mixed views on protests by popular committee members. We can conclude that there is diversity and variation in the approach to protest by the popular committees. Protest tends to create tension, uncertainty and disruption in the functioning of existing committees, especially if viewed in the light of ad hoc protest committees taking the lead.

Photo 3.12   The leader of the Makause Community Development Forum in Associated Mining and Construction Union shirt at the forefront of a march to the Johannesburg mayor's office. (Photograph by author)

RELATIONSHIP OF COMMITTEES TO EACH OTHER

Understanding the committees in shack settlements requires us to take into account the simultaneous co-existence of different committees in a particular setting. The question of the relative power and influence of each of the committees in operation arises. In 25 settlements visited (54 per cent) there was more than one committee in operation. Where there was only one committee in operation in a settlement, it was the people's committee, in existence alone in 16 settlements (35 per cent). This committee co-existed with a ward committee in 9 settlements (20 per cent), and in 6 other settlements (13 per cent) it existed with one or more of CPF, CDF and ANC committees (see Table 3.4). Besides co-existing with a people's committee, the ward committee co-existed with one or more of CPF, CDF, ANC and headman committees in 10 settlements (22 per cent). The picture that emerges is of the prevalence of people's committees followed by the ward committees, and the widespread co-existence of different categories of committees. What form does this co-existence take in practice? What are the implications for theory?

The size of the settlement and the level of organisation coincide. The existence of multiple committees occurs in large urban settlements such as Duncan Village in East London, Bhambayi in Inanda and Zenzele in Randfontein. There exists a high level of organisation, with co-ordination and co-operation between the different committees realised through regular meetings and a system of communication. Smaller settlements will have simpler and fewer structures. The life cycle of some popular committees in the large settlements preceded the new democratic order. For example, Duncan Village had street, block and area committees during the heyday of the civics in apartheid times.

We cannot establish the political character of the committees from their type or category. For example, the CDF in Itireleng in Pretoria is an independently formed committee that is highly critical of the government, the ANC Branch Executive Committee (BEC) and local councillor, while the development committee (CDF) in Bhambayi in Inanda was formed with the blessings of the ANC authorities and is integrated into a system of committees hegemonised by the ruling party. The dominance of the ANC influences the *raison d'être* of the committees. For example, in the Bhambayi, Duncan Village and Zenzele informal settlements the ANC committee dominated all the committees and everyone appeared agreed on, or acquiesced to, the pursuance of the common goal of achieving ANC hegemony in their areas.

In rural areas run by traditional authorities there will be a headman committee and a ward committee. There was peaceful coexistence in the operation of these structures in the areas visited, and co-operation took the form of a representative from the one structure attending the meetings of the other.[54] Disillusion with slow service delivery seemed behind the rivalry that developed between the traditional and municipal authorities in one rural settlement.[55] Studies into the operation of traditional and municipal institutions that explore their *modus vivendi* suggest that the common objective, besides development, is hegemony over the people, with chiefs keen to keep their power on the allocation of land secure while municipalities prioritised party political dominance.[56]

Photo 3.13   Community office in Zenzele, Randfontein. (Photograph by author)

ACCOUNTABILITY OF COMMITTEES TO THEIR COMMUNITIES

The committees claim to act on behalf of the communities they serve. This suggests that they ought to be accountable to their constituency. What mechanisms ensure this accountability, and what is its extent? Almost all the *amakomiti* I came across made the claim that they are accountable to and get their mandate from the people. The method of becoming a committee member differed, from election to self-appointment. In some instances regular elections were held, while in other cases terms of office were more or less a lifetime in scope; for example, in Thembelihle the committee conducts annual general meetings, while in Nhlalakahle the main leader had been holding this position since the establishment of the settlement more than 20 years ago. However, every few years he would ask for a new person or persons to be elected to help him.[57] With some committees, it was clear that the leaders were recallable, and during disputes or dissatisfactions it was common for community members to threaten to recall leaders.

The accountability of leaders can take many forms and be procedurally formal or informal. In Thembelihle the committee has a constitution and calls regular meetings, including weekly general meetings and monthly or bi-monthly 'mass' meetings, whereas in Graaff-Reinet the leader visited people in their homes in executing his duties and would call a meeting according to need. Trust appeared to be an important currency in the operation of the *amakomiti* with people expressing their trust in leaders by seeking their assistance or opting to take their problems somewhere else if they had little confidence or trust in a particular leader or committee. Accountability and trust was reflected in the attendance of meetings. Leaders enjoyed legitimacy if their meetings were well attended. Poorly attended meetings suggested little confidence in the leadership, but also meant that the leaders were accounting to a small section of the community they claimed to lead. For this reason, the methods of calling meetings were important, including the use of loudhailers, the time and venue of the meeting and the topics to be discussed; these factors could affect attendance.

Accountability of the leadership to the people was demonstrated when leaders met with external bodies in the name of the community. Accountable leaders take a mandate in community-wide or committee meetings and report back. In some instances community members would be suspicious of leaders, accusing them of 'working for themselves' in the sense that when they met external authorities, they sought personal gain as a priority. Leaders could be accused of 'selling out' when they took the side of the enemy or external entity in return for money or favours rather than carrying out the people's mandate. In Nkaneng the local leadership rebelled against the ANC because it objected to nominating a ward councillor candidate who was viewed as an opportunist in this sense. There is also accountability with respect to resources (money, goods, property) that leaders were in charge of on behalf of the community. Leaders proved their mettle by being honest and desisting from abusing such resources or using them for themselves.

In general, accountability of *amakomiti* to their communities did not necessarily correspond with the degree of formality of procedures such as written constitutions and regular elections of leaders. However, these mechanisms were important safeguards and markers of the seriousness with which *amakomiti* and their constituency regarded accountability. Demanding and enforcing accountability is easier when one can point to procedures and processes that have been agreed upon and are known by all.

RELATIONSHIP OF COMMITTEES WITH THE STATE

The relationship of the popular committees to the state is complex, diverse and dynamic. With respect to the people's committees, their relationship to the state varies from antagonistic to symbiotic in ways and permutations that do not fit neatly within the invited versus invented spaces theorisation.[58] Relations tended to be adversarial where the settlement was established by way of land invasions.[59] The people's committees that lead invasions are fighting committees that are antagonistic to the state. Nonetheless, at some point (the 'consolidation' phase of the settlement) the community turns to the state for assistance in the provision of basic services. The state may be uncooperative and only provide water tanks or install communal taps as a constitutional obligation. Alternatively, the state might accept the de facto existence of the informal settlement and later develop plans to formalise the settlement, provide services and build houses. But even so, it might take a long time to provide the most basic of services. In the informal settlements surveyed, 30 out of 46 (65 per cent) shared communal water taps, 32 (69 per cent) had no access to electricity, and 18 (39 per cent) were not provided with sanitation irrespective of de facto or de jure recognition by the state.

Engagement with the state may lead to a loss of independence or autonomy in the long term. In some areas, we find people's committees that work very closely with the local ANC councillor, the ward committee, the CPF and the ANC BEC such that they can be seen as part of the architecture of ANC hegemony and state control. Other people's committees will jealously guard their independence and continue to play the role of demanding services from the authorities. Maintenance of adversarial relations with the state may eventually translate into withdrawal of electoral support for the ANC, as happened in Jeffsville and Thembelihle, where the community organisations ran independent candidates in local government elections.[60]

In most cases, the relationship of the people's committee to the state, or to the ward councillor as the government's local agent, is ambiguous or ambivalent, as the following two quotations suggest:

> Sometimes our councillor comes, she talks well and she makes promises. She too will finish her term without doing anything [like the others before her]. But she might do something, we don't really know.[61]

There is no *toyi toyi* here because we think for our councillor. You see, we grew up together, she is our *sisi* [big sister]. But we clashed one day in a meeting. I asked her why when she formed her committee she did not include us [from the informal settlement]. We also clashed over water. I told her we don't want disrespect and that I had trusted and hoped for much better [from her].[62]

The relationship of ward committees to the state is not straightforward, even though they are established by the state. The ward councillor is central in the operation of the ward committee, both as chairperson of the meetings and as the lynchpin between the committee and the municipality. Some ward councillors were reported to be doing well in ensuring the successful operation of ward committees and fostering healthy relations with the communities they served. In other instances, some ward committee members were in constant conflict with the ward councillor and there was disaffection in the community. In one case, the ward councillor stopped attending ward committee meetings for four months, at which point the community broke out in protest and, among other things, burnt down the councillor's house.[63] This incident took place in a township sharing a ward committee with Top Village, an informal settlement in Mahikeng. Shack settlement inhabitants may be drawn to support such action since they have grievances of their own, but often their ward representatives find themselves conflicted. They need a stable structure and reliable communication channels to convey the many needs and grievances of their community to the state, and may be less interested in power struggles involving people living in brick and cement houses that they may view as ANC 'politicking'. Some ward and people's committees members positioned themselves neutrally in relation to such fights, hoping that a working relationship with the councillor was a more certain route to bringing development to their areas.[64]

The relationship of the CDF to the state depended on whether the community formed the committee autonomously or because of state prompting. In Itireleng settlement, the autonomously formed CDF was in competition with the ANC for control over resources, development projects and community support. In contrast, in Bambayi, the 'development committee', formed with state sanction, worked well with all structures and seemed to police the project work, making sure it did not stop and no materials were stolen. From another perspective, one can be critical of such a role and see it as falling short of the RDP's expansive vision of the CDF as a conceptualiser and overseer of projects on behalf of the community – 'people driven and people centred development'.[65]

Photo 3.14   Members of the community development committee in Bhambayi, Inanda, Durban, at the local projects office. (Photograph by author)

The Itireleng CDF demanded the right to a more expansive role in development – a challenge supported by the community – but this led to a total breakdown of relations with the (ANC) ward councillor, who then refused to call or attend any public meetings in the area.[66] Although CDF structures were originally conceived as politically non-partisan, in Itireleng, Makause and H39 it is not so. The attempt to keep alive the vision of popular participation in development as espoused by the RDP is a struggle against the top-down model currently in operation, whereby the state conceives, develops and finalises projects, and the people must accept the outcome. Sometimes even the ward councillors did not have much say over development. Often the only thing left for communities was to protest in order to register their development preferences.

PROTEST IN THE SETTLEMENTS

Protests are widespread in South Africa.[67] A significant proportion of the protests take place in the shack settlements, as Table 3.6 indicates. About 13 per cent of households live in 'informal dwellings'; this means shack dwellers are overrepresented in protest action.[68]

Table 3.6   Protests in South African informal settlements as a percentage of total number of protests

	2004	2005	2006	2007	2008	2009	2010	2011	2012	*Total*
No. of protests	1	31	12	36	32	66	59	39	99	375
Percentage	7.7	29.2	24.2	24	19.5	21	23.4	18.9	21.1	21.5
Total no. of protests	13	106	50	168	162	314	252	206	470	1,741

Source: B. Maruping, Z. Mncube and C. Runciman (2014), 'Rebellion of the Poor Quantitative Data Analysis Report', unpublished internal report of the Research Chair for Social Change Protest Monitoring Project, University of Johannesburg, adapted by author.

In my survey of settlements, I did not witness a protest, but my informants told me about one or more protests that occurred in their area. Table 3.7 indicates the number of informal settlements that had protested within the previous five years.

Table 3.7   Incidence of protests over the previous five years

Incidence of protests	*No. of settlements*	*% Where N = 46*
Settlements that protested	25	54
Settlements with no protest	17	37
Unknown	4	9
Total	46	100

Source: Compiled by the author based on field research.

The protests took the form of marches and/or disruptive action such as blocking the roads with burning tyres. There was a more or less even split between these two forms of protest. The high frequency of protests reflected in Table 3.7 is broadly in line with the protest monitor studies referred to earlier.

I asked my informants what the protests were about, and they mentioned the protest issues in Table 3.8. There is a commonality between these protest issues and those identified by the Research Chair for Social Change Rebellion of the Poor protest monitoring project (see Figure 3.1).

Table 3.8   Protest issues

Service delivery	4
Against councillor	4
Water	3
Houses	3
Waste removal	2
Electricity cuts	2
Roads	2
Recreation facilities	1
Sewer project stopped	1
Jobs .	1
Crèche	1
Employment in project	1

Source: Compiled by the author based on field research.

Why did some informal settlements protest and others not? Questions of leadership and organisation – in short, agency – appeared to be critical in this respect. There is a lot of dissatisfaction in the informal settlements, as Table 3.9 indicates, but organising a protest requires leadership and a specific conjuncture, and depends on the response of the authorities. What seems pivotal is the role of the ANC. Well-organised settlements and those in which the ANC is dominant tend to have fewer protests. It moves quickly to quell protests by persuasion or threats, facilitated by having its ear to the ground. However, sometimes people will protest regardless. Table 3.9 lists issues that irked informants about their living conditions irrespective of whether or not there had been protest in their area.

Shack dwellers are unhappy about many things. Researchers have suggested that the notion of dissatisfaction with the 'quality of democracy' appears to capture and crystallise the underlying causes behind the protests.[69] Viewed together, the protest issue 'against councillor' in Table 3.8

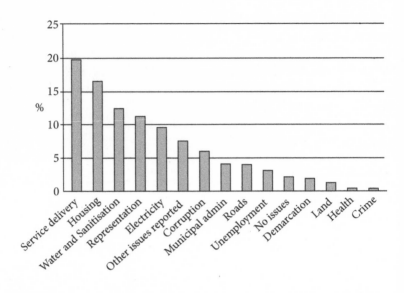

Figure 3.1 Issues in South African protests, with housing second on the list of grievances

Source: P. Alexander, C. Runciman and T. Ngwane (2013), *Media Briefing, Community Protests 2004–2013: Some Research Findings*, Johannesburg, South Africa: Social Change Research Unit, University of Johannesburg, 12 February, p. 8, https://issafrica.s3.amazonaws.com/site/uploads/Public-violence-13March2014-Peter-Alexander.pdf (accessed 21 October 2020).

Table 3.9 Issues that residents are unhappy about (disaffection)

Issue	No. of times mentioned
Housing	38
Services	18
Development	17
Electricity	11
Water	9
False promises	6
Schools	4
Toilets	3
Clinics	2
Status/future unclear	3
No hope	3
Jobs	2

Source: Compiled by the author based on field research.

and the grievance 'false promises' in Table 3.9 corroborate this view. People want substantive democracy that brings positive material improvements in their lives.[70]

COMPLEXITIES AND VISIONS OF *AMAKOMITI*

The existence of a multiplicity of committees run by the people themselves in the shack settlements of South Africa is phenomenal. It needs explanation. I have suggested the concept of 'democracy on the margins' as a heuristic device to grasp the specificity of this form of self-organisation and self-governance. In this chapter, we have seen how different communities have different combinations of committees in existence, how a specific category of committee does not operate the same way from one settlement to another, and sometimes from one period to another in the same settlement. We have also seen how the co-existence of committees in different combinations and permutations gives rise to relationships between the committees that shape the character and operation of each committee. Furthermore, the entry of the state into the sphere of the committees introduces new dynamics with the possibility of a variety of outcomes. The complexities involved suggest that there are no 'ideal typical' committees; there is a lot of unevenness between committees, power dynamics, instability, success, failure etc. All committees must respond to the specific conditions and challenges they and their communities face.

Committees are shaped by the conditions and challenges they face on the one hand, and the manner in which they respond and act upon these conditions on the other. It is hard to predict what they will become. Some may turn out badly, as we have seen, and others not. 'Democracy on the margins' is underpinned by the belief that, however we judge *amakomiti*, for shack dwellers they exist as part of the struggle to control and change their reality in order to meet their needs. As such, it is best to study them inspired by a vision of developing knowledge systems that contribute to the cause of human emancipation.[71]

4

Fatal Embrace by the ANC in Duncan Village

There are more shacks than formal houses in Duncan Village, a township in East London, in the Eastern Cape. There are backyard and stand-alone shacks, with the ratio of shack to brick house estimated as three to one.[1] What is perhaps unique about *amakomiti* in Duncan Village is that their operation reveals a close connection between shack dwellers and township residents. The connection goes back many years, into the days of the struggle against apartheid. In this chapter, I tell the story of how the area committees, the dominant 'people's committee' in '*eDuncan*', the embodiment of 'democracy on the margins' if you like, lubricate and cement this unity of shack settlement and township. We will see how shack committees are shaped by specific historical, political, social and economic conditions found in particular localities and intersecting with broader societal and global processes. A major finding and conclusion that I came to after my research was that the area committees of Duncan Village are an essential component in the construction and maintenance of the hegemony of the ANC as a movement and as government in the area. 'People's power' during the height of the anti-apartheid upheavals in the 1980s gave birth to the area committees that were then a component of the militant civic, the Duncan Village Residents Association (DVRA). Today, these committees are part of the complicated architecture of ANC hegemony whose key aims are maintaining law and order, organising local development and winning elections in the new democratic order.

SHACKS, SHACKS AND MORE SHACKS

Duncan Village is a very densely populated township with an extensive shack-land situated a handful of kilometres away from East London, a coastal city in the Eastern Cape. Housing consists of standard apartheid 'matchbox' council houses, single-sex hostels, post-apartheid Reconstruction and Development Programme houses and new housing estates built by Mercedes Benz and other companies for their workers. Everything else in between, behind, in front and across the houses consists of shacks and more shacks. There is the congestion, chaos and ultra-vibrancy of a multi-layered, poorly planned and overcrowded township. Understanding Duncan Village's history helps in making sense of and connecting with the place by giving meaning to the physical structures and images that flood the eye.

According to estimates, about 100,000 Duncan Village people live in 6,000 formal and 15,000 informal dwellings. The latter are divided into 11,500 free-standing and 3,500 backyard shacks.[2] In 1994, Duncan Village was identified as a Presidential Priority for the Reconstruction and Development Programme; however, nothing much seems to have happened with the area, plagued by high unemployment rates (55 per cent), poverty and lack of adequate facilities, especially for the thousands of households living in informal dwellings.[3]

THE DUNCAN VILLAGE RESIDENTS ASSOCIATION

White police attacked a Defiance Campaign meeting called by the ANC in 1952, leaving nine people dead.[4] This happened in the East Bank area, the precursor to Duncan Village, a place which apartheid also killed in 1960. The state demolished the people's tin houses and relocated them by force to Mdantsane, in what was to become the Ciskei Bantustan, 25 kilometres away. Some residents relocated to Duncan Village, but only those meeting the apartheid-stipulated criteria of employment, male-headed households and length of time living in the city. Life in the slums of East Bank had been hectic but exciting, like Sophiatown,[5] and people knew each other well. The economic circumstances of the people in Mdantsane and Duncan Village worsened, and gradually, starting in the factories and later spreading into the living spaces, the smouldering embers of struggle flared up.

Both Mdantsane and Duncan Village experienced a growth in community activism and resistance to apartheid in the 1970s, and especially in the 1980s. The loss of South African citizenship by Mdantsane residents made people very angry.[6] Also, apartheid's 'border industries', meant to employ commuters from the bantustans, did not take off, and in any case, labour conditions there were repressive.[7] At the forefront of the resistance was the community-oriented and militant South African Allied Workers Union (SAAWU), whose leadership strived to unite labour and community struggles.[8] It had a major influence in the formation of community organisations in Duncan Village, Mdantsane and other townships. A civic structure, the Duncan Village Residents Association, organised the residents and youth into a fighting force against apartheid, and its impact changed the course of history in this small township.[9]

With its antecedents in 'the old anti-removals committee', the DVRA had organised functioning street, block and area committees by 1984.[10] It borrowed its model of organisation from Matthew Goniwe, the leader of the Cradock Residents Association (Cradora), about 280 kilometres away, as did many other townships in the country, modifying it to suit local conditions.[11] The power of the DVRA on the ground suggested 'a peculiar form of dual power'.[12] At the height of the struggle, some commentators were describing the 1985–1986 political situation in many South African townships in these terms, albeit with some qualification.[13]

INSURGENT TOWN PLANNING AND YARD SOCIALISM

The DVRA took aim at what was arguably the rampart of grand apartheid's urban segregation policy, namely its housing and influx control policy. The apartheid regime faltered momentarily as the relentless *amaqabane* ('comrades', 'militant youth') deposed the local government councillors, seen as regime stooges, leading to a retreat of the local state and leaving a power vacuum. In an unprecedented move, the DVRA, taking advantage of the situation, encouraged thousands of rural and urban folk to flood the area and occupy backyard and stand-alone shacks – something that apartheid's influx control laws had expressly prohibited.[14] This was partly revenge for the historical forced relocation of people to Mdantsane in the 1960s – something the apartheid local state was apparently still intent on doing with respect to some people of Duncan Village in the 1980s.[15] By so doing, the DVRA revolutionised the built environment in Duncan Village. Its method included allowing tenants to set up shacks in people's yards, sometimes against the will of the homeowner, and with the tenant not necessarily required to pay rent – 'yard socialism'.[16] People also set up shacks in open spaces. The quid pro quo was 'joining the struggle' – that is, among other things, supporting the rule of the DVRA and *amaqabane*, which included subjecting yourself to their justice (people's courts) and participating in the people's governance structures (street, block and area committees). This revolution against apartheid urban planning and private property fundamentally changed the demographics and the socio-spatial configuration of Duncan Village, leading, for example, to a fourfold increase in the population of the township, which had a great impact on social relations. Greg Ruiters has described it as a form of 'insurgent town planning'.[17]

The DVRA was arguably 'hegemonic' in Duncan Village during the height of its powers. It managed certain aspects of township life according to its own improvised laws. In addition to being in charge of allocating space to erect shacks, it also took care of crime prevention and ran a people's court to deal with offenders. As one informant said:

Crime was not reported to the police. Some people resisted subjecting themselves to people's justice. I remember someone who refused to present himself to a people's court; he left Duncan [Village] and never came back because he knew he had erred. Some people left like that, we said *uwel'ulwandle* ['he crossed the ocean'] [laughs].[18]

The DVRA was, from the struggle point of view, an expression of the power of the community *vis-à-vis* the apartheid local state. It contested the state police and justice system's power over the community. It was thus also a power over the community, in the sense that residents had to heed and yield to its power, as the quote above suggests. At the local level, as Trotsky would put it in his definition of dual power, the DVRA had, 'although not yet master', indeed 'actually concentrated in its hands ... [a] share of the state power'.[19]

FREEDOM!

Hardly a few years passed, and following a period of intense repression, the apartheid government relented and bowed down to the pressure. In 1990, it unbanned political organisations, freed political prisoners and initiated negotiations to prepare for a democratic transition.[20] During this transition, the civic and the popular committees continued to operate in Duncan Village, but priorities changed fundamentally with the changing political context. The ANC successfully put itself at the head of the mass movement, and its presence opened up new debates about the strategic orientation and role of the civic structures.[21] The debate was about the role of civic structures *vis-à-vis* the ANC. One outcome was the formation of a national civic structure, the South African National Civic Organisation (SANCO), in March 1992. The ANC-SACP leadership viewed SANCO as best suited to play the role of a supportive development partner to the envisaged ANC government, rather than 'playing a watchdog role' as suggested by some civic leaders.[22] The DVRA became a local structure of this new national body called SANCO.[23]

The period from 1990 to 1994 was one of negotiations and political re-alignment and reconfiguration of organisational structures. The ANC emerged as the leading political organisation, and became stronger with the formation of the ANC-SACP-COSATU Tripartite Alliance in which SANCO participated as the 'plus one' of the trio. SANCO structures got busy in local negotiations, preparing the ground for the new local government, including sorting out some sticking points such as rent boycotts and racially defined municipal entities.[24] In 1995, it was able to nominate comrades to run as ANC candidates in the first democratically elected local government structures in the country.[25]

The activism of comrades during this period and their unity cemented by the 'Tripartite Alliance plus one' meant that many leaders would wear many caps – that is, be members of two or more of the Alliance structures – giving rise to the 'two hats' debate.[26] SACP cadre in exile had always worn two hats because they operated in the ANC, but hid their communist party membership.[27] Oliver Tambo, the ANC patriarch in exile, developed a leadership ethos whereby cadres serve the organisation selflessly and gain seniority through the length and distinction of their service in its various structures as directed by the leadership. Just like the members of the movement, the cadre, were seen as part of the 'ANC family',[28] so were, arguably, the different components, branches and divisions of the broader movement perceived; they were all part of the family. The driving force behind the democratic transition was a movement consisting of many organisations striving for more or less the same ends.[29] In practice, the most active comrades would be members and leaders in all the structures of the 'Tripartite Alliance plus one' (ANC, SACP, COSATU and SANCO).

Table 4.1 Timeline of committees in Duncan Village

Name of committee	Description	Term of office
South African Allied Workers Union	The union played a key role in mobilising the community	1980s
East London Youth Organisation	Formed by SAAWU to organise and mobilise township youth, giving rise to the *amaqabane* ('young lions') of the DVRA	Formed in 1982
Duncan Village Residents Association	A civic structure that organised and oversaw the formation and operation of yard, street, block and area committees	Formed in 1984, disbanded in 1993
Area committees	Operating mainly in Duncan Village's informal settlements	Formed in 1984, in operation today
ANC committees	The ANC 'took over' the political leadership of Duncan Village when it was unbanned, with the co-operation of the DVRA leadership; five ANC branch committees operate in Duncan Village, corresponding to municipal ward demarcations	Unbanned in 1990, and still operating today
South African National Civic Organisation	The formation of this national body of civics signalled the beginning of a period of crisis for the DVRA and other civics in the country as they struggled to redefine their role in the face of ANC political hegemony	Formed in 1992, and still operating today
Ward committees	Statutory structures that work closely with elected ward councillors in Duncan Village's six wards; they mostly work closely with and under the direction of the ANC committee, including other committees such as the community policing forums, but other political parties participate now	2006–present

Source: Compiled by the author based on primary and secondary sources.

The explanation of the wearing of many caps is important in understanding the nature and character of the committees operating today in the shack-lands of Duncan Village, in particular why many committee members serve or have served in different committees and do not see this as a problem. The different categories of committees operating in Duncan Village are: (a) area committees, (b) ward committees, (c) ANC committees and (d) development committees, CPF and other committees.[30]

'I LIVE IN AREA 8, AT ZIPHUNZANA'

Area committees are the main category of popular committee, the most prevalent and most active in Duncan Village. They are the original people's committees that were set up during the heyday of DVRA people's power, and have survived into the democratic era with features traceable to the anti-apartheid days. Other committees from this era, such as street, block and branch committees, have not fared well in the new order, with many becoming defunct and their functions taken over by area committees and by the new committees such as ward committees, ANC committees and community policing forums.[31] There is a consensus among the committee members who were my informants that area committees are the closest and most representative of community interests. They are part of a glorious history, and they represent the community 'as a whole', that is, along non-party political lines, in the spirit of the old civics.[32]

Where did the area committees fit in the old civic structures and committees? The organisational template developed by Matthew Goniwe in Cradock had to be adapted to different local conditions.[33] Moreover, some civics were in existence before Goniwe's model.[34] There were the backyards with shacks and the stand-alone shacks. Activists took yard problems to the street committees. A handful of streets combined to form a block, and each block elected representatives that would join with others to form an area committee. An area committee consists of 15 members. As a former DVRA committee member recalls:

We had committees in the yards, and a rep was elected from each yard. About 50 yards would elect ten people to represent them in the area committee, for example, Area 5. The ten reps met every Sunday to discuss issues pertaining to life in Duncan, challenges and developmental issues. In Duncan [Village] Proper, we designated eight areas.[35]

We should note that Duncan Village consists of several areas: Duncan Village Proper, Ziphunzana, Gompo, Bebelele, C-section, D-section etc. These areas have different features – for example, D-section consists of the former single-sex hostels, while another area will consist of mainly of stand-alone shacks interspersed between clusters of formal houses. This means that the basic organisational structure of the civic is modified to suit each area. The 'area' might have become important as a unit because it more readily suits the adjacent location of a combination of formal houses and backyard shacks that are clustered behind them, and streets where the houses stand in rows and clusters of shacks occupying the open spaces of the townships. 'Blocks' were probably harder to define in areas characterised by stand-alone shacks, thus an area was defined as a handful of blocks adjacent to each other. One area I visited had about 200 stand-alone shacks.[36] The DVRA divided Duncan Village into about 20 areas, with each allocated a number, for example Area 1 or Area 2.[37] Even today, if you ask someone where they live, the answer is: 'I live in Area 8, at Ziphunzana.'

POLITICAL ORPHANS

Area committees are elected in a general meeting held mostly annually; by-elections are sometimes held to replace members who have stopped being active. Area committees call regular weekly meetings when operating optimally.[38] The old area committees united under the 'branch', the DVRA, which was run by an elected central committee. The DVRA became a SANCO branch probably in 1993, after the formation of the national civic structure during the transition from apartheid to democracy.[39] Internal power struggles led to the demise of the SANCO branch, and today the area committees do not have an umbrella body that unites and co-ordinates their operation. There are, however, instances when adjacent area committees meet to discuss issues of common interest. Once a quarter, the ward councillor of a particular ward will call a general meeting and all the relevant area committees will attend. Without a branch, the area committees report to their constituency and to ANC structures, the ward committees and the councillors.[40] In township struggle language, 'the area committees do not have a mother body'.

WARD COMMITTEES

In Duncan Village there are five wards, each with its own ward committee.[41] The ward committee members receive a stipend of R1,000 from the municipality. To become a ward committee member, you need to self-nominate through a process involving the collection of signatures from people who support your candidacy. Securing nomination inside the ANC can involve competition that requires the aspirant candidates to win the support of several structures such as the area committee and the relevant ANC committee. Many informants decried the competition among comrades, contrasting it with the altruism and sacrifice associated with the anti-apartheid struggle:

> The Freedom Charter says 'the people shall govern'. This means that when your turn is over, there is no need to fight, your term has expired. If we don't want to elect you because you haven't done much, give us a chance to elect someone else who we think will do what we want. But due to incentives, comrades kill each other, beat each other, burn down your house for the position.[42]

There is not a lot of benefit from being a ward committee member, but being on the committee could possibly increase one's chances to get other positions or benefits, for example gaining employment in the various state-led local economic development projects, having a say over who gets employed, or being considered for nomination as a candidate councillor. Many informants suggested that to qualify for nomination, comrades must prove themselves through long and loyal service.[43] They have to work themselves through the various structures of the ANC and community.[44]

Ward committees work closely with the ward councillor, who chairs the monthly meetings. Members are required to sign a code of conduct that prohibits them from acting independently of or against the councillor or the municipality.[45] In Duncan Village, there is also a regulation that ward committee members cannot call community meetings, these can only be called by the area committees.[46] This is an interesting improvisation, but

Photo 4.1   Member of a Duncan Village ward committee soup kitchen team preparing to cook. (Photograph by author)

it hampers independent political action by ward committee members: 'We signed a contract that we cannot meet without the councillor – she is an ex officio, we can talk but we cannot meet without her.'[47]

On the one hand, the ward committees are there to facilitate public participation in local government; on the other hand, various mechanisms are in place to limit and hamper their independent political action. The new structures appear to diminish rather than enhance the grassroots participatory democracy of the DVRA days. The following quotation suggests the ascendancy of control over participation in the operation of the ward committees:

So when ward committees started, the street committees died off because it was understood that the people in the ward committees will do every-thing, but they don't. ... You find that it is only those who support the councillor who are part of the ward committee.[48]

'THE ANC LEADS'

There are five ANC Branch Executive Committees in operation in Duncan Village because of the alignment of ANC branches to local government voting ward demarcations. All popular committee members are members of one or other local ANC structure. I did not come across one non-ANC member among all the committee people I talked to. A comrade could be a member or office bearer (for example, chairperson, secretary) of the ANC Branch Executive Committee, the ANC Women's League or the ANC Youth League. Councillors often hold elected positions on the ANC BEC, and if not, they are ex-officio members – that is, they sit on the BEC because they are councillors. The ANC BEC is pivotal in the Duncan Village power structure or good governance model, according to my informants. It was the lynchpin between the ANC as government and as movement, the local political centre.[49] One BEC member insisted that a councillor could not do anything without the BEC.[50] The all-ANC personnel and the importance of the ANC BEC suggest the ubiquitous influence of the ANC on Duncan Village's popular committees. Since the ANC branches coincide with wards, the ANC organisation is closely in touch with developments on the ground while politically aligning the ANC as a movement to the ANC as government. The slogan of the ANC-SACP-COSATU Alliance is 'The ANC Leads', and this is clearly the case in Duncan Village, as all the important decisions affecting the community emanating from the government are first filtered through and cleared by the ANC structures.[51]

I spent a few hours at a ward councillor's office wherein were kept work tools (shovels, rakes, wheelbarrows, etc.) for a public works programme cleaning project. Workers came in to collect the tools during the conversation I was having with the councillor. A supervisor guided the process and took instructions from the councillor, who was sitting at her desk. Later, when I had a chat with the supervisor, she told me that she was an area committee chairperson. This suggested that in Duncan Village, there is close co-ordination between state processes and civic matters as far as the operation of popular committees and state-driven local development projects are concerned. This process is facilitated by the dominance of the ANC, and as a corollary, the fact that the opposition political parties are very weak and that SANCO no longer enjoys an independent existence because it does not have a branch structure. Without a branch, there is no central locus of power, thus leaving its constituent structures (the area committees) to get direction from the ANC. Meanwhile, the operation of ANC structures tends towards close alignment, and even symbiosis, between the ANC as government and as movement or party. The result is near total hegemony of the ANC over local politics, and no doubt this furthermore assures ANC victory at the polls.

OTHER COMMITTEES IN DUNCAN VILLAGE

There are other committees in operation in Duncan Village. I was able to interview one committee member of the Community Policing Forum that links the community and the police in the fight against crime. These structures meet according to a state protocol and under the direction of the police. There are also people active in the community under the title of 'community development worker' who are employed by the provincial government to facilitate development issues and improve liaison between the state and the people, for example by helping social grant applicants. There was a sentiment expressed that these structures did not fit properly into the operation of the popular committees, and there was some confusion about how they were supposed to work with the other committees.[52]

COMMITTEE RELATIONS

The area committees are the structures that are closest to the ground, calling weekly meetings attended by ordinary residents. They deal with everyday problems such as minor disputes among residents, developmental or service delivery issues such as problems with water, electricity and housing, and may nominate people for employment in state-led projects. They are expected to feed the councillor with information about the needs of the people, and in theory this is done through the ward committees or through the quarterly ward general meeting, but in practice some councillors attend the area committee meetings themselves when they deem this necessary or are called upon to do so by the committees. Since many area committee members are also members of the ANC branch committee, they give reports of their work there and get information that they pass on to their constituencies:

There is cooperation between ward committees and area committees. Area committees are on the ground, ward committees only have ten people, they can't service 10,000 people. Area committees help with communication on the ground.[53]

The area committee takes up issues like service delivery to the upper structures. Issues like crime, dirt, electrical poles, jobs, housing .... We want to know why we are still living in shacks but we voted in 1994. We have our meetings as the [area] committee, and general meetings with residents on Sundays. We get their needs, and then we go to the councillor, and then we report back. There are 154 legal shacks in my area and about 50 illegal ones.[54]

The relationship between committees is not always smooth or clear. For example, some committees are viewed as more important than others, and sometimes protocol is not followed. In one instance, a ward councillor expressed a very low opinion of ward committees and preferred to work directly with area committees.[55] He was a stalwart local leader from the days of the DVRA, and exuded a confidence and independent-mindedness based on experience and a legendary struggle pedigree. He could arguably get away with his defiant attitude and breaking of party policy because of power derived from his seniority in the movement. He was not the only informant who had a dim view of the ward committee as a structure.

Payment or 'incentives' can create problems in committee relationships. The incentives can serve as a disincentive, in that, for example, area committee members are not paid at all, but some of them may feel that they do an equal amount of, if not more, work than the ward committees. An examination of the life history of a committee member suggests that among some comrades there is a personal career strategy involving waiting for one's turn to get onto a paying committee or gain employment in a local project.[56] Long service on a non-paying committee creates an expectation that eventually the party will reward the comrade. One area committee chairperson who landed a paying job as a toilet attendant said that other people competed with her for the position, but she felt she had been hard-working in her service to the community and as such deserved the job.[57] She was unhappy about accusations that committees allocate jobs to themselves or to comrades, family and friends.[58] It is plausible that, whether by accident or design, the committee members through their interaction soon get to know each other and will collude and/or compete with each other when opportunities appear.

Community and political work that comes with payment, called a 'stipend' by the comrades, includes work in a ward committee, being a ward councillor, employment by the municipality, employment by the provincial government, a job as a community development worker, or a job in the Expanded Public Works Programme (EPWP) or Community Works Programme. Payment levels differ considerably. Community development workers are hired by the provincial government and are paid better than ward committee members. They are facilitators or liaison officers who connect the township people with the provincial offices. Workers in the EPWP receive standard rates that are on the low side. The Department of Transport and Public Works, in conjunction with other departments, employs large numbers of people on a temporary basis to carry out specific infrastructure and maintenance jobs locally. In 2008, the state initiated the Community Works Programme as the second phase of EPWP. Workers earn about R65 a day for at least eight days a month.[59] Municipalities identify work needs in specific wards, thus creating the job opportunities. In Duncan Village, the local structures are the ones that identify potential workers through the area committees, ward committees, and are supervised by the ward councillors, who in turn are instructed or supervised by the ANC branch structures.[60] The power to provide lists of workers for employment is important in the life of the various committees in Duncan Village.

COMMITTEES AND THE MASSES

Members of the community who are not part of the committee structures tended to express a lot of dissatisfaction with the operation of the committees.[61] There exist unbearable socioeconomic challenges in Duncan Village related to unemployment, poverty, inadequate housing, overcrowding, crime etc.[62] The committees serve to provide a channel for community grievances, and one can go to them if one has a problem. They also provide the necessary information about developmental issues. But development is slow, with many shack dwellers impatient to get houses. The building of new communal toilets, the promise of electricity connections, the provision of a soup kitchen and so on, do placate the masses and keep their hopes up, but impatience is growing. It was apparent that one of the main jobs of the committees was to explain government programmes to residents, showing how development was both happening and in the pipeline, partly as a mechanism for preserving the legitimacy of the government. The committee members complained that some residents did not want to understand processes, that they did what they liked, for example erecting shacks in areas where they are not supposed to, and that some of them tried to instigate protests and revolts against authority:

> The people who cause protests are those who don't attend meetings, maybe there will be three or four of them. They like turmoil/violence. ... People just put up a shack anywhere without a plan or in the wrong area. If you try to stop them as committees, they want to build by force. They are ungovernable, and this leads to protest.[63]

There were suggestions of political motives behind protests, such as the following allegation: 'That ward councillor used to organise protests. Now he got the position he wanted. But today he is facing protests [against him].'[64]

An ordinary resident who had been very active in the DVRA in the old days felt that dissatisfaction was high because today there was less grassroots democracy. What passed for participatory democracy in the form of the various committees was not genuine or enough. It looked like the people were participating, but the decisions were actually made at the top:

> Yes, it is participatory democracy from above. They [committees and government officials] must be fed by us, we must tell them what we want, not that it is them who tell us what we want. Even if I am hungry, it doesn't mean that I want bread. Maybe I want *umnqushu* [samp, crushed maize], which will make me full. Maybe I am allergic to red meat, but that is what you give me. You must ask me: 'What can I do for you?' Or even better: 'What can we do together?'[65]

Protests are widespread in South African townships and informal settlements. In Duncan Village, protests appeared to be rare, and confined to particular sections of the township when they did occur.[66] Some researchers suggest that the rate of protest might be increasing in recent times.[67] The committee members emphasised how transparency, constant communication with the people and timeous response to grievances was important in stemming the tide of protest. Some were proud of the fact that there were few protests in their ward, connecting this to their co-operative work with their councillor despite the ward having the largest number of shacks in Duncan Village:

> There is very little protest, we are united in this ward, we love each other. If someone [a comrade] is not there, we phone each other and ask: 'Where are you?'[68]

> It is not usual to have protests here. Our councillor works with the people. As soon as we hear that there is something not going well, we say, 'Councillor, please go and explain to the people about this or that.' The councillor moves quickly to solve that problem.[69]

In an incident where a young man called a meeting agitating for a march, he was reported to the police, who came and warned him against calling an illegal protest. The protest did not happen:

> The police told him [the would-be protest leader] that he had no permission to stage a march. We supported the protest issue – houses. There are no houses here. But we don't want something illegal. That boy wanted people to go to the municipality and cause chaos (*ukumosha*) there. We wanted a legal protest. In South Africa, unless you stand up, nothing will happen. People were happy with the call for protest because it was about housing.[70]

It was also suggested that where councillors did not work harmoniously with their committees, whether ward or area committees, there was always the possibility of factionalism and the instigation of protest action.[71]

Photo 4.2 shows a Duncan Village resident connecting electricity wires to the shacks. I spent the whole day with a team of five young adults busy making new connections and sorting out old connections with problems. They connect to transformers located high up on poles or streetlights. They did this openly, and no one accosted them. They had no problem with my videotaping the whole exercise and interviewing them on record. Some committee members, including one ward councillor, made it clear that they disagreed with illegal connections, but they could do nothing because the people needed electricity. Clearly, on this frontier, the masses have managed to push the state back, and current discussion of the issue revolves around the envisaged government project to electrify the shacks.

Photo 4.2 Connecting shacks to the electricity grid in Duncan Village, East London, without state sanction. (Photograph by author)

THE ANC BEAR HUGS *AMAKOMITI*

'I can't breathe!' the area committees might be feeling as they struggle to fulfil their historical mandate from DVRA days of representing and fighting for the needs of the masses. This is because of the apparent symbiosis between the ANC as movement and as government with the community structures. Cross-cutting membership and the political histories of individual comrades suggest this. It seems the power of the ANC lies in aligning its political structures closely with state and civic structures. The bond is strong and it goes back in time, as the case of one ward councillor I interviewed suggests. She is a female councillor who was born in the area, and worked her way up through the ranks of the block and the area up to branch level. She knew her area well, actively co-ordinated the work of the various committees, and attended as many area committees as possible to keep in touch with residents.[72] Her modus operandi suggested the desire and the ability to synthesise the work of the ANC as government and as movement on the ground. Her political practice is interpretable, from one point of view, as indicating the manner in which the ANC has effectively taken over the political position and symbolic space once enjoyed by the DVRA and successfully united this with its role as ruling party. The councillor said that her focus was on development, and she thought of the government as not only governing, but having a mission to improve the life conditions of the people. As she explained:

> You can't solve the problems of this area [as a ward councillor] when you never lived through them. I grew up in the shacks. Those area committees were there during apartheid, there were no ward committees then. The ward committee cannot know all the needs of the people, there is a need for area committees to channel people's grievances.[73]

And as one informant explained, referring to the councillor under discussion here:

> You must make an agenda when you call the councillor. But the councillor is not allowed to attend our meetings, but she attends because she is a resident, she is a child of this ward, she was born here. She can attend, and I don't think she can get into trouble if she does that.[74]

The councillor was a busybody. She had an office that was located in a double-storey building located on a busy street in Section C in which the state rents the first floor. An ANC Youth League office bearer and secretary of the ward committee managed her office. He received residents who came with their concerns and problems seeking help. At certain times in the morning during my observation of the operation of this office, several other ward committee members came in. They sat in the office that had about ten chairs along the walls and the secretary's desk at the far end. They talked about their work and got involved discussing a problem brought by a resident concerning housing. Soon after, the councillor came and was briefed on developments, and she in turn gave a report on some errands run and matters attended to at the municipal offices in town. After about an hour of discussion with me, the circus moved to another room in the building where there were piles of food to be prepared for a soup kitchen apparently run by the state. Ward committee members and some other women who were all comrades did the peeling and cooking in an adjoining kitchen. The councillor gave some instructions, then took me to another room where we conducted the interview.

As we talked, her role image, in my mind, changed seamlessly from politician to social worker, to civic leader, to ANC leader, to ANC Women's League leader, to mother etc. In other words, she embodied the complex and dynamic intersection and overlap between the various roles and spaces occupied by the ANC on the ground in Duncan Village. She arranged for people to be interviewed, and all of them had good things to say about her, especially how she worked hard and involved everyone. She made it clear how careful she had to be to balance and cultivate all the interests and forces in operation in her sphere of work, including higher government and party structures. Being a 'good' councillor requires a lot of skill, energy, patience and a positive attitude, it seemed to me.

In the course of our conversation, she acknowledged the pressure involved in her work. She also pointed out how she had to keep her ear to the ground, be in touch with comrades, area committee leaders etc. She also talked about the need to walk about and talk to ordinary people to keep in touch, identify problems and be accessible. She had her hands full because delivery was slow: for example, her ward had the biggest number of shacks in Duncan Village. She did her best under the circumstances, keeping people informed of developments, searching for and implementing 'soft' delivery programmes such as the soup kitchen, making sure that her ward accessed government programmes such as the Community Development Programme etc. However, the power to change people's lives lay somewhere else: 'As councillors, our hands are tied, we see parliament on TV like everyone else, we have no power.'[75]

The ward councillors appear to embody and to be the lynchpin at the point of overlap between the ANC as government and as movement. In Duncan Village, two of the ward councillors I interviewed, the one discussed in this section and another one, had a long history that went back to the days of the DVRA and the struggle against apartheid. Both talked a lot about the importance of the people, but were very clear on the need to maintain support and always project the ANC positively. The councillors are the ambassadors and key organisers of ANC hegemony in the local sphere. Their location in government and in the community made their interaction with Duncan Village's committees arguably pivotal in shaping and cementing ANC hegemony.

SLIPPAGES, OPENINGS AND POSSIBILITIES

It is hard to understand Duncan Village fully without reference to its history as a township organising and fighting against apartheid in the 1950s and the 1980s. Its very physiognomy as a shack-overrun area reflects this. As one resident opined in her autobiography, the proliferation of shacks turned her beloved Duncan Village into 'a virtual squatter camp', and that was an observation about the late 1950s,[76] before the DVRA's 'insurgent town planning' that increased the shacks fourfold. To maintain law and order and guard its hegemony over the area, the ANC government has developed a tightly interwoven system of committees that includes modified structures from the DVRA days, new structures such as ward committees, ANC party structures and state structures co-operating in keeping it together, as it were. This is a Herculean task in the light of the great developmental challenges and apparent shortage of state resources to significantly and quickly improve the conditions of the people. My research revealed the centrality of this mission and the role of the different actors in carrying it out: ward councillors, ward committee members, area committee members, ANC BEC leaders and state structures. It is a daily and arduous task for some, and brings to mind Gramsci's insight that as a process, hegemony is concrete, contingent and conjunctural.[77]

The picture I have painted of the architecture of ANC hegemony is of a somewhat cast-iron grip over local state and community political processes. I have referred to instances where protest action has been pre-empted and prevented because of this. However, I would argue that a closer reading of my account reveals both constraints and possibilities. As Gillian Hart has argued, it is possible to identify 'the slippages, openings, and possibilities for emancipatory social change in this era of neoliberal capitalism, as well as the limits and constraints operating at different levels'.[78] I referred to a committee member who had opposed protest action because it involved *ukumosha*, but had also stated that 'in South Africa unless you stand up, nothing will happen'. Pithouse is in agreement with Hart on the importance of 'the local state' and 'the local' as key terrains for challenging policies and structures that serve the minority, and not the majority.[79] With respect to the politics of the committee members, their role as informants in the course of my interviews probably constrained them in painting a more positive picture of their work and their party, the ANC. However, we cannot be categorical because 'political subjectivities can neither be read off the structure of socio-economic relations nor deduced from hegemonic discourses'.[80]

An aspect worth noting is that daily political practice in Duncan Village, its links to the political history of the place and the present enmeshment with the ruling party suggest the existence of a specific political culture that defines the place.[81] As a researcher, I felt this in that after a few days in the area and talking to committee members in particular, I started to 'tune in' to the dominant discourse and outlook, namely the acceptance and promotion of the ANC as government and movement even as comrades were aware and willing to talk about its shortcomings. However, people made critical comments 'appropriately'. Conversations with ordinary community members, and especially those who were politically active (outside or on the margins of the framework of the committee system), revealed perennial and sharp criticism of the ANC, especially in relation to its housing delivery record. These observations suggest the importance of the twin concepts of 'political culture' and 'ANC hegemony' in making sense of the operation of the popular committees in Duncan Village. I will revisit these concepts in Chapter 7.

Is the concept of 'democracy on the margins' useful in making sense of local democratic practices and the operation of committees in Duncan Village? An important difficulty is the entanglement of people's committees – the area committees – with party and state structures arguably in the context of a legitimising ideology that supports a social order characterised by inequality. This suggests that the democracy of the marginalised is subordinate to and supports the ruling elite. Some features of 'democracy on the margins', as theorised in this book and related to the daily struggles of the people, may be reconfigured and diluted by their association with the hegemonic practices and purposes of the power structure. The dynamism of grassroots forms of democracy are stifled by the mechanisms of state control that require predictability and continuity rather than the unpredictable effervescence and insurgency of popular action.

The revolving doors and conveyor belts of the Duncan Village committee structures facilitate comrades' upward trajectory from grassroots structures in which they are volunteers into state bodies that pay stipends and salaries. In other words, the voluntarist ethos of 'democracy on the margins' lives and works side by side with the corporatist ethos of the (capitalist) state (bureaucracy). Similarly, area committee members who answer to their constituencies have to contend with state structures that require loyalty and accountability to themselves. All these considerations arguably serve to redefine 'democracy on the margins' in Duncan Village. However, we should note the 'slippages, openings and possibilities' that occur in the process of exercising hegemony.[82] The power structure arguably maintains area committees because their 'democracy on the margins' characteristics are necessary in the legitimisation of the status quo and its political processes. The existence of these characteristics leaves open the possibility of challenging the dominant order by activating the insurgent elements of 'democracy on the margins'.

The popular committees in operation in Duncan Village are similar in structure and function to committees found in other South African informal settlements, but there are certain historical and contextual specificities that influence their operation. In Duncan Village, the ANC has continued to maintain its hegemony over local politics and the committees, although protests are beginning to proliferate. The background to this is the history of the popular committees and their operation going back to anti-apartheid struggle days, when the DVRA briefly exercised a kind of 'dual power' and pursued policies that fundamentally changed the socio-spatial dimensions of the area. The ANC has been able to take over this legacy, including maintaining the operation of the same structures and personnel as in the old days. This has helped it to be hegemonic despite failing miserably to address the developmental needs of the area, including housing, electricity and employment. The popular committees, in particular the area committees, are part of this architecture of hegemony, but they are not mere conveyor belts for the ruling party and the state. The dynamics of the situation, including insurgent attitudes and actions, the rising anger and frustration about lack of improvement in people's lives, and the increasing combativeness in the mood of the working class are such that the committees act as barometer, lightning rod, brake and safety valve of this mood. For example, they work to pre-empt protest, and this requires a close ear to the ground. Their adoption of an attitude of acceptance to the practice of electricity self-connections suggests retreat in the face of mass pressure. They are not immune to the general mood, and they share the hardships of life in the shacks. As such, they occupy an ambiguous and dynamic place between the 'invented' and 'invited' space dichotomy, where the former suggests a greater degree of political autonomy *vis-à-vis* the state, and the latter incorporation into the state's political and developmental agenda.[83] The 'democracy on the margins' ethos which informs the operation of people's committees such as the area committees finds itself in a contest with the dominant liberal democratic form. Recent political developments in Duncan Village such as the rise in protest action suggest that the balance of forces between the two is constantly changing.[84] The area committees might escape the suffocating embrace of the ANC after all.

5

Iinkundla of Nkaneng:
The Rural in the Urban Dialectic

The contrast between the abject poverty of the Nkaneng shack settlement and its location in the platinum belt with its large amounts of platinum, chrome, tin and other minerals is disconcerting.[1] The Rustenburg landscape boasts the highest density of shack settlements in South Africa, with most located next to specific mine shafts and some adjacent to built-up recently constructed working-class townships.[2] The shacks multiplied in the area when many miners left the single-sex apartheid-era mine compounds and erected shacks not far from their workplaces. Invariably, the shack settlements that emerged sprouted *amakomiti*.

In this chapter, I discuss a unique type of committee that the platinum miners living in the shacks have created which is modelled on traditional local governance structures found in the deep rural areas of the Eastern Cape: *iinkundla*. The words *inkundla* (singular) and *iinkundla* (plural) are isiXhosa language for an African chief's court in the rural areas. These committees appear to be an improvised elaboration of the documented 'homeboy' and 'homegirl'[3] (*umkhaya*) social networks migrant workers historically relied upon to mediate access to the urban centres to which they migrate.[4] There is Inkundla yaseLibode, meaning 'the *Inkundla* of Libode', Libode being the name of a village back home. Other villages will have their own *inkundla*. These structures exist side by side with other more modern forms of committee, namely ward committees, ANC committees and community policing forums. *Iinkundla* not only raise interesting questions about the relationship of the traditional to the modern, and the rural to the urban, they also underline the agency of shack dwellers, who clearly tap on their past experiences and world view in order to put their stamp on the type of *amakomiti* they form.

A HOME FROM HOME ON THE PLATINUM BELT

Rustenburg is a city located in a platinum mining area 112 kilometres north-west of Johannesburg. The main and dominant economic activity is mining. Mining has contributed 23.3 per cent of North West Province's economy and comprised 22.5 per cent of the South African mining industry.[5] It is painful that despite its 'rich array of natural resources ... the North West Province is one of the poorest provinces in South Africa'.[6] The Gini coefficient 'is above 0.6 in the Province, placing it among the most unequal regions in the world'.[7] Unemployment in the province stands at 40 per cent, while Rustenburg city's year-on-year growth for the five-year period up to 2012 was 10 per cent.[8] Most of the country's platinum comes from Rustenburg and Brits, with South Africa meeting 70 per cent of global demand.[9]

The population growth in Rustenburg is higher than the country average due to in-migration of job seekers, mainly from other parts of the province and to a lesser extent from other provinces (10 per cent from the Eastern Cape), and 7 per cent from South Africa's neighbouring countries.[10] According to municipal figures, 17.6 per cent of the population live in the town's 24 informal settlements,[11] while independent researchers put this figure as high as 41 per cent.[12] Poverty levels are high in Rustenburg, with 50 per cent of the population recording zero monthly income, 11 per cent earning less than R800 and 38 per cent recording less than R3,200.[13]

By the end of the 1990s, the number of unemployed migrants swelled; thousands of employed and unemployed lived in informal backyard and stand-alone shack settlements.[14] Rising unemployment levels have resulted in 'an even more desperate reserve army of labour than in the early days of migrancy', creating conditions for the continuation of the super exploitation of labour.[15] Contracting out, labour broking and various labour cost-saving machinations by mining capital have resulted in 'unacceptably low wages, poor conditions and low union levels [affecting] at least a third of labour hired by mines'.[16] The mining companies did not share with workers the profits from the 2000–2008 commodities boom.[17]

The settlement called Nkaneng, also known as Bleskop, is found along the D108 road on the way from town to Marikana. It is called Nkaneng ('by force') because it was born of a land occupation.[18] It is called Bleskop because of its location next to the Bleskop Vertical Shaft, owned by Anglo American Platinum (Amplats). The settlement consists of approximately

4,000 structures with an estimated population of 11,879.[19] Right next to the settlement is the Bleskop mine compound or hostel. The settlement is on flat ground to the west of a hill and is situated about 3 kilometres away from Photsaneng, a small formal township that is partly controlled by the Royal Bafokeng Administration, the traditional authority. It is important to note that since the 2006 local government demarcations, Nkaneng and Photsaneng, an informal settlement and a built-up township, fall under Ward 33, and as such share a ward councillor, ward committee and an ANC branch committee.[20]

The settlement lacks basic services such as electricity, proper sanitation, piped water and community facilities. The road infrastructure is poor yet designed in a grid format, and each shack has its own yard. The shacks are mostly made of corrugated iron. Poverty and uncertainty about the future of the settlement discourage residents from using brick and mortar for building; there is a hope that the state will build houses for the informal settlement dwellers. Some shacks have ventilated pit toilets courtesy of a government project that ran out of funds before completion. Water is ferried into the settlement, and at certain times on certain days, residents can be

Photo 5.1   Crèche in Nkaneng owned and run by Ms Gladys Kani. (Photograph by author)

seen queuing with their vessels waiting for the water truck. The several fixed green water tanks that are elevated above the ground seem not to be in use. Privately owned *bakkies* (small trucks) roam the settlement's roads selling water to community members. The advantage is that residents can get the water at their gates. People rely on wood, coal and paraffin for their energy. At night, it is very dark because there are no streetlights.

There are no community facilities such as halls, sports grounds and parks. Community gatherings and meetings happen in an open space marked by a thorn tree in the midst of the shacks. Church services take place in people's shacks, with some built slightly larger than normal for this purpose. There are a few ramshackle general dealer stores built of brick and mortar; there are numerous *spaza* ('informal') shops in the form of shacks that have a big 'window' on a side wall that serves as a counter.

The people who live in the area represent a cross-section of the working class. The majority appear to be unemployed, self-employed and/or under-employed workers. Mine jobs are preferred, but increasing use of labour brokers exposes mineworkers to precariousness.[21] Many residents are migrants, in that they maintain strong ties with their homes and families in the rural areas. However, many recent migrants could not secure formal employment and find themselves 'in an increasingly marginal position economically, reliant on informal activities, or on poorly paid and insecure work in the formal sector (e.g. security and domestic work)'.[22] Many come from the 'deep rural areas' where poverty levels are high and employment prospects slim. Cox, Hemson and Todes provide a list of these areas defined in terms of poverty, geography and rural status.[23] Some areas mentioned in the Eastern Cape are Libode, Ngqueleni, Qumbu, Mqanduli and Lusikisiki. It is from these areas that the members of the *Iinkundla* of Nkaneng come from.

HISTORY OF THE COMMITTEES IN NKANENG

Nkaneng, like many informal settlements in the area, sprang up at the birth of the democratic South Africa during the relaxation of influx controls and when the platinum mines were expanding phenomenally in response to the increased global demand.[24]

Many workers took advantage of the freedoms bestowed by the post-apartheid Constitution and made their own way, rather than through the recruitment agencies such as Teba, to booming towns such as Rustenburg to

Photo 5.2   Nkaneng settlement with the Bleskop hostel visible in the background.
(Photograph by author)

seek employment. They had to arrange accommodation for themselves, and many rented backyard shacks in established townships such as Photsaneng. Nkaneng informal settlement emerged by way of a land invasion that at first was a trickle of people who walked away from their rented accommodation in Photsaneng, crossed the mine railway line and set up the settlement on a bushy plain next to the Bleskop hostel. The major pushes were the unbearable high rents and a desire to escape the control of landlords and enjoy some freedom and personal space:

I came here in 1994, I think May. I was there on the first day of this settlement. The committees cut enough space for your shack, they didn't use any string. We came in numbers like pigs released out of a sty, we all came out. We escaping [*sic*] the oppression of the landlords in Photsaneng. We paid R70 rent, R20 if my brother and his wife visited me for one night. You had to clean a toilet you didn't use, sweep the yard. We were oppressed.[25]

We came here because of suffering. I came in 1996. I came here looking
for a job but never found it. We came because we are free in South Africa,
we can live anywhere we like. But there is discrimination here, they say
this is the land of the Bafokeng. I cleared the bush to erect my shack, I got
permission from the committees. Yes, they were ANC committees, the
leader was Cairo.[26]

The move also represented liberation from Lucas Mangope, the then
Bophuthatswana Bantustan president, whose police often raided workers
at night demanding permits to be in the area. Many interpreted this
enforcement of influx control laws as a form of tribalism. The bantustan
was officially the 'homeland' of SeTswana-speaking people. Many miners
were migrants from the Eastern Cape and other parts of South Africa and
Southern Africa; SeTswana was not their home language.[27] The release of
Nelson Mandela from prison and the ANC taking power also defined the
moment. Indeed, on 18 October 1997, Mandela came to address the locals
at the Bleskop Stadium.[28]

The exodus to the promised land was led by a young man named Cairo
who was an ANC supporter. He appears to have been an early ANC organiser at a time when the party was still establishing itself and had no problem
with people invading land and establishing settlements. The land invaders
had to cut down the bushes and clear the ground in order to erect their
shacks. Even though life was hard and there were no basic services provided
in the new area, the people felt free and to some extent in control of their
own destiny:

Cairo never wanted money, he sat down and said, 'This is what I think.'
He asked you what you think as the community and mostly we agreed
with him. He forced [matters] to get us this area. No one can kick me out
from here. I will tell them it is Cairo who gave me this area. He called
it 'All Nation Village'. We are free here, we got independence in South
Africa. Mandela said we can live anywhere we want.[29]

This highlights the interaction between local and national politics, including the development of a national identity. Cairo and his comrades allocated
land to the people who came over to join the few shacks that had been set up.
Each household received a piece of ground sufficient to accommodate the

size of a shack. Some people say it was free, and others say they were happy to pay the R5 that was required.

Cairo's committee was the first one in the area. It was an ANC committee-cum-civic because at the time the only organisation was the ANC (later, the United Democratic Movement [UDM] made inroads into the area). Subsequent committees have had a tumultuous history. Several years after the settlement was established, Cairo began to experience opposition to his role as leader of the settlement. Some employed miners in the area indicated their dissatisfaction with his regime, slandering him as a loafer (he was unemployed) who spent time with their women while they were at work.[30] Cairo soon left the settlement, and people say he set up another one near Marikana. Since then, several committees have been established at different times with varying lifespans whose birth and ascendancy often involved tensions, and sometimes violence. These committees are: a civic-type 'street committee', the Five Madoda committee, the ANC committee, the community policing forum, the *iinkundla* and the ward committee.[31] At any given time, two or more committees have mostly co-existed in the settlement, namely a people's committee (civic, street committee or Five Madoda), an ANC committee and (later) a CPF. However, at one point a Five Madoda committee and a civic or street committee co-existed in parallel and in competition – that is, two 'people's committees', according to my definition. The ejecting of Five Madoda from the settlement resolved the tension. With the *iinkundla* committees, there are at least five structures operating simultaneously based on the five towns or villages that people originate from in the rural areas. Table 5.1 provides a summary and timeline of the various committees in past and present Nkaneng, including a brief description of each committee's history and role. There is a lot of overlap in the periods of existence of the committees because they often existed simultaneously.

Commentators have noted that organisations that 'are involved in state-like performances such as security enforcement' in fact engage themselves 'in a perpetual renegotiation of the boundaries between state and society'.[32] This is true of all the committees that have gained ascendancy in Nkaneng. The first committee run by Cairo allocated stands, engaged in matters of 'development' such as water provision, resolved disputes and fought crime.[33] The state was largely absent. The overthrow of Cairo's committee was because of the emergence of the Mouthpiece Workers' Union in 1995, a rival of the National Union of Mineworkers (NUM), which started infiltrating

Table 5.1   Timeline of committees in Nkaneng

Name of committee	Description	Term of office
Cairo's committee	Established the settlement; acted as the first people's committee or civic	1994–1999
Five Madoda	Associated with the trade union Mouthpiece; operated a powerful dictatorial people's court; dissolved violently in 2004	1998–2004
Street committee or civic	A civic structure related to Cairo's original committee; a people's committee, it allocated stands and ran a people's court; it was eclipsed by Five Madoda, but later re-emerged; today defunct, and its functions were taken over by the CPF, *iinkundla*, ANC and ward committees	2004–2011
ANC committee	The ANC enjoyed support early in Nkaneng; an ANC local committee engineered the ousting of Five Madoda; today, the Ward 33 Branch Executive Committee spans Nkaneng and neighbouring Photsaneng	2002–present
Community policing forum	Initially fighting crime and serving as a people's committee or street committee, its notoriety led to its restructuring in 2006 with reduced powers, today supervised by the police and by other committees in the area	2007–present
Iinkundla committees	Hometown networks; initially focused on burials, but later acquiring dispute resolution and crime fighting powers; acted as political broker during 2012 by-election	2002–present
Ward committee	Statutory structure, working with ward councillor; focuses on development; once a strong ANC base, but now less partisan after the disastrous 2012 by-election	2006–present

Source: Compiled by the author based on field research.

and setting up structures in the informal settlements around the mines.[34] The new union contested the NUM at the workplace and at the workers' living quarters, in particular in the hostels. Targeting living spaces was an NUM strategy, and its dominance of the hostels helped it recruit.[35] The struggle for dominance in the workplace reproduced itself in the workers' living spaces.

Mouthpiece set up a Five Madoda ('five men') committee that made inroads into Nkaneng as soon as it had a secure foothold at the hostel.[36] A power struggle ensued, with Five Madoda building their own office/court next to the one operated by the ANC-aligned 'street committee', the latter a continuation of Cairo's original committee.[37] This continued for a couple of years, but later the street committee stopped operating.

The people's court took place in a special shack called the 'Tin House'. The Five Madoda lost their power after the demise of Mouthpiece, and eventually ANC-aligned community forces drove them out violently.[38]

Afterwards, there was the revival of the 'street committee' under the leadership of Comrade Ntohololo; he also operated the Tin House in addition to other activities. The focus then, as with the Five Madoda, was on crime prevention; this involved night patrolling, imposing curfews on shebeens for the sake of order and resolving disputes at the courthouse.

IINKUNDLA PLAY THEIR HAND

Ntohololo died, and leaders with hard hands took over. They were accused of being abusive in their application of people's justice; it was said they handled cases with partiality, they 'arrested' people, levied fines and used torture.[39] This provoked a reaction from the community, with *iinkundla* committees, which hitherto had focused on burial issues, beginning to demand extension of their powers to include dispute resolution, a move designed to protect members from the harsh justice of the Tin House.[40] Another solution by the community was the setting up of a CPF structure. The latter fell into the hands of leaders who tried to transfer the activities of the street committee to the CPF using the newfound authority of this statutory structure. Night patrols continued, the Tin House continued, curfews continued, there were allegations of a protection racket extorting the Somali-owned shops, etc. It took a woman to solve the problem, when Nkaneng's first ward councillor led the community to restructure the CPF, excluding the rogue elements from the new structure.[41]

The fall from grace of the CPF and its problematic leadership came at the same time as the rise of the ward committee that, in the context of Nkaneng, assumed the functions of a developmental structure and a people's committee. It focused on development issues linked to local government and addressed local problems and social issues. However, some residents still feel the vacuum created by the absence of a 'civic' or 'street committee':

> After they closed down Mouthpiece, new committees were operating, then that was stopped because of infighting. They closed down the house where the cases were held. They used to solve our problems. We are suffering because the Tin House was closed down. The men of *iinkundla* closed it down. We are in the location [urban area or township], not in Idutywa [a rural town in Eastern Cape], we are from different areas. We need [people's] committees.[42]

Meanwhile, the *iinkundla* committees became increasingly important in the political life of the settlement, moving from social functions to jurisprudence. They increasingly sought to limit the power and jurisdiction of the people's court, and had the support of many residents in this effort. The *iinkundla* committees proffered an alternative cultural, juridical and procedural foundation for solving local disputes and crime prevention that contrasted with that of the Tin House. They called for a traditionalist and rural communal approach to dispute resolution and dealing with victims and perpetrators of crime. Their strategy was to claim jurisdiction over residents who came from a particular area's *inkundla*. They said the Tin House had no jurisdiction over such people and only the *inkundla* from their village or town (using the law of that village) could judge them. If a dispute involved people from different villages, then the relevant *iinkundla* committees had to meet to find a solution. If a culprit faced the justice of another *inkundla*, his or her *inkundla* should be present and represent the person. This contrasted with the justice of the Tin House community court that tried and sentenced people as individuals by 'self-appointed' judges and prosecutors.

When in 2006 Nkaneng nominated and voted for its own ward councillor, the ever-changing, ambiguous and constantly negotiated relationship of the popular committees with the state was reconfigured. The new councillor had been a community worker for about a decade before her nomination.[43] She tells her story, saying she swung into action trying to bring development to the area and stabilising the tumultuous operation of Nkaneng's popular committees:

The green water tanks you see were installed by me. I got support from Xtrata [mining company], they installed 12 tanks. I started with the roads, talked to the government. I got a grader to scrape the roads. Some Portuguese set up a clinic in a container. We also set up three crèches, one of them is still operating. I came with the toilet project, I signed for it. It was done only half-way. It was the municipality, you know, they go this way and that way, chowed the money. In 2010, I pushed to get land for the settlement because we are living under the [Bafokeng] king. The municipality promised some land near Karee, but then my term ended in 2011.[44]

She left office when in 2011 the ANC nominated a different candidate to become councillor, this time a comrade who resided in Photsaneng, who unfortunately very soon died of illness. The ANC nomination process to replace the deceased in the 2012 by-election was very controversial and has marred local politics to this day.[45] It divided the local ANC into two. The Rustenburg ANC Region, led by the mayor, imposed an unwanted candidate on the community, the same disgraced leader of the CPF and people's court. He had even run against the ANC on a Democratic Alliance ticket when he failed to win nomination as candidate in 2011. To make matters worse, the ANC branch members had already nominated their candidate. The blunder by the ANC Region was due to factionalism in the ANC that tragically revealed itself when a whistle blower, Moss Phakoe, was murdered:[46]

We were told that when we go out [end our term of office as councillors], we'd be catered for, for example be given a job to clean offices. Moss Phakoe was killed for anti-corruption. The mayor was stealing cars. He was shot in September 2009, it was on a Saturday. From then on, there were two cores [factions]: the mayor's and Phakoe's. Phakoe tried to help us. We who were Phakoe's core were kicked out. Today, I can't do anything because I belong to Phakoe's core.[47]

The result was that the community was force-fed the unwanted candidate. The ANC branch revolted and urged its candidate to run as an independent candidate. The independent happened to be the ANC Youth League chairperson in the ward. The *iinkundla* committees were persuaded to support the independent candidate. He won.

To conclude, this section shows the historical entanglement, mutual influence and competition among the popular committees in Nkaneng. We can also see the influence of broader processes such as the role of the ANC Region, the power struggles between unions and the creation of state-community structures such as the CPF. It would be very hard to understand the twists and turns in the physiognomy of the committees without some knowledge of the history of local politics in Nkaneng.

IINKUNDLA AS PEOPLE'S COMMITTEES

The *iinkundla* are important in Nkaneng, although they are not necessarily the most active, influential or popular committees. They are not centrally involved in development matters; this role is allocated to the ward committee. Their involvement in crime fighting and dispute resolution is recognised, but is somewhat contested by the existence of a CPF and police hostility to the running of people's courts. They earned their role as key political players in the area during the election of the independent councillor, yet they are not politically partisan, as their members tend to belong to different political parties.

There are at least five *iinkundla* committees in operation in the community: the Libode, Mqanduli, Ngqueleni, Qumbu/Mount Frere and Lusikisiki/Flagstaff *iinkundla*. Each name refers to an area in the Eastern Cape where the migrants come from. Workers from Southern African countries also group themselves according to their country or province of origin: for example, Mozambicans in the settlement have meetings where they collect money needed in the event of a death or other serious calamity, with the balance shared out at the end of the year.[48] To be a member of an *inkundla*, you have to be a 'homeboy/homegirl'. You must also participate in the affairs of the *inkundla* by attending its meetings and paying the financial contributions required. Collectively appointed or approved male elders manage each *inkundla*. Women are active as secretaries of dues and membership records in some *iinkundla*. The different *iinkundla* have separate meetings unless there is a need for a joint meeting.

Iinkundla concern themselves primarily with deaths and dispute resolution. They operate a burial scheme whereby you make regular or one-off money donations to subsidise transportation and funeral costs of a deceased *umkhaya* ('homie'). They also engage themselves in dispute resolution and in criminal matters, where they apply a form of restorative justice. Serious crimes are referred to the police.[49] Support for the independent candidate in 2012 redefined and extended their role as significant political players in Nkaneng. The independent councillor consults with *iinkundla* in his work, thus they appear to be increasingly playing a developmental and political role.[50] I was able to attend two *iinkundla* meetings in the course of my research: the Mnqanduli and Libode *iinkundla*. The meetings showed how *iinkundla* instil and appeal to a sense of belonging and tradition while carrying out very practical and mundane functions.

Photo 5.3 Inkundla yaseLibode ('the *Inkundla* of Libode') meeting. This meeting consisted of goat owners worried about and discussing the problem of stock theft in the area. (Photograph by author)

More than 100 people attended the Mnqanduli meeting, held on a sunny Sunday morning under the protective shade of the bus shelter next to the Bleskop hostel. There were tables and chairs to the front for the leadership and the many secretaries-cum-treasurers to sit, including special guests. The spirit of the meeting was celebratory and buoyant, as if people relished being together with their fellow villagers even though the subject of the discussion was sombre. Indeed, after the meeting, about a quarter of the crowd, consisting of the key people, office bearers and special guests, remained behind and crates of beer and cool drinks were brought for refreshment. Some people used the post-meeting commotion to meet people they had not seen for a while, and others to inquire about their membership dues.

The Mnqanduli *inkundla* general meeting was discussing plans to transport the body of a young person who had died. A funeral undertaker was present to discuss coffin and transport prices. Pointed questions were directed at the undertaker, the leadership and the crowd, and answers provided – all done with a delicate, sensitive and impressive use of language, including huge doses of rhetorical flourish, debating skill, humour, irony and idiomatic expression. This helped the meeting to grapple with and make decisions in a public and democratic fashion on issues such as what type and price of coffin to choose. The leaders of the Mnqanduli *inkundla* clearly regarded the meeting as a success, and perhaps a broader triumph for their leadership and/or the collective. Unity, compassion and competence appeared to be important values. The meeting appeared to affirm collective identities.

In contrast, the Libode *inkundla* meeting was much smaller, consisting of ten men and two women who sat in a half-circle in a shack yard on wooden benches and improvised seating. The focus of the meeting was the problem of stock theft in the settlement. Some members of the *inkundla* reared goats, and someone was stealing them. The meeting discussed steps to be taken to curb the problem, including approaching the police and requesting them to set up roadblocks and not allow the transportation of livestock unless papers were produced proving ownership. The meeting was kind enough to dedicate about 30 minutes of its time to a group interview, answering my questions about the *iinkundla* system. The answers underlined the genesis, rationale and development of the *iinkundla* in the area. What the speakers emphasised was exasperation with the crime situation in the area, the excesses of the so-called crime fighters who themselves acted criminally, and the reign of terror residents had been caught up in. This led to the search for an institution that would help the community deal with the problem in an effective and sensible manner. The chosen institution was the generations-old tried and tested *inkundla* system. The system facilitated a collective approach to the problems while providing a moral and social foundation as a guideline for the practice:

We don't belong here, we came to work. When we saw the problems here, we remembered where we come from, that we belong to different kings, we are together, but we come from different areas. We were reminded when we saw people dying. We thought the best way is how we live at home. The kings co-operate with each other. So if there is a killer, we call each other as members from towns to find out what is going on. If there is a case and there is no one from your area, it is as if that person is being prejudiced, you must come with people from your town.[51]

The *inkundla* system came into existence as a challenge to the 'street committee', an institution whose idea originated in the (urban) township civics. Its detractors label it as a backward-looking, rustic institution that should not operate in an urban area.[52] Their leadership is illiterate and lacks understanding of developmental issues, said someone who claimed a benign attitude towards the institution.[53] One interviewer responded when asked about *iinkundla*: 'Oh, you mean the traditional leaders.'[54] However, when I asked them about their vision for the informal settlement, the Libode *inkundla* responded in a forward-looking manner that married rural and urban developmental goals:

Where you work, it is like home, it is even bigger than home because we live here for 12 months and only spend one month at home. It must be a good place to live in, and not like what it is now, like it is for sheep. It must have electricity, they must build houses, there must be water to drink besides that which is brought in by the municipality [in tanks].[55]

The *inkundla* members also distinguished clearly between their role and that of the ward committee, which they saw as a conduit for local government, but not a people's committee representing the community: 'You need *iinkundla*, a committee to look after the people and the community. The ward committee is about service delivery, it is not about governing this place.'[56]

In conclusion, while the origins of the *iinkundla* committee system as a social institution are traceable to the rural areas, it is my contention that in both form and content it differs significantly from the rural version because it fulfils different needs and is implemented in a different sociocultural and economic context. For example, none of the leading members of *iinkundla* were chiefs or of royal blood. They began their operation in the informal settlement as 'homie' networks and social support groups in the event of emergencies and bereavements; they extended the scope of their work in order to have some control and protection in the social and communal life of their members in the urban working environment. Kinship and common village origins, and the importance placed on these, are the political and cultural foundations of the *iinkundla* committee system on the one hand, while practical and useful tasks such as organising funeral collections, solving disputes, fighting stock theft and other crimes provide the material basis for the recognition and authority of the *iinkundla* on the other hand. The trajectory of the *iinkundla*, as the narrative above suggests, is understandable in the context of the political culture in Nkaneng, especially as it relates to migrant workers trying to have some control over their living spaces. We can see the flexibility and adaptation of traditional social institutions to changing circumstances and their ability to traverse the urban–rural spatial divide and past–present temporalities.

WARD COMMITTEES

Ward committees are an innovation introduced by the ANC during its second term in office by legislation to enhance participatory democracy at local government level.[57] In Nkaneng, as in other parts of the country, this had the effect of forcing these new structures to jostle for space in a context where popular structures of grassroots representation were already in existence. The ward committee works with the ward councillor, who chairs it, thus connecting poor working-class communities to the government for the development and improvement of the area. Ward committee members occupy 'portfolios' such as healthcare, water and sanitation that correspond to government functions and departments. The ward committee thus operates in a manner that is analogous to a 'cabinet' of the ward councillor on local government and developmental matters – it is there to help the councillor and the government to get the job done. In Nkaneng, this allowed the other committees to continue carrying out their functions while surrendering the developmental space to the ward committee.

In theory, the ward committee ought to be non-party partisan because development must benefit the 'whole' community. But the committees tend to reflect local power dynamics. The by-election in 2012 threatened to destabilise the status quo, with the ousting of the ANC and replacement by an independent ward councillor. However, the old committee members continued in their positions, giving a toehold to the ANC. But the ANC branch was irrevocably divided by the by-election because the branch voted for the independent. The bigger problem facing the ward councillor is that as an independent and ANC 'renegade' (having stood against the party's candidate), he expects obstructionism rather than support for his development projects from the ANC-dominated municipality. Eventually, he decided to join the Economic Freedom Fighters (EFF), an opposition party. The ward committee, a developmental structure, thus finds itself caught up in the local political jostling and has to adjust to rapid political reconfigurations. Some people were not happy:

> We got lost by voting for the independent. The ANC Region forced us to vote for Comrade X. We know him, we can't vote for him, we can't just vote for anyone. But this new councillor takes us nowhere, he is in EFF now. How is he working with the ANC Municipality? He is doing nothing.[58]

ANC COMMITTEES

The ANC has enjoyed dominance and hegemony in Nkaneng for long periods, but at times this has been severely shaken. The rise of Five Madoda shook it, and so did its recent defeat by an independent in the by-election. The Marikana Massacre has also not endeared the ANC as government to the miners who live in Nkaneng, and opposition political parties such as the UDM, DA and the EFF have muscled into the picture out of concern, and are no doubt seeking to take advantage of the situation.[59] The *iinkundla* leaders are associated with the Associated Mining and Construction Union (AMCU), the rival union to the NUM, and while the green AMCU T-shirt is visible and worn by workers around the area, no one dares to wear the red NUM T-shirt. However, the ANC has managed to keep part of its base through the interventions of the ANC Region using the state to call *iimbizo* (community meetings) and implement small-scale developmental projects – for example, the distribution of paraffin burners and free paraffin to residents, the grading of streets, ID and voter registration mobile units and so on, all carried out by locals wearing ANC T-shirts, and always at the helm the Region's preferred candidate, who is apparently a tireless organiser. Given all this, the ANC committee has political traction in the area, but it is fighting a battle for its political survival in Nkaneng: 'There is a new ANC that pushes us old ANC back. We are now sitting down, not because we crossed the floor, but because you don't know how to contribute.'[60]

THE SIGNIFICANCE OF THE MARIKANA MASSACRE

For an economically depressed and poorly serviced area, there has been little protest activity in Nkaneng compared with other informal settlements in South Africa. There appear to have been two major protests in the settlement in the past five years. Disaffected youth led one, with unclear outcomes, and the other was allegedly organised by the ANC Region's preferred candidate in an attempt to whip up support against the newly elected independent councillor.[61] The police quashed the protest quickly, and a public meeting denounced the instigator and threatened him with expulsion from the area.

A significant development that had an impact on the local political culture is the Marikana Massacre. The death of 34 miners working for Lonmin and on strike for better wages had reverberations in Nkaneng. Most miners left the NUM to join the AMCU. At nearby Bleskop hostel there seems to have been a total rout of the NUM, with all the workers deserting it and the hostel committee wholly taken over by the AMCU.[62] While the massacre does not seem to have directly influenced the by-election results in 2012,[63] its timing was enough to lead some journalists to link the two events in a causal relationship.[64] We can expect this momentous event to influence the popular consciousness and political culture in Nkaneng because platinum mining and its associated struggles are crucial for the settlement. Some informants underlined this link, relating wage levels to the local economy and small business prospects.[65] The AMCU blames the ANC government for the massacre, and this has implications for ANC hegemony. The EFF is a wild-card entry in the match.

THE 'RURAL IN THE URBAN' DIALECTIC

The theoretical significance of *iinkundla*, judging by the successful intervention in the 2012 by-elections, might be that migrant cultures maintain the 'rural in the urban' symbolically, and they may re-invent and invoke a virtual rural imaginary in order to 'press claims for their right to remain in the city'.[66] In other words, we should focus on the 'urban' concerns of *iinkundla* rather than believe their detractors, who accuse them of being rustics who are pre-occupied with and only know 'rural' things. The reconstitution of the 'rural in the urban' dialectic is 'an urban rather than a rural resistance ideology, which has come to exist outside the circuits of rural social relationships and political identities'.[67]

The concept of 'democracy on the margins' appears to shed some light on the analysis of *iinkundla*. They are structures that were marginal to democratic processes in Nkaneng, but found a way of extending their sphere of activities into dispute resolution and later into electoral power broking. Despite denouncing *iinkundla* as run by traditional leaders and saying they do not fit within Nkaneng's 'modern' political culture, the dominant local structures have had to recognize and accommodate these *amakomiti*. Their traditional versus modern dichotomy was inadequate in understanding and dealing with *iinkundla*. The dynamism of the *iinkundla* and their ability to adapt to changing circumstances and challenges have brought them closer to the 'mainstream' of local politics of Nkaneng, turbulent as it is. 'Democracy on the margins' as a concept seeks to legitimise and cater for and express grassroots views and needs which might be neglected or excluded by the dominant forms of democracy. *Iinkundla*, with all their contradictions, such as their patriarchy, illiteracy, particular village identities, anti-urban ideology and so on, suggest that the concept of 'democracy on the margins' is useful in understanding these processes of adjustment, adaptation and self-assertion of the excluded (and perplexed) through self-organisation aimed at meeting their needs.

A sober analysis of the *amakomiti* of Nkaneng suggests that they were all in turmoil in the period covered in this chapter. Some disappeared, some lost their dynamism, some were discredited, and some were struggling to find their bearings. Apparently operating in the realm of 'democracy on the margins', the *iinkundla* committees seem to be the only ones that emerged stronger from the political turmoil. Their challenge is to redefine themselves further in the eyes of the community if they are to win and be trusted with the additional powers they appear to seek. Whatever happens to them, the story of this structure challenges binary and structural-functionalist theoretical approaches and points to a need for dynamic theorisation that grasps the uneven and combined development of political consciousness, organisation and culture.

6

Thembelihle Settlement:
A Vision of Hope

Bhayiza Miya spent three months in Sun City, also known as the Diepkloof Prison, supposedly 'awaiting trial' after being arrested for leading a major protest action in Thembelihle, an informal settlement in Lenasia, south of Johannesburg. This was not the first time he had been a victim of state repression for involvement in the struggle of this community for housing, services and a decent life. Twenty years before this protest which sent him to jail, he had lost all his front teeth from a rubber bullet fired at point blank range by a policeman in an attempt to quell the community's opposition to forced removals. In between these bad experiences at the hands of the ANC state's law enforcement agencies, Miya never stopped being an active member and leader of the Thembelihle Crisis Committee (TCC), the social movement organisation that led both the struggle against relocation two decades ago and the month-long protest action for housing, electricity and other services that turned Miya into a jailbird.

For two decades, the TCC has been at the forefront of the Thembelihle community's struggle for recognition ('proclamation') of their informal settlement and provision of basic services.[1] The TCC operates in the same space as an ANC committee and a ward committee. Researchers have struggled with how to characterise this committee because of its unique features and the peculiarities of the political process in this community.[2] The socialist-oriented committee regularly leads the Thembelihle community in protest, and is arguably a main contender for local power and influence, challenging the political hegemony of the ANC government and party by pressing forward the community's demands for development. In this chapter, I will examine the dynamics behind the emergence of the TCC and the factors that shaped its politics. I will do this by tracing the evolution of the committees and organisations that operate in this settlement from past to present.

I will explore the argument that it is the TCC's grounding in the Thembelihle community's radical participatory democratic practice that has allowed it to keep in touch with the needs and views of its constituency, making it possible for it to play a more or less dominant role in local politics for about two decades.

THE PLACE OF GOOD HOPE

Thembelihle is an informal settlement situated cheek by jowl with Lenasia, a suburb that was designated 'Indian' under apartheid's Group Areas Act.[3] Lenasia is located 30 kilometres south of Johannesburg's central business district. Thembelihle's shacks lie between Extensions 9, 10 and 14 of Lenasia. There are between 7,000 and 8,000 households cramped into 6,775 shacks, with 3,597 being primary dwellings and 3,178 occupied by sub-tenants.[4] The settlement layout is a square grid town planning pattern with many of the roads wide enough to allow easy access for pedestrians and motor vehicles.

The roads are unpaved except Capella Street, the access road running through the settlement north to southeast, and another road that runs east to west through the southern part of the settlement. There is a water tap in every yard, but the water pressure is low and many taps run dry during peak hours. There are no flush toilets, you have to dig your own pit toilet; the government recently installed some ventilated pit latrines, but the project was not completed. Communal and recreational facilities are almost non-existent except for a dusty football ground where Bhayiza Miya is often to be seen – he is a keen soccer player and administrator.[5] In the 1990s, local schools were refusing to accommodate students from Thembelihle, but they agreed after a 'Right to Education' campaign spearheaded by the TCC and supported by the University of Johannesburg's Centre for Education Rights and Transformation.[6]

Community meetings take place at SA Block, two brick buildings that were once a brick-making factory. The complex consists of run-down offices and a monumentally long 'hall' that was built for other purposes and whose interior is dark because of its small windows and cavernous nature. In front of the buildings is a parking lot that serves as the venue for Thembelihle's open-air community meetings. Meetings also take place at the taxi rank toward the north of the settlement. The street running east to west near SA Block is Thembelihle's main and busiest street. It is a long road along which there are rows of shacks on either side. About half of these shacks operate various small businesses, taking advantage of the human traffic. These *spaza* (informal) shops sell basics such as cool drinks, bread, paraffin, meat and beer. A few artisan-type businesses are in operation, such as a shoemaker, tailor and hair salon. About five years ago, a mall was built a kilometre or two away to the east of the settlement that provides a wider range of goods, entertainment and job opportunities for the locals.

An important factor in the life of the community has been the installation of electricity in the area by the residents themselves.[7] Most shacks now enjoy electricity which is self-connected and against the laws of the municipality. Self-connection started slow, but really took off around 2010, when reputedly everyone wanted to watch the World Cup on television.[8] At first, comrades connected to the few high-mast 'Apollo' street lights in the area, but this tampering cast the settlement into darkness. Connections are now made to the electrical transformers serving Lenasia. Complaints by Lenasia residents and the practice by City Power, the municipal electricity company, of periodically cutting and confiscating the people's cables invariably provokes street protests, such as the one on that happened on 25 June 2014.[9] A winning tactic employed by Thembelihle residents is retaliating by sabotaging Lenasia's electricity supply, plunging parts of the suburb into darkness[10] – a devious trick they learned from informal settlement comrades in Protea South, Soweto. Thembelihle residents feel that they are entitled to the electricity. One argument proffered to justify self-connections is that people have died as a result of shacks burning down because of the use of unsafe energy.[11] The authorities claim that they cannot install electricity because the township is not proclaimed and their policy is to relocate the people:[12]

Oh yes, we have electricity, can you see how smart we are? So we all have electricity cables underneath and others dug deeper, so that no one can steal them. It is a real cable and it works well …. The last time I used gas, it was back in 2011, if not 2010.[13]

The [September 2013] protest helped us because we have electricity now. The Indians know very well that this is not 'land Asia', this is Thembelihle. They know very well that when they cut off our electricity, the mall also gets its power cut off, too.[14]

At 59 per cent, the rate of unemployment in Thembelihle is higher than Statistics South Africa's 38.8 per cent expanded definition of unemployment.[15] Many Thembelihle workers are precariously employed, earning low wages and with little job security.[16] There is a perception that local Indian employers pay less.[17] Many workers can walk to work, but there are kombi taxis to help you reach Lenasia Central Business District, which is 7 kilometres away. Thembelihle is a poor working-class residential area because many people are reliant on or aspire to employment as their main source of income.[18] The government social grants are probably an important source of income. Working appears to be an important aspect of the lives and identities of Thembelihle residents, as the following quote from a man who survives on collecting scrap for recycling and once owned a spaza shop suggests when he looks back on his life spent in the area: 'This place taught me how to be a man, moreover I was working at that time.'[19]

Ithemba means 'hope' in the isiZulu language, and *elihle* means 'good' or 'beautiful'. 'Thembelihle' therefore means 'a place of good hope'. The name was given to the settlement early in its life by the first committees operating in the area, to convey the sense of hope that gripped the residents then. The place was 'baptised' after an episode of violent conflict in the area. The name thus represents a tenacious hanging on to the dream of building a new community against all odds, including internal fights and external threats. It seems that this determination to realise the dream became an important element of the Thembelihle collective identity:[20]

> In 1990, this place was further established, [but] up until Section F [came into being], then more chaos erupted. There were disagreements and no understanding. We ended up going to the [ANC] Region. At the Region, we talked and discussed things .... We were told to name this place, and then Bab' uMakopo said: 'We have a beautiful hope that this place will be beautiful' – that is how this place was named Thembelihle.[21]

But as you move around the area today, there are empty stands where the tenants have moved away to Lehae, a new housing development about 4 kilometres away to which people are being 'voluntarily' relocated by the authorities. It appears as if there is erosion of this hopeful identity:

> [We have] to think questions of identity, either social or individual, not in the wake of their disappearance but in the wake of their erosion, of

their fading, of their not having the kind of purchase and comprehensive explanatory power they had before ....[22]

The empty spaces and absent neighbours arguably represent the power of the state to impose its decisions on the people and its refusal to develop the settlement. It also represents the surrender of hope and the stripping of the place-based collective identity as people relent and give up on keeping on living in their beloved Thembelihle in exchange for a brick 'RDP' house in the new area.[23] The battle is not altogether lost, because an overwhelming majority continue to live in Thembelihle and, as we will see below, the government has very recently relented on its relocation policy:

> I don't want to leave a place I'm used to, to go and start all over again. Have a new neighbour that I don't even know. Where I live I know all my neighbours and we are used to each other.[24]

But the hope of *in situ* development is being eaten away as if by termites each time a family pulls down its shack and moves to Lehae.[25] It is as if the territorial stigmatisation or 'blemish of place' that the community had managed to largely conquer through its resistance to forced removal is being resuscitated and the process of 'dissolution of place' has begun; authorities will vilify and stigmatise 'slums' until the residents themselves tragically internalise this, resulting in: 'the loss of a humanized, culturally familiar and socially filtered locale with which marginalized populations identify, and in which they feel at "home" and in relative security.'[26] Hence the old guard's lament:

> You see our community used to be very strong but now we are very weak because as many as we are, we no longer have hope for our place like before.[27]

> I wish this community can be developed, we love this place.[28]

STRUGGLE YIELDS VICTORY

The story of Thembelihle might have a happy ending after all. A two-week-long protest by the residents demanding development took place on

23 February 2015. The TCC organised the protest, which saw 60 people arrested.[29] The protest attracted media attention, and the government did not come off well when it later raided the settlement under its Operation Fiela, a crime-prevention crackdown that was condemned as displaying elements of xenophobia by critics and, with respect to Thembelihle, political repression.[30] As if in response to the pressure emanating from the bad publicity, on 28 April 2015 the government issued a media statement that read in part:

> Thembelihle will now receive dedicated government support, provision of services including housing and related infrastructure such as water and electricity following the approval and formal registration of Thembelihle as a housing project under the Department of Human Settlements.[31]

By all accounts, this represents a victory for the community, because for more than a decade, as we will see in the account below, the government's policy had been to relocate the community, hence its refusal to provide basic services. It could be that the dream of the old guard will be realised after all and the struggle of the community led by the TCC will at last bear fruit.

HISTORY OF *AMAKOMITI* IN THEMBELIHLE

For the sake of clarity and analysis, I will divide the history of Thembelihle committees into two periods. First, there were the committees that were active during the establishment of the settlement and early consolidation of community life in the settlements, and secondly, a later period when the committees had to respond to the threat of forced removal of the settlement, a decision taken in 2002 by the municipality. Thembelihle was born in 1989. The settlement was established several years earlier by a small group of workers employed at the SA Block brick-making factory who occupied the open veld nearby. The area suddenly grew in size, thus earning the new settlement the name Esigangeni ('in the bush' or 'the open veld').[32] There appears to have been little threat of forced removal.[33] Nelson Mandela visited the settlement in 1994 – a proud moment for the residents.[34] His new democratic government extinguished the flame of hope he had kindled in residents' hearts when it later earmarked the settlement for relocation. For

Table 6.1 Timeline of committees in Thembelihle

Name of committee	Description	Term of office
Sofasonke Party committee	Party leaders from Mshenguville in Soweto ran the committee, allocating stands and resolving disputes; it co-existed with other committees	1989–1991
Community committees	Established by residents to organise settling in at Thembelihle; broadly democratic and accounting to assemblies that met almost every day in different parts of the settlement	1989–1991
Popular community committee	After the inter-committee conflicts reached crisis proportions, the community elected a single committee to unify the whole settlement	1991–1999
ANC committee	The ANC gradually gained influence, and its leaders worked in the popular community committee	Unbanned 1990
Masibambane, Masakhane, PAC, Inkatha Freedom Party committees	Other committees existed, competing for power and influence with the dominant committee; some committees represented political parties	1990–present, but some have declined
	ANC Government Relocation Plan divides community	1998
Thembelihle Crisis Committee	Formed to lead the struggle against relocation plans by the ANC government; socialist-oriented	Formed in 2001, the leading committee today
Landless Peoples Movement	A national social movement that established structures in Thembelihle, but has since declined	2003–2008
Ward committee	Statutory body advising ward councillor; dominated by the ANC, with the TCC holding one seat on it since 2012	2006–present

Source: Compiled by the author based on field research.

two decades after this, the people of Thembelihle lived under the threat of eviction.[35] The character of the committees reflects this turning point.

During apartheid days, various committees existed in the settlement. They vied for dominance, but forged a fractious unity around the establishment and consolidation of the settlement; disputes were around how to do this and who should be in charge. During the early period, competition among the committees turned violent. Peaceful methods of contestation prevailed once the violence dissipated. Under the ANC government, the relocation threat became a focal point, and the contestation among committees was about whether and how best to resist the relocation. Furthermore, with the dawn of democracy, the electoral process and access to state power became important even as other mechanisms of competing for local power and influence remained important. Winning arguments at the community general meeting, called the 'mass meeting', became a very important platform in the local politics of the settlement.[36] Organising and leading protest action was another mechanism and a reflection of power and influence.

Before 1990, political parties such as the ANC, Pan Africanist Congress (PAC) and Azanian People's Organisation were banned by the apartheid state, and only those willing to collaborate with the apartheid state were allowed to operate, namely the Inkatha Freedom Party and the Sofasonke Party.[37] Yes, the party formed by the great Sofasonke Mpanza, the 'grabber' of municipal land and father of Soweto, over time became increasingly collaborationist with the apartheid state. The ANC was nowhere when the settlement was established. However, it acquired a halo after its unbanning in 1990 and its victory at the first democratic elections in 1994, since it was the party that defeated apartheid and brought freedom. It won support in Thembelihle and became dominant, pushing aside or absorbing committees and organisations that had helped to establish and govern the early life of the settlement. In 2002, several years after gaining local dominance and state power, the ANC government adopted the policy of relocating Thembelihle.[38] This thrust the ANC, both as government and as movement, into a collision course with the community and led to the emergence and rise of the TCC as an oppositional committee that soon challenged ANC dominance in the area. The TCC challenge arguably contributed to the drop in electoral support for the ANC in two local government elections.[39]

For a fuller understanding of the political history of Thembelihle, one needs to address the background stories, the less-documented facts and events, and the forgotten committees and personalities that provide the rich context within which the political contenders in the foreground find their meaning and battle it out. The next section presents some of this less-known history, focusing on the past committees that operated in Thembelihle.

THE SOVEREIGN VOICE OF *UMPHAKATHI*[40]

The number of shacks in Thembelihle exploded from the small cluster of retrenched workers' shelters around the factory buildings given to them by their employer.[41] By 1989, large groups of people were coming to Thembelihle, many coming from areas around Johannesburg and some migrating directly from the rural areas, as happened in other areas.[42] Many people came in semi-organised fashion from nearby Mshenguville, a Soweto informal settlement closed down by the authorities and its residents relocated to Orange Farm, more than 30 kilometres away:[43]

> During those years, I can say in less than seven to eight months, people were piling up because I came here in June 1990 …. Yes, they came in numbers because they heard that a new place had just opened up. I also heard there is a place in Lenasia, and I was not happy where I was staying, then I decided to move.[44]

Committees to supervise the influx and settlement of people were set up. A leader of the Sofasonke Party, Nongeleza, led one of the first committees. The focus was on the allocation of stands and dispute resolution. Later committees, apparently founded on broadly democratic principles, were set up for the different sections:

> The committee was elected at the community grounds. The committee members were called and then we were elected. I can say the committee met every day in the afternoons. The cases were mostly about people fighting and disagreements within the committee. I can say it was an everyday thing.[45]

It was a rough-and-ready direct form of democracy, as this informant recalls:

> They would elect a person when we were having a mass meeting. We would ask each other questions as a community, and if you came up with

a great idea of how to help the community, then they would elect you right away …. Yes, just like that. They wouldn't ask how many people want this person to be a committee member, no, no, that was a waste of time.[46]

Conflict soon erupted in the settlement as different groups and committees vied for power and influence. It was a fight between leaders and between different sections of the settlement, namely sections D, F and N:

What I remember the most is our struggling. The struggle to get water, until we officially had taps. It was a struggle. Before that, there were fights between Section F and Section N.[47]

If I remember well, this was in 1989. This is when the different sections were cut out. Section D was cut, this was in December. Then in 1990, Section N was cut. When Section N was cut, that is when the chaos erupted. A man got injured, his name was Elliot. He stayed there at Section D. It was very chaotic. Some people got arrested, and when that happened, the cutting of the sections had to stop.[48]

The work of cutting out stands was done at some point by a man called Elliot and another man who spoke TshiVenda.[49] Elliot developed the grid structure that exists today. However, a dispute arose around his town planning scheme. He had left some land for communal, business and recreational use. But some local leaders began to allocate people into these empty spaces, apparently motivated by self-enrichment, charging people for the irregular allocations:[50]

The committee that I was part of is the one that ruined this place. It was planned that this place starts from here and it ends there up to the grounds, but because we didn't listen to each other, it ended up badly … someone from the committee started making money from cutting and selling stands [in the reserved place]. Then the fights broke out.[51]

Some informants pointed to an ethnic dimension to the conflict: 'The Xhosas arrived and they were demanding. Hey! They wanted seats in the committee.'[52] Replacing force with democracy apparently restored peace:

123

After that [the fights between different sections], a committee was elected, by law we were electing street committees; I was one of them, there was Mbanga, there was Mcithi, and we were all from Section N. From Section D there was Bab' Khumalo and Sam.[53]

A period of co-operation followed this rough patch in the history of the area as residents and their committees focused on improving living conditions in the area.[54] During this period, the ANC enjoyed some authority in the area and used it effectively:

The ANC was now active in the area and when the fight got out of hand the committees went to the ANC Region who ruled that for the sake of peace allocations be allowed in all the open spaces.[55]

By 1993, the community had successfully put pressure on the authorities to install communal water taps in the area. The state installed a battery of taps at one corner of the settlement from which people could fetch water. Feeling inconvenienced, the people organised to buy pipes and laid them out to connect every yard to the main pipe. The various committees in the area organised money collections and bulk buying of the plumbing materials. Bringing the water closer united the committees:

Then we came together as Section F and Section N, the fights had stopped and we also got our pipe. It was a struggle, a real struggle, but in the end we got the water.[56]

Some Xhosa man said, 'Johannes [interviewee], we should sit down and talk. This is not helping us.' Indeed, we called everyone, the Tswanas, but mostly it was the Sothos and Xhosas, and we got together. We said we have to build Thembelihle so that we can be in the papers and be well known everywhere. We should be the beautiful hope we always intended to be.[57]

But the political jostling did not stop. There was instability, as no group was consistently dominant and people could usurp and sway decisions to suit their agendas.[58] Meanwhile, the ANC and the 'comrades' were becoming dominant. Dan Bovu was the key local ANC leader and, with the support

of 'the ANC Region and the Indians', as some informants put it, his committee became influential in the area. Although many people later detested
him because as ward councillor he supported the relocation of Thembelihle,
even those informants who disliked him conceded that during his heyday he
was resourceful, enterprising, innovative and a hands-on leader.[59]

Dan – as he is popularly known in the settlement – was branch chairperson, and hence leader of the ANC comrades. The ANC apparently soon
took over the key tasks of running the settlement from the earlier committees or dominated in these structures. Apparently, the ANC's attempts to
establish SANCO structures in Thembelihle were unsuccessful.[60] One of the
tasks SANCO, as a civic structure, would have been in charge of was crime
fighting. Like many settlements experiencing rapid expansion, Thembelihle
saw crime levels rise:

> People were complaining about crime. At SA Block there was a place
> where you could go and complain about anything, then they will help you
> resolve it. There was a Crime Prevention Unit, there were people called
> 'comrades'. When you go complain to them, they would go to that person
> and beat them up first … even when you have not finished explaining
> what you have done or not done.[61]

> There was a man that used to work at SA block, named Tshawe. He was
> making things strict, but he would really embarrass you. He would make
> you walk the streets naked. If you had raped, they would undress you and
> hit you on your penis [in public] … it was disgraceful.[62]

Dan's ANC was deeply involved in community issues. In 1995, Dan became
the ward councillor on the ANC ticket, no doubt further increasing his and
the ANC's power and influence in the settlement. The overwhelming victory
of the ANC in the first national elections held in 1994 saw it repeat the feat in
the local elections a year later; it is likely that this further eroded the power
of other political parties such as the PAC and Inkatha Freedom Party in
Thembelihle. However, the local committees and political actors continued
to fight for their space. The local community organisation Masibambane, for
example, appeared to have competed with the ANC for influence.[63] Another
earlier committee was Masakhane.[64] Despite ANC dominance, there was a
tradition that the voice of the people, of the community – *umphakathi* –

was sacrosanct, and that this voice was expressed in the community mass meeting. This must have kept the door open for other political actors to vie for influence.

THE STRUGGLE AGAINST RELOCATION

Mandela is reputed to have admonished the Indians to learn to live with black people. He praised the well-laid out stands in Thembelihle and called for the new government to build houses for the people during his visit in 1994.[65] The residents' hopes were shattered when the Johannesburg Municipality announced the impending relocation of Thembelihle because the area's terrain was dolomitic and could not sustain residential housing.[66] This policy provoked strong opposition and pitted Bovu, in his new role as ward councillor, against the people.[67] The Thembelihle community contested the suggestion that it was unsafe to build houses in the area.[68] For years, in my recollection, the TCC and the community were obsessed with dolomite, including commissioning geological studies to counter the government's plans. One informant told me how she stopped being active in an ANC committee and joined those opposed to the relocation:

> I was young, I was young, but what they were telling me, I couldn't see it [the dolomite and the need to relocate]. It's as if they were telling me to hold a wall that's falling and that I must not get sleepy because it will fall on me if I do. But then if you do sleep, you find that wall still standing. So it's something that is not there. Crisis [TCC] opened our eyes.[69]

Why did Bovu adopt a position that was so unpopular in Thembelihle? It seems he was caught between the policy of the ANC as government and the wishes of his constituency; he decided to listen to the ANC. This discrepancy between the mandates of the ANC as government and as (popular) movement created costly political contradictions for the ANC.

The unpopularity of Dan Bovu and the ANC in Thembelihle reached a climax when on 21 June 2002 the hated 'Red Ants' invaded the settlement with bulldozers.[70] In the build-up to this momentous event, a new leader and committee had emerged in Thembelihle known as i-Crisis ('the Crisis'). The TCC was born in 2001 expressly to organise the struggle against the impending forced removals.[71] The dominance of the ANC and the decline of other political parties and local organisations, combined with the ANC's sudden loss of popularity due to the relocation policy, created political space for a new organisation. The TCC's bold opposition to relocation won it supporters and activists from various local organisations, with some leaving their political homes as these responded inadequately to the crisis.[72] The objective was clear and unambiguous: no to forced removals, no to relocation. They demanded *in situ* development.[73] At the head of this new organisation was a new leader, the wily and forceful leader Mzwandile Mdingi. At the height of his power, as one informant commented: 'Mzwandile was king in Thembelihle.'[74]

Mdingi had a strong character, charisma and a bold style of leadership that appealed to the desperate Thembelihle community. A man of action, Mdingi's simple plan was that everyone in Thembelihle, especially the men, would wake up early in the morning and join the fight to drive away the Red Ants.[75] Activists called regular meetings to mobilise the people behind the campaign. The TCC also organised legal assistance in aid of the cause. But on D-Day, it was Mdingi's plan that won the day:

> Ah no, Mdingi had a strong gang, his own gang. There was no gathering, you would hear a loud bang on your roof and someone shouting, 'Get out!' You would hear a man saying: 'I'm still getting dressed.' The response would be, 'You are only getting dressed now?' You got dressed on the way there, and you wouldn't even have a weapon to protect yourself with, but you will get it when you get there.[76]

Although some people's shacks were destroyed and 647 families agreed to relocate to Vlakfontein 8 kilometres away, Mdingi's lieutenants mobilised the masses and put up a good fight on the day. After some pitched battles involving police rubber bullets (some hitting Miya in the mouth), stone throwing and no doubt a lot else, the authorities had to stop the forced removal.[77] The residents' victory was decisive. The new spirit of triumphant defiance put wind in the sails of the TCC, catapulting it forward as a leading organisation in the settlement. It directed the momentum to banish Dan Bovu from the settlement. Thousands of residents ransacked his offices at the SA Block community centre, chasing away his assistants. I was there to see this 'festival of the oppressed' – there was exuberance, joy and lots of laughter.[78] The community saw no reason for Bovu to have offices in an area that he wanted obliterated. This action amounted to a political coup against the ANC as the TCC, in the name of the people, put itself at the head of the mobilised community.

Local political contestation in Thembelihle became further complicated when a year or so later, Mdingi split the TCC and aligned himself to the Landless Peoples Movement (LPM). The TCC had earlier joined the Anti-Privatisation Forum (APF) as an affiliate.[79] The LPM was mobilising for land in the urban informal settlements in addition to its rural base.[80] Over time, after a tense modus vivendi, the LPM lost its power and Mdingi left the settlement, leaving the TCC to carry on with the fight:

> Mzwandile [Mdingi] really tried, but he was uneducated. Mzwandile only understood what is being said, but when it came to words on paper, he would want you to read it for him. And if you read it for him, you also have to translate. But now Siphiwe and the others used to translate untruthfully because they wanted to be in control also, they wanted to end Mzwandile's time in power. That is how Mzwandile's reign ended and Bhayiza [Miya] took control.[81]

For several years after the failed forced removals, the TCC continued to enjoy a degree of dominance in the area, but the ANC was busy clawing its way back into the hegemonic spot, with Bovu able to slowly recapture lost political ground in the settlement.[82] Despite his unpopularity, as ward councillor, his position was secure because in South Africa there is no legal mechanism for a community to recall a councillor from office against the wishes of the political party. He finished his term of office, and in 2006 was promoted onto the City of Johannesburg's mayoral committee and put in charge of housing. A new ANC ward councillor, Janice Ndarala, took over.

Meanwhile the TCC, together with other social movement-type organisations affiliated to the APF, had formed the Operation Khanyisa Movement (OKM), an electoral front based on a socialist platform to run in the 2006 elections. It contested in Thembelihle, and though it lost to the ANC for the ward councillor position, it won about 4,000 votes that yielded one proportional representation seat on the City of Johannesburg Council. The OKM managed to retain this seat in 2011 with an increase in the number of votes won in Thembelihle.[83] Thus the TCC challenge to the ANC became both electoral and on the ground; the ANC is challenged in its two capacities as ruling party in government and as a movement. Researchers studying the OKM have pointed out the smallness of the electoral challenge and the almost negligible impact one seat in a big city council like Johannesburg has; however, they emphasise the significance of this for local political dynamics in Thembelihle.[84] In addition, the TCC decided to run candidates in the ward committee elections in 2012, and managed to win the housing portfolio seat.[85] These initiatives illustrate the dynamic and multi-pronged nature of the methods used by the TCC in its struggle for the development of Thembelihle.

ANC LEGITIMACY CRISIS IN THEMBELIHLE

The ANC branch at Ward 8 consists of comrades from Thembelihle, Lenasia, Lehae and Lawley. The ANC in Thembelihle sometimes meets separately to address local issues. The ward councillor is an ex officio member of the BEC. She has come under fire for denouncing the electricity self-connections despite having joined the march for electricity organised by the TCC before she became a councillor.[86] As a new councillor, she was at the receiving end of a march making similar demands. Some informants did not have a high opinion of her, associating her closely with Dan Bovu:

> If you ask her about Thembelihle, she will tell you that Dan said this. As people are going [to Lehae], it is now that I have realised that she is not a councillor but Dan's employee .... The councillor we have now is dead. We don't have a councillor, I don't want to lie to you. We say bad things about Dan but there are too many things he did and we liked them.[87]

As housing member of the mayoral committee, Bovu is in charge of the exodus of Thembelihleans to Lehae; he controls the lists that allocate people to houses. This has led to accusations of nepotism and corruption, with local ANC members accused of selling stands left vacant by people moving out.[88] The close identification of the ANC with the council and councillors seems related to the legitimacy crisis it faces in Thembelihle. Some residents have very little trust in its intentions, plans and processes:

> I'm not saying I hate ANC, I don't hate it, but I want to tell the truth, ANC has crooks. ANC is very good, but it is infiltrated with crooks. You are trying to live your life, but they keep on sucking you left and right.[89]

We take people as our superiors, but they don't do anything for you, they are doing it for their own wellbeing. You will be poor for ever, and they are eating in their houses.[90]

BHAYIZA MIYA AND THE WARD COMMITTEE

The democratic participatory shortcomings of the ward committee system are a hackneyed truth among local government observers in South Africa.[91] In Thembelihle, the majority of ward committee members are ANC, including the ward councillor, its chairperson. The TCC won a seat on the ward committee, and Miya occupies it.[92] A researcher assessed his role positively in a structure many analysts have almost considered irredeemable.[93] A Thembelihle resident seems to agree with this assessment:

The ward committee has ten people on it. Bhayiza is the one that is working there, and the others are not. I can tell them in their faces, they know me. Bhayiza calls meetings, he will gather a few cents, take a car and organise a [loud] speaker and go around to inform us about what is going on.[94]

Photo 6.1   TCC youth leader (centre, with arms outstretched) leading a song in a demonstration in support of the platinum miners' strike at the Chamber of Mines building, Johannesburg. (Photograph by author)

RESTORING HOPE

Amakomiti have to be in step with the wishes of the community, otherwise their popularity, power and influence decline. This was the downfall of Bovu and the ANC when they adopted the position in support of relocation. Despite this, Bovu's support base did not evaporate. An astute politician, he came back to give reports as the ward councillor and to take mandates, a process the TCC probably had no choice but to allow. It is likely that from the point of view of the rank and file, the TCC is watched and critically evaluated, as is the case with the ANC and other parties. An informant displayed skepticism at Miya, the TCC leader, becoming a ward committee member:

> [These days,] he is always travelling, he goes to Marikana and things like that. Don't bother to call him when he has just received his salary from the ANC; he is no longer able to run, he is this big [fat] …. Yes [the strongest committee is Bhayiza's], but you can see that corruption is there, but it is not bad because they are not doing it straight in [front of] our eyes.[95]

Each committee orients itself to the masses, keeps in touch with popular sentiment, and develops its political programmes and positions accordingly. The TCC has managed to maintain its position of leadership and influence in the community in this way. This is not always easy. Issues addressed can be complicated. The TCC also has to contend with the competing interventions of its political rivals. A case in point is the move to Lehae, where the TCC was caught between its position of no relocation and the reality that houses were being built less than 5 kilometres away from the settlement. Agreeing to move to Vlakfontein had been denounced as a 'betrayal' by the TCC.[96] In the end, the TCC adjusted its position to saying that people were free to live where they wanted, and those who wanted to leave should do so while those who wanted to stay in Thembelihle should also be allowed to do so.[97] With respect to the latter group, the TCC reiterated its original demand for *in situ* development of Thembelihle and the provision of basic services; it also demanded transparency and fairness in the allocation of houses:[98] 'Now the change that is there is that people are moving. I have been complaining, and I'm even tired of complaining that people are moving to Lehae but I am still here.'[99]

The TCC's two-pronged approach has not saved it from a bigger problem. The struggle to establish and improve living conditions in the settlement, and later the struggle against relocation, were key in forging a Thembelihle collective identity. However, 'the place of hope' has not yet seen the realization of its hopes. An informant remembered the great hope they had for the place, and said that none of all the committees that have existed have been able to get the area developed.[100] The move to Lehae, although it is in fact a trickle, symbolises a loss of strength and resolve, both important components of Thembelihle's collective identity among the old guard. Some feel defeated:

> They are moving people to silence us. No one remembers why we were protesting, we were protesting for houses to be built here and that they should provide us with electricity. That is the main reason of the protest, but now people are excited because they are moving away.[101]

> But this place is not going backwards or forward, it is on a halt.[102]

However, the recent announcement by the government that Thembelihle has been proclaimed as a housing project and will be developed will no doubt remove the pessimism and restore the hope of the old guard.[103] Indeed, after a bureaucratic-length interregnum, the authorities began to install electricity in the settlement. This has resuscitated hope among those who remain. It will no doubt shift the terrain of struggle significantly for the TCC.

The struggle of the TCC and the Thembelihle community continues. The state must build the houses it promised, it must let Comrade Makama rest in peace in his grave. Yet the TCC has given the community of Thembelihle something more valuable, namely the leadership and organisation to help shape a local politics and political culture that create democratic spaces wherein residents can exercise some control over their destiny and resist the impositions of the powerful. This was not a gift of TCC to the community; the Thembelihle political culture of direct democracy and of respecting the voice of *umphakathi* allowed the TCC to rise and shine. A 'democracy on the margins' was developed over time, with its various dimensions and components progressively added and fine-tuned until it became what it is today. The TCC case dispels many shibboleths about the politics of South African informal settlements and the social movements found therein, including problematising some concepts used to describe and understand these movements. It gives a glimpse of what is possible with a grassroots politics that seeks to effect immediate and systemic change in its challenge to the power of the powerful.

7

Amakomiti: A Vision of Alternatives

Life in the informal settlements is not easy; there are many challenges. Nonetheless, we have seen that those who live there have no choice but to rise up to the challenge and take action to make a life. They learn to do things for themselves, including creating new 'housing developments', drawing up 'town planning schemes' and turning open spaces into places people can call home. In this book I have focused on how they organise themselves into committees and assemblies (general meetings, mass meetings) in order to find collective solutions in the struggle to satisfy their needs. Can we learn anything from this practice? Can people who live in shantytowns, shacks and favelas teach us anything about democracy, about how to govern society in a way that is inclusive, participatory and addresses popular needs? These questions led me to conduct research into this field in the first place. In this chapter, I revisit them in the light of my research findings and locate them within broader theoretical, historical and political parameters. I want to delve into a wider field beyond the shack, the locality and the needs of the shack dwellers for decent housing. My inquiry concerns the human condition. As far as possible, I want to inquire whether and to what extent our understanding of the self-organisation practices of the shack dwellers presented in the previous chapters can contribute to finding political answers to some key questions facing humanity today.

Let us begin with a recap of my key findings. I found committees, called *amakomiti* (in isiZulu) or *dikomiti* (in Sesotho), in operation in 45 out of 46 shack settlements in the course of a research tour of settlements in four South African provinces. More than one committee operates in the majority of settlements. I identified a minimum of seven categories of committees in existence: people's, ward, ANC, community policing forums, community development forums, and headman and ad hoc protest committees.

The most prevalent committee is the people's committee, defined as an autonomously formed committee, and it operates in three-quarters of the settlements; the next in prevalence is the ward committee, a statutory structure, found in just less than half of the settlements. In many instances there is interaction between the different categories of committees in operation in any given context, some co-operative and some antagonistic. History, politics and personnel in each settlement shape the character of the committees, their operation and their interaction with each other. The political culture of a settlement and the nature and extent of ANC hegemony were important variables in the committee dynamics. Influence over and control of the shack committees is contested terrain and a central aspect of the battle for political hegemony over shack constituencies. These internal struggles affect the quality of what I call the 'democracy on the margins' practised by *amakomiti* in the settlements. This concept aims to convey the groundedness of democratic practice in the settlements, neither romanticizing it nor disparaging it. The intersection of structure and agency shapes it on the ground. Struggle shapes 'democracy on the margins'.

In order to broaden our horizon and avoid South African exceptionalism, I will begin with a brief history of the squatter movement during the Iran Revolution in 1979. What happened there is that at the height of the revolutionary upheavals, squatters occupied city buildings with the approval of the Mullahs (theological leaders). It is important to note that these occupations took place during an upsurge in struggle and that the occupiers formed committees, the *shuras*. I hope this Iranian story will illustrate the common experience and significance of *amakomiti* across national borders. It will also help to examine some key concepts and debates that will be useful in the discussion that will follow, namely my presentation of a revisionist history of the squatter movement in South Africa. I believe that a new history is necessary in order for us to recognize the true potential of *amakomiti* and the movements of shack dwellers. My argument is that squatter movements are working-class movements, but this is a conclusion I will be working toward as we delve into the discussion below.

THE SQUATTER MOVEMENT AND THE REVOLUTION IN IRAN

Something amazing happened in Iran in 1979. There was a revolution. The Shah of Iran was overthrown, and a new Islamic regime, headed by Ayatollah Khomeini, took over. Less well known is that hundreds of buildings in the big cities were taken over by the homeless under cover of the political turmoil. The occupation of buildings was extensive, with 4,500 villas taken over in only three neighbourhoods in the first months of the revolution.[1] The occupation of buildings by the burgeoning squatter movement was an expression of the revolutionary fervour and action that gripped the country. The squatters formed committees, the *shuras*, which joined the Popular Organisations, an array of organs of the revolution that organised and led other sectors of society in the revolution. The homeless were able, as part of the revolutionary forces, to get their housing needs met. In line with insights by Marxist scholars, the political organisation of the squatters in Iran, like that of the working class elsewhere, flourished during upsurges in struggle.[2] Indeed, Leon Trotsky even suggested that 'apart from revolution they [soviets] are impossible'.[3]

The role of the squatters during the revolution is well documented and theorised by Asef Bayat, a leading scholar in the field.[4] In Chapter 1, I touched upon some of Bayat's work. Of particular interest here is that in his account of the squatter movement in Iran, he grapples with the question of the class identity of the squatters, theorising the divergence in the political orientation of the poor, the unemployed workers, slum dwellers and squatters *vis-à-vis* the working class and the radical middle classes.[5] To understand where Bayat is coming from, we have to complete telling the story of the occupations of city buildings in Tehran.

The Islamic revolutionaries supported the struggle of the squatters as part of undermining the authority of the old elite, which opened the door for the Mullahs to take power.[6] The squatters' committees organised the provision of basic services and worked at making the occupied buildings habitable once successfully occupied.[7] The broader movement formed Islamic consumer cooperatives and neighbourhood councils. These served 'as the most effective link between the revolutionaries and the underclass communities'.[8] Indeed, in the post-revolutionary period, the new Islamic Constitution recognised the councils, structures that were effectively organs of people's power during the height of the revolution. However, the new Islamic regime's enthusiasm for 'councillism and decentralisation' soon disappeared as the proliferation of grassroots forms of autonomous organisation was found to be at odds with 'the monopoly of power and paternalistic and selective mobilisation of pro-government individuals'.[9] The Mullahs tightened their grip on power, and council activities were attenuated, with many members becoming victims of state repression.[10] Although it took many years and met with mixed success, the authorities were able to remove many squatters from the buildings.[11]

This sorry ending in the unity in action built between the poorer sections of society, the squatters and the revolutionary theologians echoes some of the criticism some researchers have levelled at the ANC-led democratic government, whose housing programmes have not been extensive enough to provide decent houses for all.[12] For Bayat, this outcome shows that the class interests of the squatters and of the poor do not coincide with those of the middle and working classes. The big barrier between these classes is that the politics of the poor is concerned with 'immediate' issues and is 'non-ideological'. There is an echo here of how some commentators have characterised the movements of South African shack dwellers as apolitical or not ideological, maintaining that they do not share a common interest with trade unionists and township people who live in built-up houses. Others have used class analysis to argue that the poor of South Africa, especially unemployed workers, are an 'underclass' with divergent or peculiar interests.[13]

It is interesting that in his account of the squatter movement in Iran, Bayat includes a sociological analysis of the occupational life circumstances of the squatters. He quotes a study conducted in 1971 in Iran which concluded that 'over 80 per cent of squatters were involved in unskilled or semiskilled jobs, including construction, street vending, and low-paid government employment', noting that 'Slum dwellers seemed to have higher incomes and job security .... Many of them had been born in the cities.'[14] This suggests that the slum dwellers constitute a section of the working class. They are workers, albeit poorly paid and suffering from high job insecurity.

Finally, Bayat specifically mentions South Africa to corroborate his argument that political upheaval and the undermining of state authority creates favourable conditions for squatter movements to thrive and take the offensive.[15] Indeed, it was the upsurges of the 1980s and the wavering of the apartheid state that emboldened squatters to organise land invasions and establish shack settlements *en masse*. Most informal settlements I visited were established between 1990 and 1994 (see Table 3.1). Following Bayat, I propose that the workers' movement spearheaded the upsurge in struggle, thus creating space for the squatters to occupy land in the period covering the late 1980s to the early 1990s. At the same time, the shack dwellers were fighters who constituted an important section of the working-class army, and as in the 1940s, their antics and bravery were a source of inspiration: 'The Africans in the squatter camps became international front-page news, with their courageous resistance against the state's deportation schemes.'[16]

Shack dwellers are workers. Class analysis must be grounded; Alexander and Pfaffe suggest that the 'patterning of class' – that is, how it is constituted, shaped and expressed – 'varies from country to country shaped, in particular, by different histories of class formation and classed culture.'[17] As happened during the 1940s, working-class interests and needs drove the land invasions and settlement formations of the 1980s, with workers taking action to secure a place to live in the cities and towns of South Africa:[18]

> The persistence of squatting, despite the efforts of the state to eliminate it, sometimes by ruthless measures such as bulldozing squatter shacks, is testimony to the determination of people drafted into the industrial workforce to achieve *de facto* ownership of land in the vicinity of industrial development.[19]

In South Africa, 'the longer term interests of the poor … are nearly always bound up with those of workers.'[20] This conclusion allows us to employ Marxist tools of analysis with some confidence when assessing the political condition of the shack dwellers and understanding *amakomiti*.

A SHACK DWELLER'S HISTORY OF
THE SOUTH AFRICAN STRUGGLE

My purpose in this section is to revisit the history of the struggle in South Africa, locating the place of informal settlement dwellers in it. It is a re-evaluation of South African urban history from the vantage point of the squatter movement, which has arguably played an important role in the struggle for social justice and economic equality not often fully appreciated by researchers. Besides the well-known and lamented demolitions of historical residential areas such as Sophiatown and District Six, including 'slums' and 'transit camps' such as uMkhumbane (Cato Manor) and Crossroads, there are many smaller and less-known black areas which suffered the same fate and have only been tangentially dealt with by historians. We should note that some important realities and ideas that we ought to know about and appreciate were blotted out when the Nationalists took over in 1948 and declared war on squatters, interracial areas and 'black spots' in a spate of evictions and forced removals.[21] Class analysis was confounded as the apartheid regime used a blunt instrument, smashing anything and everything black, thus necessarily privileging race over class in historical analysis. Questions such as the class identity of squatter camp dwellers, their political practice, economic circumstances and their relationship to other classes or class fractions became secondary to the need for unity of the oppressed in the face of a ferocious and frenzied apartheid monster. Apartheid severely curtailed the development of political organisation and consciousness in the squatter camps by making these places cease to exist.

The apartheid experience has tended to obscure the specific class dimensions of the relationship of petty bourgeois political elements to the mostly working-class-led squatter movement of the 1940s in Johannesburg. When we lift the unifying quilt of nationalism from the oppressed, we find important divergences in political orientation, strategy and style that arise out of the class differences among them. The squatters did not readily gain the support of organisations such as the ANC, ANC Youth League and the SACP because of the circumscribed class political outlook of the leaders of these organisations. Nor was the potential power of the squatters as allies in the national liberation movement fully appreciated. There were many lost opportunities.

My historical investigations suggest that the 1940s squatter movement exhibited aspects of working-class self-management and self-rule that find an echo in the Marxist classical treatment of the subject. Some of these aspects are evident in today's *amakomiti*. A tradition that emerged in the squatters' movement, and which *amakomiti* appear to perpetuate, was of leaders and their followers taking control of their lives, taking matters into their own hands, turning to each other and organising themselves to satisfy their needs. Camp leaderships were apparently in touch with the needs of the camp residents, and came up with plans to meet these.[22] Indeed, 'the movements reveal powerful reciprocal relationships of authority and trust between squatter leaders and their followers.[23] Regular meetings were held, and at the head of each camp were committees such as the Sofasonke Party, the Pimville Sub-Tenants Association and the Alexandra Tenants Association.[24] The camp management arguably embodied 'a state within a state' – a form of working-class self-rule, or at least its seeds. In my research, it became clear that every informal settlement in post-apartheid society had a history of formation that included spawning its own James Sofasonke Mpanza, Comrade Jeff of Jeffsville in Pretoria, Mr Boyana of KwaBoyana in Vryheid or Comrade Cairo of Nkaneng in Rustenburg, for example. Although keen to negotiate with the state in order to secure basic services, many of the informal settlements went through a period of operating like 'liberated zones' where police and state officials had no jurisdiction. It was the self-organisation of the working class in their living spaces with the aim of meeting its own needs. This is an aspect that Marxist theorisation arguably ought to pay more attention to and study the empirical features of this model of working-class self-rule, just as Marx did with respect to the Paris Commune.

The phenomenon of self-organisation by informal settlements happens in other parts of the world. Manuel Castells has argued that the *barrios* and *favelas* are sometimes more organised than built-up areas.[25] Other researchers have noted this self-organisation in other countries.[26] It behoves Marxist theoreticians and organisers to find ways of strengthening these organisations and bringing them into the broader working-class movement, as appears to have happened in South Africa at the height of the struggle against apartheid in the 1980s. These alternative forms of organisation enable the masses to participate in processes of decision-making that correspond with their aspirations;[27] they may strengthen the workers' movement because they embody the embryo of workers' control in day-to-day practice while in certain respects laying the basis for a future socialist democracy.

With respect to the Thembelihle Crisis Committee, it developed a socialist outlook and practice not in isolation, but in close association with other organisations, including with the Soweto Electricity Crisis Committee and the Anti-Privatisation Forum, among many others. As such, a bridge was built between the struggles of shack dwellers and township residents, overcoming the artificial barriers by focusing on the differences between these constituencies. My interpretation of the evidence from this study is that where working-class politics is at the forefront, as in the case of the TCC, it is more likely that shack residents and their movements will be part of the broader movement of social change. This happened in the 1980s during the struggle against apartheid, for example in Etwatwa, Benoni, where employed workers came out in support of the shack dwellers' resistance to the demolition of shacks by the apartheid municipality.[28] Where petty bourgeois politics is at the forefront, such as when 'Trevor Manuel later defended the neglect of Khayelitsha by comparing the victims of these forced removals with scabs who take the place of workers on strike',[29] or when the United Democratic Front supported the apartheid warlord Ngxobongwana in Crossroads,[30] an apparent contradiction emerged between the squatter movement and the broader movement. Leadership, organisation and class outlook are important factors in this regard. In the 1940s, there were connections between the squatters' struggle and other struggles of the working class as a whole: 'industrial action, transport boycotts, and food riots, as well as in the development of support for wider political movements'.[31] The connection was also there in the 1980s.

There was interpenetration of workplace and living space struggles in the 1980s. Trade union leaders such as Moss Mayekiso and other worker leaders and ordinary workers strove to unite township and factory struggles.[32] At work, a form of worker control developed whose building blocks were the shop steward committees and later the joint shop steward councils.[33] Eddie Webster's research into the iron foundries in the 1980s revealed the creation of 'the embryo of a working class politics in South Africa' that involved:

> the growth of an organized challenge on the shop floor which has widened the negotiable issues, pushing forward the invisible frontier of control in the workplace.
>
> These demands extend beyond the workplace to include issues concerned with the reproduction of the workforce such as housing and pensions.[34]

Webster refers to the 'November 1984 stayaway when over half a million workers stayed away from work in protest over issues in the schools, townships and factories'.[35]

There are many ways to understand worker control, but in the context where Webster is writing, it was about how workers sought to have more say over the production process and the related terms and conditions of work. Workers were pushing the 'frontier of control' by contesting the power of the bosses, the managerial prerogative, to dictate how things were run at the workplace. The logical conclusion and triumph of this struggle from the point of view of the workers was that they themselves should take over and run the factories – that is, the socialist organisation of production. Moreover, as Sakhela Buhlungu observes: 'Union democracy was not merely an end in

141

itself but also a means to a greater end, namely, political democracy and working-class leadership in society.'[36]

The tradition of participatory democracy that was the hallmark of trade union practice spread out and infused the many structures of the growing movement in the workplaces and living spaces, in the civics and youth organisations, in church and women's groups, and in the townships and squatter camps. What was happening, according to Jonathan Grossman, was the development of 'a subversive progressive tradition, very powerful and at moments dominant within the unions and the movement of struggle more broadly'.[37] This was the development of a 'working class politics'[38] and of a 'workers' movement',[39] and it threatened the capitalist ruling class.

Neville Alexander has identified a set of factors that led to the successful negotiated settlement in South Africa.[40] One of them was the willingness of the ANC leadership to co-operate in what Huntington,[41] the theorist of democratic transitions, has termed a 'transplacement' type of transition whereby both the ANC and the apartheid government were crucial in initiating and sustaining it.[42] At the heart of this transition was the abandonment or significant toning down of the radical demands of the workers' movement for change, such as the call for '"nationalization" of mines, monopoly companies, banks, etc.' contained in the Freedom Charter, a document the ANC lauded for decades as its vision and policy framework.[43] The dispensation the ANC leadership co-midwifed 'first and foremost, serves the interests of the capitalist class'.[44] This entailed 'bloodless battles' inside the ANC with respect to policy positions, and 'there can be little doubt that … the radical forces suffered an almost irreversible defeat'.[45] It is within this context that the civics, shop steward councils and other organs of workers and people's power, including the UDF itself, were neutered. Cajoled and seduced, they came to support and be part of institutional state relations designed to curtail 'the ANC's ability to redistribute opportunity, infrastructural resources, access to productive activity and institutional power in favour of the popular classes'.[46]

At the workplace, the demand for worker control turned into calls for co-determination whereby the unions would co-operate with management in developing medium- to long-term productivity and profitability targets and ways to meet them.[47] Geoff Schreiner, a National Union of Metalworkers of South Africa official, advocated leaving 'complex substantial decisions' to individuals, not structures,[48] a position contested by Rob Rees and others.[49]

Increasingly, trade union leaders and labour analysts began to see the radical tradition of 'militant absentionism' or 'ungovernability' as counterproductive, and the call for 'reconstruction' (of a non-racial capitalist economy) drowned out the calls for the 'destruction' of the capitalist system.[50]

At workers' living spaces, the township civics suffered the same fate. Ideas of people's power came under attack, both frontally and underhandedly. The 'painstaking participatory democracy, built through direct mass action, almost always illegal, in struggle against often vicious repression' was undermined and eroded as 'leaders' were elevated above the movement.[51] The ANC leadership used its authority to control and contain mass struggle and militancy in the townships.[52] With the connivance of UDF leaders themselves, it shut down the UDF and other organisations that had become living embodiments of the radical mass participatory form of democracy.[53] Using the SACP, it sponsored debates about the need for the civics to play a 'reconstruction' role instead of a 'watchdog' role over the new post-apartheid government (just in case it 'sold out').[54] The idea of people's power was arguably sacrificed on the altar of class collaboration between the ANC as leader of the national liberation movement and big capital represented by the De Klerk regime.[55]

Since then, civic structures have become weak, and remain so in the postapartheid order.[56] Organisation in the shack settlements has not escaped this general weakening of civics. Nevertheless, as my research arguably shows, if we compare the fate of the shop steward councils, the civics and the shack settlements as grassroots structures of self-management, selfrule and mass participation, then the shack settlements have at least kept one arrow in their quiver. Some observers have argued that the negotiation settlement ignored the interests of informal settlement dwellers, probably requiring them to continue with the struggle, thus being less responsive to the mood of demobilisation prevailing then, and benefiting from the reduction in state repression.[57] Political conditions and the compromise made between the national liberation movement and capital denuded the ideas of worker self-organisation, self-management and self-rule, in the civics and the unions, of their revolutionary content. These ideas survive in somewhat diluted form in the people's committees, ward committees, school governing bodies, health committee, CDFs etc. It is, however, the shack settlements and their *amakomiti* – despite the absence of a workers' movement providing a centre of authority and albeit themselves largely shorn of revolutionary content – that exhibit characteristics classical Marxism would faintly recognise as aspirant forms of workers' 'self-management'.

AMAKOMITI AND MARXIST THEORY AND PRACTICE

What are the implications of the study of *amakomiti* for the Marxist theory of working-class self-organisation? Marxist theory prods us to pay attention to the political economy of shack settlements, noting their location within the configuration of capitalist urban space. Informal settlement dwellers are often workers or job seekers who want to live in areas close to employment opportunities. However, not only do city planners not prioritise the needs of working people, South African apartheid geography has relegated many workers to areas far from the central business districts and industrial nodes. In the new South Africa, little has changed as the market has replaced racism in the marginalisation of working class residential areas. Land values and property prices are some of the main mechanisms that exclude workers.

The Marxist emphasis on the unity of interests of the working class is also important in making sense of *amakomiti*. Recent theoretical trends in academia tend to focus, elaborate and put emphasis on social difference rather than commonality. For example, postcolonial theory appears to put an impenetrable barrier between workers in the Global North and Global South.[58] Differences must be explored, but for what purpose? My research suggests that workers living in built-up areas and those inhabiting slums can and do develop different priorities and even different political orientations. But if I had approached the field with a theory that seeks to elaborate on difference, I think I would have missed the existence of countervailing tendencies, some of them not arising out of the structural conditions, but from conscious interventions aimed at building unity in struggle in the face of 'objective' difference.

I noted that some informal settlements are located very near to or even within the perimeters of an existing working-class township. What emerged is that relations between shack dwellers and township residents – that is, the degree of proximity and integration between shack and council house – depended on historical factors. For example, in Duncan Village the process of setting up shacks was organised by a township civic as part of the struggle against apartheid spatial planning. In fact: 'By the early 1990s … spontaneous invasions were followed by planned land invasions, spearheaded by township based civic organizations in townships such as Wattville on the East Rand.'[59] This history of establishment of the shack settlements created a bond between shack and township resident. In some North Western informal settlements, such as Siyahlala-Huhudi in Vryburg and Baipei-Ikageleng in Zeerust, I found co-operation between residents of the newly established settlements and the adjacent built-up townships, largely because many of the post-apartheid land invaders were 'children' and relatives of the township folk who had established the new settlements due to intolerable overcrowding. In these cases, the new communities were allowed to use the formal township's services, such as water and sanitation. In other townships, the shack dwellers are sometimes made to pay for the use of such services, for example in the Duma Nokwe A and B settlements in Mdantsane in East London and Vrygrond in Graaff-Reinet.

Sometimes there is a distant relationship between the host community and the shack dwellers: for example, in Thembelihle and Nhlalakahle the settlements are located next to 'Indian areas'. In both these settlements, the electricity self-connections have created tensions between the formal and informal residents. This is not necessarily a racial issue, as the Protea South shack dwellers have had clashes over self-connections with Soweto residents where their informal settlement is located. However, the relationship is complex and multi-faceted: for example, many shack dwellers do business with the host community, and there are often associational links that might be political because both communities fall under the same ward. The TCC has a conscious policy to develop good relations with its Lenasia neighbours. The 'Indians' provide the TCC with meeting venues, donations for specific events etc. An important intervention of the TCC leaders since its formation was to 'educate' the residents not to use the word *amakula* ('coolies') because it is derogatory and racist. They have also fought against the idea that the ANC government wanted to relocate the settlement because the 'Indians' did not want them. In Chapter 1, I tell the story of how the TCC fought in defence of African immigrants during the xenophobic violence of 2008, 2011 and 2015 – a feat recognised and rewarded by the government. Human agency, education and emancipatory political projects can overcome objective constraints when they address prioritising unity rather than division. This is easier if our theory opens rather than closes doors between people.

It is not possible to have fundamental social change without mass participation. But for this to happen, organs of struggle and of self-government are

145

necessary, such as the 'soviets' during the Russian Revolution. The ultimate defeat of the Soviet workers' state, including its distortion and degeneration on the road toward self-destruction, should not blind us to important lessons about the soviets and the centrality of self-organised structures to facilitate mass participation in lasting social change. To illustrate my point, let us consider briefly the classical debate (often caricatured) between Lenin and Rosa Luxemburg. Lenin was the man of the vanguard, 'better fewer, but better', while Luxemburg believed in the mass strike, the revolutionary spontaneity of ordinary workers. My treatment of this important debate will be sketchy due to space constraints. During periods of political upsurge, Lenin adopted an 'expanded definition' of the working class that came closest to the position of Luxemburg, who had a profound belief in the 'organic capacity of the working class' to make its own revolution. Not only was it Lenin's task to persuade fellow Bolsheviks of the importance of the soviets, but he did so because he thought that during revolutionary upsurges, the key movers of history were the broadest layers of the popular classes. This position, it can be argued, would accommodate the self-organisation of the shack dwellers. Luxemburg supported all forms of organisation created by the working class in the course of struggle, and would undoubtedly embrace *amakomiti*. In other words, given a generous vision and a discerning theory, we can see *amakomiti* joining other sections of the working class and co-operating with workers' councils, soviets, shop steward councils etc. It is possible to imagine *amakomiti* having a role in the institutions of self-rule in a democratic workers' state.

An objection might arise that soviets and factory councils are organisations based in the factories, while shack committees operate in workers' living spaces. My submission is that the Marxist theory of self-organisation has to take on board class organisation at the workplace as well as at the living space. Soviets were 'purely class founded, proletarian organisation[s]' precisely because employed workers formed them.[60] However, workers also need organisation in their residential areas, and it might have been an oversight of the Bolshevik leaders or the particular circumstances in Russia that led to representation not being formally extended beyond the workplace. There are numerous examples in history of residential organisations involving themselves in working-class action: for example, the neighbourhood councils of the Portuguese and Iranian revolutions, and the South African township civics. The problem of non-working-class elements joining and possibly politically dominating these structures needs to be addressed, not only in the living spaces, but also at the workplace.

We should follow workers home and regard them as rounded beings. They are workers at work and at home, at their workplace and their living space. There is no Chinese wall between the exploitation and hardships of the workplace and those of the living space, because there is an underlying and living connection between the two in the functioning of the capitalist system itself. As Harvey puts it:

> [C]apital dominates labor not only in the place of work but in the living space by defining the standard of living of labor and the quality of life in part through the creation of built environments that conform to the requirements of accumulation and commodity production.[61]

Harvey hastens to add that this does not mean that labour cannot fight back, and indeed it does fight, mainly because:

> The built environment requires collective management and control, and it is therefore almost certain to be a primary field of struggle between capital and labor over what is good for accumulation and what is good for people.[62]

In this fight, labour or working-class communities can sometimes win against capital on particular issues, but 'the limits of tolerance of capital are clearly defined'. Therefore, 'For labor to struggle within these limits is one thing; to seek to go beyond them is where the real struggle begins.'[63]

Just as Russian soviets and Italian factory councils were formed during upsurges in struggle, in South Africa *amakomiti* thrived during moments of political upsurge during which they organized land invasions and established shack settlements. Why do *amakomiti* continue to exist beyond the political upheaval that gave birth to them? The evidence from the findings suggests that *amakomiti* continue to exist because of the hardships of daily life in shack settlements that require standing together and organising. *Amakomiti* appear more responsive to the needs of their constituencies; they change their form and character in order to address these needs. Informal settlement dwellers do not have many other avenues to put forward their demands and cater for their interests, so there is always an objective need for *amakomiti* to exist. In South Africa, for example, some commentators note that people with more money can 'opt out' of state services or supplement them through paid private provision (healthcare, education, security etc.). But for many workers, this is not an option.

There is a debate about 'new organisational forms' in the workers' movement. These are supposed to replace 'traditional' working-class organisations such as political parties and trade unions. The question is where *amakomiti* fall: do they belong to the old or the new forms? This question arises because traditional organizational forms are having a hard time adjusting to changing conditions, technology and composition of the working class. They are also perennially letting down workers, failing to defend their interests, and have developed a bad reputation for making decisions 'from above' rather than 'from below'. With respect to unions, workers will continue to need them as long as the capitalist class continues to exploit. Without a union, the employer would have too much power over workers. The solution lies in increasing the power of unions to push the boss back and win workers some gains. Strengthening the element of self-organisation of ordinary members at the lowest level can be a basis for resisting the trade union bureaucracy, compelling it to do what workers want. The same logic applies to political parties of the working class. This is easier said than done and there are no shortcuts, but we can take heart in the self-organisation that is already taking place in workers' living spaces, such as that found in the shack settlements in the form of *amakomiti*. If these grassroots structures are viewed as part of the tradition of grassroots democratic participation in the day-to-day life and struggle of the working class, at work and at home, then they can contribute to the Herculean effort needed to revitalise democratic practice in working-class organisations.

Buhlungu has argued that during the 1980s there was a dynamic cross-pollination between democratic principles and practices occurring at the workplace and in workers' living spaces in the townships. He observed that:

> the democratic tradition of unionism owes its origins to a very wide range of influences and sources, among which were cultural, traditional, political, and intellectual influences ... [it] was a complex composite of the lived experiences of egalitarianism and grassroots participation shared by black workers and the intellectual contributions of activists from different social and political backgrounds.[64]

He identifies several influences and sources of participatory democracy, such as from the churches, schools, sports clubs, unions, civics, youth organisations and women's groups. In practice, organised labour became the backbone of the workers' movement and one of the main custodians of this progressive democratic tradition. Buhlungu argues that there has been a 'decline' in the democratic tradition of the unions and 'the erosion of worker control'.[65] The workers' movement needs examples and instances of self-organisation. If we look hard enough, we can find these in the most unlikely places, sometimes in places where we never thought to look. The workers' movement can learn from *amakomiti*.

The decline in the relevance and attractiveness of Marxism as a political ideology and guide to action is a shortcoming. Marxism needs to inform the shack dwellers' movement. Bayat has argued that slum dwellers are 'non-ideological',[66] with the implication that a political ideology such as Marxism might not be relevant to the struggles and concerns that preoccupy shack dwellers and their committees. In South Africa, this argument has found support among important organisations and commentators in the shack dwellers' movement. Sometimes, it takes the form of claiming that shack dwellers have developed a unique politics that is distinct from, is an improvement upon, and eschews concern with ideological issues and approaches that preoccupy 'the Left'.[67] This is an important argument that has implications for issues such as whether shack dwellers can be part of the workers' movement, whether they would or should support a working-class party, and whether their movements should adopt socialism as their vision.

In my research findings, the concept of 'political culture' emerged as very important. The reason the TCC has been able to thrive as a leading organisation in Thembelihle, for example, has a lot to do with the political culture of open debate, participatory democracy and respect for the collective voice of the rank and file that characterises political practice in this settlement. Every important decision, including questions of ideological orientation and general strategy, is taken to the general meeting. This is arguably a political method based on the understanding that ordinary working-class people, be they shack dwellers or union members, have knowledge and intellectual life, and that questions of ideology, theories, principles, strategies and tactics belong to the rank and file, and not just to the leaders or the organic intellectuals of the movement. In other words, no idea is too big or too abstract for the general meeting. No special people have a mandate to think on behalf of and decide without the mass of residents of Thembelihle.

'Nothing About Us Without Us' is the powerful slogan of Abahlali baseMjondolo.[68] But in the shack dwellers' movement in South Africa there has at times been expressed the idea that some issues are not immediately relevant to the immediate struggle for houses, water and electricity – that is, there is a separation being introduced between political-ideological questions and 'bread and butter issues'. It is true that there is little reason nor time for shack dwellers' forums to discuss ideas that have no bearing on building stronger organisation for self-activity and mobilisation around the everyday problems facing shack dwellers. But issues of struggle, political power, the state, ideology, strategy and so on are relevant. Although this can be difficult or time-consuming, they must still be brought to the general meeting for discussion, rather than *a priori* defining them to be 'above the heads' of the rank and file and confining their discussion to groups of specialists inside or outside the movement. We must avoid the policing of ideas whereby gatekeepers decide which ideas can or cannot be discussed in the movement. Defining shack dwellers as inherently 'non-ideological' justifies intellectual gatekeeping.

Workers are first and foremost 'producers, not wage-earners, the slaves of Capital'.[69] Luxemburg believed that it is the millions and millions of workers who must struggle for and create the society without exploitation of the future.[70] No leader or group of leaders can do this for them. This means that ordinary workers, including the mass of shack dwellers, must be engaged in the debate about which are the best radical political alternatives that must be fought for in order to build a new, just world. They are the ones who must constitute the power necessary to turn these into reality; nothing that will affect their future must be discussed without them. They themselves, and not a special corps of intellectuals, must realise that their problems emanate from the way that society is structured, and that any lasting solutions will require radical transformation. Without them, there can be no revolution.

A vexed question in the politics of transformation is the role of political parties. My research suggests that local shack dwellers' committees will work with, support and join political parties and other civil society organisations in order to augment their influence and organise support for their struggles. Sometimes, as in the case of Duncan Village and many other settlements, they look toward and work with the ruling party, the ANC. In

other cases, such as in Thembelihle, they throw in their lot with anti-capitalist and pro-socialist movements and organisations, some of which are
working toward overthrowing the capitalist state and replacing it with a
workers' state. Organised labour and township civics in South Africa mostly
align themselves with the ANC. It is only recently that NUMSA, the metalworkers' union, opted to withdraw its support and called for the formation
of a working-class party, thus provoking new configurations of political alignment in the country.[71] Despite the fact that some movements and
unions adopt an ideologised 'apolitical' or 'non-partisan' stance, ostensibly
to protect and project their independence, in practice, working-class formations tend to align themselves with particular political parties and to
orient toward state power in South Africa. This is a position that is closer to
the Marxist approach than the autonomist and anarchist positions that are
opposed to representative democracy and the state in principle.

There is a need in South Africa for an organisation that focuses on power
– a political party of the working class.[72] Experiences of soviets, workers
councils, factory councils and other working-class structures considered
here, especially in contexts of defeated revolutions, suggest this. These structures mostly start off addressing immediate issues and then are drawn into
struggles for power that often involve a phase of 'dual power' or something
approaching it. At this point, it becomes necessary to focus upon and prepare
for the end goal and ponder the best path to reach it. Given the failures and
mistakes of revolutionary efforts in the twentieth century, I would suggest
that the role of the party in the twenty-first century should be to ensure that
these debates and discussions are taking place in the movement as a whole,
and in a participatory democratic way. History suggests that this happens
in any case during revolutionary upsurges. The important point is that the
momentum and focus should not be lost in the midst of the chaos of revolutionary upheaval. Experiences of political parties that lose the plot by either
becoming reformist or dictatorial do not and should not distract attention
from the need to concentrate the revolutionary flame like a blowtorch on the
moorings that keep the ruling class in power. This suggests the need for a
political organisation, a party. I am not in a position to take this point further
here, but I can say with confidence that no revolutionary transformation
can be possible without grassroots self-organising by the masses, without
soviets, factory councils, street committees and so on, without structures
like *amakomiti*. It is thus not surprising that the first sign of a lost revolu-

tion is the attenuation or distortion of grassroots self-organisation, as the example of the dismantling of the *shuras* in the Iranian revolution suggests.

Shack dwellers and their committees are everywhere in South Africa, and there is no indication that they will disappear. A substantial proportion of the protests taking place in the country involve this constituency.[73] But like all the other community protests, the protest action is fragmented, with little support and solidarity across the settlements.[74] This, however, does not mean that protesting has no impact. The Thembelihle Crisis Committee, for example, after years of sustained protest, has compelled the government to abandon its relocation policy with respect to the Thembelihle settlement and commit to *in situ* development.[75] In many settlements, the ANC still enjoys a tenuous if undeniable hegemony. The vicious attack on Abahlali baseMjondolo in Durban's Kennedy Road settlement, where the members of this organisation, including its president, S'bu Zikode, were driven out of the area, suggests a two-pronged approach by the state to opposition in the settlements.[76] Depending on the circumstances, the state will use hegemonic tactics that involve influencing and taking over the local committees; but where this does not work, it is prepared to resort to naked repression.[77] This suggests that in areas where communities are 'neglected' by the state in terms of improving living conditions, the ANC will in general not bother itself with them unless they resort to protest action or somehow appear to pose a threat to its hegemony. Many settlements complained of political neglect, and informants told me how the local ANC leadership moves very quickly as soon as it gets wind of a plan to organise shack dwellers' dissatisfaction into protest action.[78] What this suggests is that self-organisation linked to the struggle for improved services directed at the state remains 'an objective need' and an important weapon in the settlements. When protest challenges ANC hegemony, it is more likely to get a speedy response, positive or negative, from the state.

The Marikana Massacre that happened on 16 August 2012 has been a 'turning point', changing political dynamics significantly in South Africa.[79] The workers' committees that organised and led the strike wave in the platinum belt were an affirmation of the importance of working-class self-organisation.[80] The massacre's aftermath exacerbated the legitimacy crisis of the ANC, shook to the core the ANC-SACP-COSATU Alliance and created huge divisions in the labour movement. NUMSA pulled out of the Alliance in 2013, withdrawing its electoral support for the ANC, and for its troubles, got expelled from COSATU despite being the biggest affiliate, with over 350,000 members. The union resolved to make common cause with struggling working-class communities and formed a United Front, a new union federation and a workers' party. This would bridge the gap created by Alliance politics that divided organized labour from working-class community movements for more than two decades.[81] Metalworkers are important in a reviving workers' movement: for example, metalworkers and their unions were always in the lead in the Russian soviets.[82] However, after 20 years in a political limbo in which it cut its ties with communities, the union has a lot of work to do. There will undoubtedly be a need to bridge the political–cultural divide that has developed between different sections and components of the workers' movement. Both organised labour, in this instance led by NUMSA, and working-class communities and their movements and organisations will need to reach out to each other and learn to work and struggle together. The interaction will without doubt raise in quite specific ways theoretical and political questions such as that of 'vanguardism', because employed and organised workers may be in a stronger position to lead and provide the resources for the movement than the unemployed

Photo 7.1   Privately owned rental accommodation (*emqashweni*). Thousands of people live in this type of accommodation in KwaZulu-Natal and other provinces. (Photograph by author)

and underemployed. It will be necessary to debate anew and to reformulate the relationship between nationalist and socialist goals informed by theoretical insights garnered from the study of twentieth-century revolutionary experiences, not least from the catastrophic dead-end politics of Stalinism, to develop and prepare *amakomiti* of the shack settlements as part of an array of embryonic structures to be used as springboards in the formation of councils, civics and soviets that will be central in the next revolutionary upsurge in South Africa. *Amakomiti* must reach out to the hundreds of thousands of other inadequately housed people such as those who live in *emqashweni* (privately owned rented accommodation; see Photo 7.1). This is important in the light of recent figures that suggest that the rental of informal housing has doubled in the period 2002–2014.[83]

As the working class faces the challenges of capitalist crisis in the twenty-first century, it arguably needs a movement and a party that will take it all the way to the dismantling of the social structures that organise and generate exploitation and oppression. Such a party, as the history I have considered in this book seems to suggest, must be a mass, socialist, revolutionary party – that is, it must take the form of a movement of millions and millions of ordinary workers and supporters. The revival of the workers' movement, its coalescence into a formidable force in the course of struggle, its revolutionary slogans, its mass organisations that will lead the struggle against capitalism and turn themselves into organs of workers power, will require a political and organising centre that will take responsibility for this work of co-ordination, education and leadership. Without such a party, the building of a workers' socialist state in Russia would not have happened.[84] The South African working class needs its own party.[85] Dwindling electoral enthusiasm and support for the ANC, as reflected in the 2016 local government elections, suggests that political space exists for such a party from an electoral point of view. From the point of view of working-class politics, such a party will have failed in its task of uniting and strengthening the working-class movement if it does not reach out to shack dwelling communities and organise them and their *amakomiti* into dependable sections of the workers' movement.

Lastly, as the capitalist crisis wreaks havoc with living standards all over the world, we see an explosion in the number of people who live in informal housing. This is the main observation made by Mike Davis in his book *Planet of Slums*.[86] He mars this important contribution on the issue with his view that slum dwellers somehow constitute a kind of lumpenproleriat, leading him to dismiss their political agency. Lenin, whose skills of organising were honed in the process of preparing for and leading a successful revolution, argued that the revolution is waged with the human material history provides, rather than what revolutionary purists require.[87] He called for a proletarian revolution in Russia, well aware of the limitations of the Russian working class, arising partly out of its location and development in a 'backward' country. We face the same problem in the twenty-first century, where the uneven development of capitalism has left many countries and many working classes unevenly developed,[88] and many places have not reached the level of economic and social development Marx had envisaged to be necessary for a socialist transformation. There was a lot of improvisation in the course of the Russian revolution: for example, the soviets found a way of accommodating soldiers and sailors into their structures.[89] It can be argued that the workers' movement in South Africa, and in many parts of the world where there are slums, will have to find ways of integrating the shack dwellers into its organs of struggle and workers' power. In practice, capitalism is doing what Marx and Engels predicted in *The Communist Manifesto*: dividing the world into two great opposing classes, the increasingly rich, tiny minority capitalist class, and the millions and millions of humanity whose conditions of work and life mean they have nothing to lose and everything to gain by involving themselves in struggles against capitalist policies.[90]

Photo 7.2   The workers' committee that led the Lonmin strike before the Marikana Massacre in Rustenburg, August 2012. (Photograph: Greg Marinovich)

CONCLUSION: *A LUTA CONTINUA!*

Amakomiti are the grassroots democratic structures set up by the inhabitants of informal settlements. They are important to study and understand
because self-activity and self-organisation provide the strongest foundation
of working-class collective political action. The role of *amakomiti* is that of
organs of struggle and of self-government. In practice, it can be argued that
they operate somewhere between Colin Barker's revolutionary perspective
of alternative political forms and the reformist formulations of mainstream
social movement theory.[91] In other words, they are not always leading
struggle, and the powers they have of self-management can be quite limited.
For example, Duncan Village's area committees are arguably a shadow of
themselves compared to their glory days during the reign of the DVRA and
people's power in the 1980s. The ANC government has not only moved to
curtail their power, it has also introduced competing and better-resourced
ward committees that seem to crowd the area committees out. Well-paid
employment in the capitalist state sucks leading comrades from the ground
like a gigantic vacuum cleaner.

This book is therefore not a glorification of *amakomiti*, and neither is it
a romanticisation of the organisations and movements of shack dwellers.
Life in the shack settlements is not ideal nor conducive in bringing out the
best in human beings. It is hard to be the best you can be while living in a
shack, being subjected to environmental racism.[92] There exist various forms
of oppression and exploitation, brutality and callousness. Capitalist individ-
ualism, nationalist xenophobia, sexist domestic violence, fear of deprivation
and many other evils that characterise society are concentrated in these
living spaces:

> Aggressive competitiveness, individualism, instrumentalism, were
> dominant parts of capitalist morality, contextually affirmed, and corrod-
> ing collectivism and solidarity inside the workers' movement. These were
> features of the life imposed on workers every day.[93]

There will be many problems with *amakomiti*. It is a struggle against
heavy odds. But look at how the workers at Marikana heroically and against
all odds continued with their strike after 34 of their comrades lay dead.[94]
Look at how in the slums, those spaces for 'warehousing the twenty-first

century's surplus humanity'[95] there is still laughter, beauty and compassion. With workers, there is always a way forward. There is a compelling drive to survive, to live, to struggle. There is a force that drove the Marikana miners to fight against all odds, that pushes squatters to take over land and face down the state police. It is the organic capacity of the working class, according to Antonio Gramsci, the limitless 'capacity for initiative and creation of the working masses':

> how limitless the latent powers of the masses are, and how they are revealed and develop swiftly as soon as the conviction takes root among the masses that they are arbiters and masters of their own destinies.[96]

The widespread existence of popular committees in the shack settlements suggests that there indeed exists a form of 'democracy on the margins' despite all the problems and in a context where many working-class structures such as township civics have more or less collapsed or been robbed of their class independence and fighting spirit. It is a democracy of people pushed aside and neglected who are fighting to have their needs addressed and their views taken on board. Different committees adopt different politics and tactics, leading to different possibilities and outcomes for the communities they organise and lead. Nothing is predetermined, there are limitations and possibilities in every situation.[97] The search for and the testing out of the best politics and strongest action continue. The learning from past victories and defeats continues. The ultimate goal is the eradication of all forms of exploitation, oppression and domination in the world.[98] I hope that my attempt at extending our understanding of *amakomiti* contributes something to that process. The sun will rise for the workers.[99]

Postscript
Covid-19 and the Shacks

2020. Covid-19. It caught all of us off guard. This book delayed publication as the pandemic wrought havoc across the world and, for once – said the perennial underdogs – it directed its attack on the advanced capitalist countries, leaving the developing and poorer ones more or less untainted, but only for a while. Still, it was long enough for silly people to say, 'Ah don't worry, it is a white man's disease.' It was only the calm before the storm, and the pandemic hit South Africa with a vengeance. By the end of August 2020, infections stood at about 639,000 and deaths at 14,000. This means that South Africa is in the top ten of countries with the highest rates of infection. It is the highest in Africa, although mercifully with a relatively low number of deaths compared to infections.

The ANC government, fresh from its election victory in 2019, acted swiftly, instituting an early, speedy and comprehensive lockdown on 26 March 2020, when the infections were few. The government, led by the State President and the Minister of Health, waged a concerted campaign to win consent from the country for what, with hindsight, were draconian steps that were harsh on the working class and the poor. As everyone was bemused, and fearful, the country's leaders ran on ahead, took centre stage, doing this and that, passing decrees and making proclamations, everyone awaiting with bated breath what the President would say next, which power was going to be wielded. The army was deployed to keep people off the streets. Resistance first emanated from and was led by cigarette manufacturers and retailers, followed by the liquor and restaurant industries, as the lockdown hit where it hurts most. Over the months, the lockdown rules were gradually reduced from Level 5 to today's Level 2, and people are drinking and puffing away gratefully.

The government measures to fight the virus exposed once more its increasing class distance from the poor as it imposed social distancing in ways which those who live in shack settlements could simply not adhere to.

The shack settlements are overcrowded, and the government set in motion plans to 'de-densify' by providing temporary shelters in certain areas, including targeting the homeless (those who sleep out in the open) and compelling them to move off the street. Unsavoury skirmishes ensued. Water tanks were provided for shack settlements as the call to wash your hands frequently proved impracticable in areas where there was no potable water.

Like leper colonies of biblical times, the shack dwellers were cordoned off and their movements monitored by the police and army with apartheid-style bullying. A few people got killed by soldiers or police and a lot more got pushed around as the bans on movement, social gatherings and alcohol were enforced. Soldiers shot and killed a man, Collins Khosa, in Alexandra Township for allegedly drinking beer in his own yard. A couple of months later, an official investigation revealed what everyone knew: the soldiers had been way out of line when they killed Khosa.

The lockdown raised memories of the States of Emergency of the 1980s, in which punishment was arbitrary and the security forces could act with impunity. Some communities protested in the streets, complaining about hunger as the lockdown forced people to sit at home without an income (while the bosses and professional workers were able to work from home). Workers, street traders and those in the informal sector who are daily fighting to survive paid the biggest price. In its wisdom, the government had decided to allow supermarket chains owned by big business to operate, but banned street traders and hawkers from trading. Later, when this policy was relaxed, small traders had to stand in queues to apply for trading permits.

The fear of the virus, of death, was the biggest bludgeon the government had to quell any opposition. Ordinary people, workers, shack dwellers, the poor and the vulnerable found themselves caught between the devil and the deep blue sea. Their precarious existence in capitalist South Africa was magnified. As one pamphlet agitating against the system put it:

Workers are scared to go to work and they are scared to be unemployed. They are scared for their children to go to school and they are scared for their children if they do not go to school. They are scared when they must get into a taxi or a bus for transport. And they are scared when there is no taxi or bus. They are scared when hunger drives some onto the streets. And they are scared when they stay in their shacks. They are scared when the police and soldiers don't stop reckless behaviour and they are scared when they see the police and soldiers approach them.[1]

The emptying out of the public health system also soon became apparent. Despite the early action by the government to stem the infection tide, harsh socioeconomic realities, including the failure of the government of national liberation to improve living conditions more than 25 years after liberation, exposed millions to the devastation of the pandemic. In South Africa, healthcare workers were fighting a virus with a health system that does not work. The country has a two-tier health system: one private, the other public, one for the rich, the other for the poor. If you get sick, it is better that you should have 'medical aid', a type of health insurance which only middle- and upper-income people can afford. Then you can be attended to at a private hospital and get good medical care at prices that will wake you up from a coma. Otherwise, you may end up in an overcrowded and dysfunctional public hospital where you are likely to catch something which you had not presented with when you came. Elderly people are known to refuse to go to hospital: 'What, you are tired of me, now sending me to the *slagpaal* [Afrikaans for 'slaughterhouse']?' A decade is ending with the ANC government singing the hymn of a National Health Insurance system that will serve all, but there has been little tangible progress and people continue to die in state hospitals.

The pandemic has ironically exposed the limitations of private healthcare, with at least three private hospitals experiencing infection outbreaks among the nursing staff. Both the private and public medical laboratories were found wanting, unable to cope with the testing workload, resulting in long delays before people could get results for their tests. But the people who should be the first to be protected from the virus, the health workers who are without doubt the frontline troops in the war to save lives and ensure health for all, found themselves struggling to get adequate supplies of personal protection equipment (PPE). How could they fight the virus without protection for themselves? Many complained about the shortage of masks, gowns, sanitiser etc. This has been their cry throughout the several months of the pandemic in South Africa. Health workers say that in the public hospitals things are so bad that when they go home, they pray that they don't infect their families.

The biggest union in the healthcare sector, the National Education, Health and Allied Workers Union, an affiliate of COSATU, the ANC's alliance partner, is mobilising health workers for a general strike after sporadic and uncoordinated action by health workers feeling the pressure. COSATU has announced a one-day strike some time in the near future. For the first time, its rival the South African Federation of Trade Unions, whose biggest affiliate is NUMSA, has pledged its support for the strike. The C19 People's Coalition, with more than 200 civil society organisations, and the most active in mobilising around the pandemic and organising relief and support for neglected communities, has also pledged its support. The coalition has held several street protests, raising various grievances and demands around the need to protect people and provide adequate support. If the unions follow the same route as the rumbling and grumbling would suggest, then this time the masses will hit the streets in numbers and C19's protests will seem like a very light warm-up before the champion boxer goes into the ring.

Meanwhile, what appears to be the straw that is breaking the camel's back and provoking mass protest is the ruling class being found engaged in an orgy of looting of funds meant for the protection of the poor. Millions of rands are being stolen from Covid-19 relief, provision of PPE etc. The spokesperson of President Ramaphosa was forced to step down after she and her husband won a shady government contract, a 'tender', to supply PPE. Apparently, government procurement laws were suspended to facilitate the response to the virus. The Gauteng Province's Minister of Health is on special leave awaiting outcome of an investigation. People's jaws fall to the floor almost every day as new and more scandalous headline stories are heard about Covid-19-related corruption. At first, it was price gouging by supermarkets, but now it is politicians and government officials setting up companies and selling PPE, some of it failing to pass quality tests, to the government at inflated prices. The latest scandal is the head of the Unemployment Insurance Fund, in charge of the government Temporary Employee/Employer Relief Scheme, who was found dipping his grubby fingers into the till, making false payments and using other machinations to steal. The 'nation' is disgusted, frustrated and very angry. Hope and trust is daily being eroded.

Covid-19 has highlighted and accentuated what many people already knew: that the working class and the poor live in danger because of the system that puts profits before people. Workers know that poverty is a danger to health, that it is an ongoing and ever-present threat to their lives. The fact that the pandemic has made this worse does not detract from the sad truth that it was like that before the virus and it will be like that after the virus. The lives of workers are at risk. Bosses force workers into work situations that are dangerous and where there is risk of infection. This is what bosses do even before Covid-19 – they force workers to do dangerous work. They will continue to do so after Covid-19 is gone. Shack dwellers live in flimsy structures which make them sick and miserable. This happened before Covid-19 and will continue after Covid-19. The yearning to return to normal means, for millions of people, going back to that life of hardship, of struggle for survival, which is the only thing the system can offer them.

But there were counter-currents. The events surrounding Covid-19 brought to the fore the power of local organisation, as the *amakomiti* in the shacks and activist organisations in the towns and townships organised local food supplies, took care of the old and stood against the excesses of the army. The people knew they were on their own, and across the country working-class communities responded with imagination and inventiveness. At a time of social distancing, the bonds nurtured through the long years of neo-liberal ANC rule once more became the line between survival and death.

While Covid-19 has changed the terrain of struggle, recent experiences have taught the workers and poor of this land that local forms of organising are important to sustain bare life. They have also learned that they have to find ways of linking with other communities of the working class. They realise that the struggle for survival in the face of Covid-19 deepens local networks, but it can also cut you off. It can isolate communities from each other as they look inward. Government restrictions on freedom of movement only make matters worse. But it seems that of late, communities are reaching out, common platforms are being put together, major actions are being planned and new strategic questions asked.

How do local defensive trenches translate into more generalised offensive lines of march? How do we challenge the system which is making us pay for its crisis? Which social force can match the totalistic power of capital?

My journey started with a simple question, '*Ngingalitholaphi ikomiti lalendawo?*' ('Where can I find this place's committee?').

I not only found a committee, but found a renewed radical optimism. I hope that in reading these pages, you too will be inspired.

Appendix 1
List of Case Study Interviews

Interview No. 1DV, community member and ex-DVRA committee member (male), 3 October 2013

Interview No. 2DV, ward councillor and ex-DVRA committee member (male), 4 October 2013

Interview No. 3DV, ANC Branch Executive and ANC Women's League committee member, 5 October 2013

Interview No. 4DV, area committee member and ANC BEC member, 5 October 2013

Interview No. 5DV, area committee member, Duncan Village, 6 October 2013

Interview No. 6DV, ANC ward councillor, Duncan Village (female), 25 February and 1 October 2013

Interview No. 8DV, ward committee and area committee member (female), 2 October 2013

Interview No. 9DV, ward committee member and ANC Youth League member, 1 October 2013

Interview No. 10DV, group interview with seven residents (five males and two females), 25 February 2013

Interview No. 11DV, area committee member (male), 3 October 2013

Interview No. 12DV, area committee member (female), 3 October 2013

Interview No. 13DV, community member (female), 3 October 2013

Interview No. 14DV, community policing forum and ANC BEC member (female), 2 October 2013

Interview No. 1NK, Inkundla yaseLibode group interview (ten males and two females), 15 July 2013

Interview No. 2NK, CPF committee member and ex-ward councillor (female), 7 July 2013

Interview No. 3NK, community members group interview, founder members of Nkaneng community (two females), 2 July 2013

Interview No. 4NK, *spaza* (informal) shop owner, Mozambican national (male), 4 July 2013

Interview No. 5NK, ex-CPF committee member, ward committee member, ANC committee member (male), 14 December and 2 July 2013

Interview No. 6NK, ANC committee member (male), 23 June 2013

Interview No. 7NK, personal assistant to ward councillor, ex-ANC Youth League committee member (male), 25 June 2013

Interview No. 8NK, ANC committee member (female), 16 July 2013

Interview No. 9NK, community member (female), 18 July 2013

Interview No. 10NK, community member (male), 4 July 2013

Interview No. 11NK, Inkundla yaseNgqeleni member (male), 18 July 2013

Interview No. 12NK, Inkundla yaseMqanduli member (male), 10 November 2013

Interview No. 13NK, hostel committee member and AMCU shop steward (male), 17 July 2013

Interview No. 14NK, hostel manager/official (male), 17 July 2013

Interview No. 15NK, municipality housing official (male), 14 December 2012

Interview No. 16NK, ANC proportional representation councillor (female), 28 June July 2013

THEMBELIHLE INTERVIEWS

Interview No. 1TL, resident from the early days and ex-ANC committee member (female), 19 December 2013

Interview No. 2TL, resident and member of early committees (male), 18 December 2013

Interview No. 3TL, resident from the early days (male), 18 December 2013

Interview No. 4TL, resident from the early days (female), 21 December 2013

Interview No. 5TL, resident from the early days (male), 22 December 2013

Interview No. 6TL, resident and TCC committee member (male), 18 December 2013

Interview No. 7TL, group interview, residents of Thembelihle (two females and one male), 5 January 2014

Interview No. 8TL, TCC committee member (female), 5 January 2014

Interview No. 9TL, community member, youth (female) 6 January 2014

Interview No. 10TL, community member, youth (male) 6 January 2014

Appendix 2
List of Research Tour Interviews and Places Visited

No.	Description of interviewee	Male or female	Date of interview	Name of settlement	Town or city
1	Headman committee member	Male	4 Dec. 2012	Top Village	Mahikeng
2	Resident	Female	4 Dec. 2012	Top Village	Mahikeng
3	Ward committee member	Male	5 Dec. 2012	Dinokana village	Zeerust
4	People's committee member	Male	5 Dec. 2012	Baipei – Ikageleng township	Zeerust
5	Youth	Female	5 Dec. 2012	Ikageleng – Dinokana village	Zeerust
6	People's committee member	Female	6 Dec. 2012	Siyahlala – occupied houses in Huhudi Extension 25	Vryburg
7	People's committee member	Female	6 Dec. 2012	Monomoto – Huhudi Extension 26	Vryburg
8	People's committee member	Male	6 Dec. 2012	Phola Park – Huhudi	Vryburg
9	Headman committee member	Male	10 Dec. 2012	Mandela Park	Mahikeng
10	People's committee member	Male	10 Dec. 2012	Rooigrond	Mahikeng
11	People's committee member	Male	11 Dec. 2012	Rooikoppies – Marikana	Rustenburg
12	Resident	Male	11 Dec. 2012	Yizo Yizo – Boitekong	Rustenburg

No.	Description of interviewee	Male or female	Date of interview	Name of settlement	Town or city
13	People's committee members (group)	4 males 2 females	12 Dec. 2012	Freedom Park	Rustenburg
14	Housing official	Male	13 Dec. 2012	Rustenburg Local Municipality	Rustenburg
15	Ward committee member	Male	14 Dec. 2012	Nkaneng (Bleskop) – Marikana	Rustenburg
16	Residents (group)	5 females	22 Jan. 2013	Princess	Roodepoort
17	People's, ward and ANC committee members (group)	4 females 1 male	22 Jan. 2013	Zenzele	Randfontein
18	CPF member	Female	22 Jan. 2013	Zenzele	Randfontein
19	People's committee member	Female	22 Jan. 2013	Spooktown – Bekkersdal	Randfontein
20	CDF member	Male	23 Jan. 2013	Makause	Germiston
21	People's committee member	Male	23 Jan. 2013	Tsakane Extension 10	Brakpan
22	People's committee member	Male	24 Jan. 2013	Jeffsville – Atteridgeville	Pretoria
23	ANC BEC member	Male	24 Jan. 2013	Itireleng – Laudium	Pretoria
24	CDF members (group)	1 male 1 female	24 Jan. 2013	Itireleng – Laudium	Pretoria
25	CPF member	Male	27 Jan. 2013	Tamboville – Glenwood	Pietermar-itzburg
26	People's committee member	Male	27 Jan. 2013	Nhlalakahle – Northdale	Pietermar-itzburg
27	Security worker – development project	Female	28 Jan. 2013	Bhambayi – Inanda	Durban
28	CDF members (group)	2 males	28 Jan. 2013	Bhambabyi – Inanda	Durban
29	People's committee member	Female	29 Jan. 2013	Barcelona 1 – Lamontville	Durban
30	Youth	Female	1 Feb. 2013	SASKO	Ulundi

Appendix 2: Research Tour Interviews and Places Visited

No.	Description of interviewee	Male or female	Date of interview	Name of settlement	Town or city
31	Ward committee member	Female	3 Feb. 2013	H39 – Madadeni	Newcastle
32	Resident	Female	3 Feb. 2013	H39 – Madadeni	Newcastle
33	CPF member	Male	4 Feb. 2013	Siyahlala (Dunusa)	Newcastle
34	Resident	Male	4 Feb. 2013	Siyahlala (Dunusa)	Newcastle
35	Residents, mostly youth (group)	6 females 9 males	4 Feb. 2013	eSiteshini – Ngagane	Newcastle
36	Resident youth	Male	4 Feb. 2013	eSiteshini – Ngagane	Newcastle
37	Ex–people's committee member	Male	4 Feb. 2013	eSiteshini – Newcastle	Newcastle
38	People's committee member	Female	5 Feb. 2013	eDlamini –Sibongile township	Dundee
39	Resident	Male	5 Feb. 2013	KwaBoyana	Vryheid
40	Public relations officer	Female	6 Feb. 2013	Amajuba Municipality	Newcastle
41	Councillor (proportional representation opposition party)	Male	14 Feb. 2013	Emfuleni Municipality	Vanderbijl-park
42	Residents	3 females	14 Feb. 2013	Sebokeng Zone 20 Phase 2	Vaal
43	People's committee member	Male	17 Feb. 2013	Vrygrond	Graaff–Rei-net
44	Residents (group)	2 females	18 Feb. 2013	Chris Hani	Somerset East
45	Resident	Female	18 Feb. 2013	Chris Hani	Somerset East
46	Resident	Female	18 Feb. 2013	Zinyoka	Somerset East
47	People's committee member	Female	18 Feb. 2013	Mahlabathini – Motherwell	Port Eliza-beth

No.	Description of interviewee	Male or female	Date of interview	Name of settlement	Town or city
48	Residents (group)	14 females 1 male	19 Feb. 2013	Ntswahlane – KwaNobuhle township	Uitenhage
49	People's committee members (group)	2 males 1 female	19 Feb. 2013	Gunguluza – KwaNobuhle township	Uitenhage
50	Residents (group)	3 males	20 Feb. 2013	Ramaphosa – New Brighton	Port Elizabeth
51	Youth (group)	3 males	20 Feb. 3013	G–West – Walmer	Port Elizabeth
52	CPF member	Male	24 Feb. 2013	Malinda Forest	East London
53	Ward committee member	Female	24 Feb. 2013	Cambridge	East London
54	Ward councillor	Female	25 Feb. 2013	Duncan Village	East London
55	Residents (group)	2 females	25 Feb. 2013	Duncan Village	East London
56	Residents (group)	4 females 2 males	25 Feb. 2013	Duma Nokwe B – Mdantsane	East London
57	People's committee member	Female	25 Feb. 2013	Duma Nokwe A – Mdantsane	East London
58	ANC BEC member	Male	26 Feb. 2013	Orange Grove – West Bank	East London
59	Resident	Male	26 Feb. 2013	Siyanda	Butterworth
60	Residents (group)	3 males 2 females	27 Feb. 2013	KwaS'gebenga (Khayelitsha) – Ngcambedlana Farm	Mthatha
61	People's committee members (group)	2 females	27 Feb. 2013	Thambula Phansi – Ngcambedlana Farm	Mthatha
62	Residents (group)	2 females	28 Feb. 2013	Sibantubonke	Mthatha
63	Ward committee member	Female	10 Dec. 2012	Imperial Reserve Township	Mahikeng

Notes

PREFACE

1. *Amagali* means 'shacks' in isiXhosa; in isiZulu the word is *imijondolo*, thus Abahlali baseMjondolo ('Residents of the Shacks'), the name of the movement of shack dwellers in South Africa. There are other names used: *amahoko*, *imikhukhu*, etc.

2. R. Pithouse (2005), 'The Left in the Slum: The Rise of a Shack Dwellers' Movement in Durban, South Africa', paper presented at *History and African Studies Seminar*, University of KwaZulu-Natal, Durban, 23 November.

3. From the Bertolt Brecht poem 'A Worker Reads History' (1936).

4. C. Barker (2015), 'Beyond the Waves: Marxism, Social Movements and Revolution', paper presented at *Alternatives Futures and Popular Protest* conference, Manchester, UK, 30 March–1 April, https://sites.google.com/site/colinbarkersite/ (accessed 12 July 2019).

5. 'The coincidence of the changing of circumstances and of human activity or self-change [*Selbstveränderung*] can be conceived and rationally understood only as revolutionary practice'; K. Marx (1845), trans. C. Smith and D. Cuckson (2002), *Theses on Feuerbach*, www.marxists.org/archive/marx/works/1845/theses/ (accessed 10 October 2020).

6. D. Harvey (2005), *A Brief History of Neoliberalism*, New York: Oxford University Press, p. 77.

7. A. Bayat (1997), *Street Politics: Poor People's Movements in Iran*, New York: Columbia University Press; M. Davis (2006), *Planet of Slums*, London: Verso.

8. See L. Sinwell with S. Mbatha (2016), *The Spirit of Marikana: The Rise of Insurgent Trade Unionism in South Africa*, London: Pluto Press.

1 INTRODUCTION: DISRUPTING PRIVATE LAND OWNERSHIP?

1. R. Teo (2015), 'The Organisation of a Land Occupation: A Case Study of Marikana, Cape Town', Master of Social Science in Sociology dissertation, University of Cape Town, p. 75.

2. Household yards or plots are called 'stands', and the *stoep* is a verandah or porch in front of the house.

3. C. Guevara (2002), *Guerrilla Warfare*, Lanham, MD: Rowman & Littlefield, p. 174.

4. Interview, Fundis Mhlongo, Durban, 5 June 2012.

5. A. Gilbert and J. Gugler (1982), *Cities, Poverty, and Development: Urbanization in the Third World*, Oxford, UK: Oxford University Press , p. 89; A. Mabin (1989), 'Land Invasion: Causes, Forms and Consequences as Portrayed in Selected South American Research', *UF Research 7*, Johannesburg, South Africa: Urban Foundation, Stellenbosch University, p. 23; Teo, 'The Organisation of a Land Occupation', pp. 54–5.

6. P. Alexander (2010), 'Rebellion of the Poor: South Africa's Service Delivery Protests – a Preliminary Analysis', *Review of African Political Economy*, 37(123), pp. 25–40; P. Alexander, C. Runciman and B. Maruping (2015), 'South African Police Service Data on Crowd Incidents: A Preliminary Analysis', Social Change Research Unit, University of Johannesburg.

7. In this study, out of 46 informal settlements, 20 (44 per cent) were established by way of invasions, 6 (13 per cent) were established through 'silent encroachment' (see Table 5.3).

8. J. Holston (2008), *Insurgent Citizenship: Disjunctions of Democracy and Modernity in Brazil*, Princeton, NJ: Princeton University Press, p. 171.

9. Statistics South Africa (2016), 'GHS Series Volume VII: Housing from a Human Settlement Perspective' (media release), 20 April.

10. The story of Duncan Village backyard shacks that were erected under the leadership of a township civic is told in Chapter 4 of this book.

11. R. Nunes (2014), *Organisation of the Organisationless: Collective Action after Networks*, London: Mute and Post Media Lab.

12. A. Bayat (1997), *Street Politics: Poor People's Movements in Iran*, New York: Columbia University Press, p. 159.

13. Teo, 'The Organisation of a Land Occupation'.

14. Ibid.

15. Teo, 'The Organisation of a Land Occupation', p. 58.

16. Bayat, *Street Politics*.

17. Teo, 'The Organisation of a Land Occupation', p. iii.

18. Bayat, *Street Politics*, p. 159.

19. A. Bayat (2013), 'The Urban Subalterns and the Non-movements of the Arab Uprisings: An Interview with Asef Bayat', conducted by N. Ghandour-Demiri, 26 March, www.jadaliyya.com/Details/28301 (accessed 18 October 2020), p. 1.

20. Teo, 'The Organisation of a Land Occupation', p. 60.

21. Ibid., p. 99.

22. Ibid., p. 101.

23. Ibid.

24. Ibid., p. 16.

25. *Baba* means 'father' in isiZulu.

26. J. Cole (1987), *Crossroads: The Politics of Reform and Repression, 1976–1986*, Johannesburg, South Africa: Ravan Press.

27. K. French (1983), 'James Mpanza and the Development of the Sofasonke Party in the Development of Local Politics in Soweto', Master of Arts dissertation, University of the Witwatersrand.

28. The Orlando Pirates, arguably the oldest professional soccer club in South Africa, are still known as *ezikaMagebhula* by fans.

29. I give more details on Mpanza and the Sofasonke Village committees in Chapter 2.

30. Bayat, *Street Politics*; Bayat, 'The Urban Subalterns and the Non-movements of the Arab Uprisings'; J.C. Scott (1985), *Weapons of the Weak: Everyday Forms of Peasant Resistance*, London: Yale University Press.

31. C. Barker (2015), 'Beyond the Waves: Marxism, Social Movements and Revolution', paper presented at *Alternatives Futures and Popular Protest* conference, Manchester, UK, 30 March–1 April, https://sites.google.com/site/colinbarkersite/ (accessed 12 July 2019), p. 19.

32. Republic of South Africa Department of Home Affairs (2016), 'The Winners of the Mkhaya Migrants Awards', www.dha.gov.za/index.php/statements-speeches/920-the-winners-of-the-2016-mkhaya-migrants-awards (accessed 10 October 2020).

33. Councillor Simphiwe Zwane occupied public office from 2011 to 2016. The 'Operation Khanyisa Movement' electoral platform was inspired by the Paris Commune delegate principle, which included the right of recall, salary at the rate of a skilled worker, leading struggles on the ground, etc. See N. Pingo (2013), 'Institutionalisation of a Social Movement: The Case of Thembelihle, the Thembelihle Crisis Committee and the Operation Khanyisa Movement and the Use of the Brick, the Ballot and the Voice', Master of Science dissertation, Development Planning, University of the Witwatersrand.

34. J. Bix (2013), 'Gramsci Comes Home', *Jacobin Magazine*, 19 August, www.jacobinmag.com/2013/08/gramsci-comes-home (accessed 1 April 2020).

35. K. Marx (1991 [1981]), *Capital: A Critique of Political Economy, Volume 3*, London: Penguin Books, p. 772.

36. E. Swyngedouw (2012), 'Rent and Landed Property', in B. Fine and A. Saad-Filho, *The Elgar Companion to Marxist Economics*, Northampton, UK: Edward Elgar Publishing, pp. 310–15, p. 313.

37. Ibid., p. 314.

38. Ibid.

39. Interview no. 26, People's Committee members, Pietermaritzburg, 27 January 2013.

40. L. Drivdal (2014), 'The Politics of Leadership Organizing in Informal Settlements: Ambiguities of Speaking Publicly and Mediating Conflicting Institutional Logics', PhD thesis, Centre of Criminology, Faculty of Law, University of Cape Town, p. 3.

41. Ibid.

42. S.J. Greene (2003), 'Staged Cities: Mega-events, Slum Clearance, and Global Capital', *Yale Human Rights and Development Journal*, 6(1), pp. 161–87.

43. M. Davis (2006), *Planet of Slums*, London: Verso, p. 201.

44. L. Zeilig, D. Seddon and P. Dwyer (2007), 'An Epoch of Uprisings: Social Movements in Post-colonial Africa', paper presented at *Fourth Historical Materialism Annual Conference*, School of Oriental and African Studies, London, 9–11 November.

45. A. Callinicos (2007), 'Swelling Cities of the Global South', *Socialist Worker*, 3 July, p. 1.

46. R. Pithouse (2005), 'The Left in the Slum: The Rise of a Shack Dwellers' Movement in Durban, South Africa', paper presented at *History and African Studies Seminar*, University of KwaZulu-Natal, Durban, 23 November.

47. NUMSA (2013), 'Resolutions Adopted at Numsa Special National Congress, December 16–20 2013', p. 6, www.numsa.org.za/article/resolutions-adopted-numsa-special-national-congress-december-16-20-2013/ (accessed 25 October 2020).

48. M. Burawoy (2009), *The Extended Case Method*, Berkeley, CA: University of California Press, p. 21.

2   'THE PEOPLE CANNOT LIVE IN THE AIR':
HISTORY OF THE SQUATTER MOVEMENT IN SOUTH AFRICA

1. C. Barker (2008), 'Some Thoughts on Marxism and Social Movements', unpublished paper, https://sites.google.com/site/colinbarkersite/ (accessed 12 July 2019), p. 1; S. Cohen (2011), 'The Red Mole: Workers' Councils as a Means of Revolutionary Transformation', in I. Ness and D. Azzellini (Eds), *Ours to Master and to Own: Workers' Control from the Commune to the Present*, Chicago, IL: Haymarket Books, p. 48.

2. *Iinkundla* are chiefs' courts in Mpondoland; more about these structures later in the text. Iinkundla zamaMpondo means '*Iinkundla* of the Mpondo People'.

3. SAHO (South African History Online) (2015), 'The Khoisan', www.sahistory.org.za/people-south-africa/khoikhoi (accessed 21 October 2020).

4. SAHO (2015), 'The First 1820 Settlers Arrive in South Africa', www.sahistory.org.za/dated-event/first-1820-british-settlers-arrive-south-africa (accessed 3 March 2015).

5. T.J. Stapleton (1994), *Maqoma: Xhosa Resistance to Colonial Advance*, Cape Town, South Africa: Jonathan Ball.

6. P. Bonner (1980), 'Classes, the Mode of Production and the State in Pre-colonial Swaziland', in S. Marks and A. Atmore, *Economy and Society in Pre-industrial South Africa*, London: Longman, p. 83; W. Van Binsbergen and P. Geschiere (Eds) (1985), *Old Modes of Production and Capitalist Encroachment: Anthropological Explorations in Africa*, New York: Routledge, p. 151.

7. M. Mamdani (1996), *Citizen and Subject: Contemporary Africa and the Legacy of Late Colonialism*, Princeton, NJ: Princeton University Press, pp. 23–4.

8. W. Beinart (1982), *The Political Economy of Pondoland 1860 to 1930*, Johannesburg, South Africa: Ravan Press.

9. *Inkundla* was also a courtyard-like space used for public cultural events such as dancing and weddings.

10. R. Abel (1979), 'Western Courts in Non-Western Settings: Patterns of Court Use in Colonial and Neo-colonial Africa', in S. Burman and B. Harrell-Bond (Eds), *The Imposition of Law*, New York: Academic Press, pp. 167–200; S.F. Moore (1986), *Social Facts and Fabrications: 'Customary' Law on Kilimanjaro, 1880–1980*, Cambridge, UK: Cambridge University Press.

11. M. Mamdani (1996), *Citizen and Subject: Contemporary Africa and the Legacy of Late Colonialism*, Princeton, NJ: Princeton University Press, p. 119.

12. Ibid., pp. 22–3; Moore, *Social Facts and Fabrications*, pp. 55–8.

13. H. Wolpe (1972), 'Capitalism and Cheap Labour in South Africa: From Segregation to Apartheid', *Economy and Society*, 1(4), pp. 425–56.

14. S. Friedman (2015), *Race, Class and Power: Harold Wolpe and the Radical Critique of Apartheid*, Scottsville, South Africa: University of KwaZulu-Natal Press.

15. Beinart, *The Political Economy of Pondoland 1860 to 1930*.

16. Ibid., p. 156.

17. As Stephen Friedman puts it: 'But as Archie Mafeje and others noted, the plans of the dominators cannot be grasped unless the response of the dominated is understood too'; Friedman, *Race, Class and Power*, p. 280.

18. V.L. Allen (1992), *The History of Black Mineworkers in South Africa*, Keighley, UK: The Moor Press.

19. Derek Hanekom, then Minister of Agriculture and Land Affairs in the post-apartheid government, said this in a meeting of shack dwellers we had organised as ANC leaders around 1998; this is based on my recollection.

20. K. Benson (2015), 'A "Political War of Words and Bullets": Defining and Defying Sides of Struggle for Housing in Crossroads, South Africa', *Journal of Southern African Studies*, 41(2), pp. 367–87, p. 370.

21. G. Ellis (1983), 'Africans in the Western Cape 1900 to 1982: A Chronology', in D. Horner (Ed.), *Labour Preference, Influx Control and Squatters*, Cape Town, South Africa: South African Labour and Development Research Unit, SALDRU Working Paper No. 50, p. 110; A. Silk (1981), *A Shanty Town in South Africa: The Story of Modderdam*, Johannesburg, South Africa: Ravan Press.

22. Benson, 'A "Political War of Words and Bullets"', p. 371.

23. P. Maylam (1983), 'The "Black Belt": Black Squatters in Durban 1935–1950', *Canadian Journal of African Studies*, special issue: *South Africa*, pp. 419–20.

24. A.W. Stadler (1979), 'Birds in the Cornfield: Squatter Movements in Johannesburg, 1944–1947', *Journal of Southern African Studies*, special issue: *Urban Social History*, 6(1), pp. 9–123, p. 93.

25. M. Legassick (2007), *Towards Socialist Democracy*, Scottsville, South Africa: KwaZulu-Natal Press, p. 189.

26. Built in 1931, Orlando and Pimville-Klipspruit were the nucleus of what would later become Soweto, the biggest black township in South Africa. See P. Bonner and L. Segal (1998), *Soweto: A History*, Cape Town, South Africa: Maskew Miller Longman, pp. 13–17.

27. K. French (1983), 'James Mpanza and the Development of the Sofasonke Party in the Development of Local Politics in Soweto', Master of Arts dissertation, University of the Witwatersrand, p. 85; B. Hirson (1989), *Yours for the Union: Class and Community Struggle in South Africa*, London: Zed Books, p. 150.

28. Bonner and Segal, *Soweto*; French, 'James Mpanza', p. 78; Hirson, *Yours for the Union*, p. 150.

29. French, 'James Mpanza', p. 293.

30. Hirson, *Yours for the Union*, p. 150.

31. Ibid., pp. 155–8; P. Bonner (1990), 'The Politics of Black Squatter Movements on the Rand, 1944–1952', *Radical History Review*, 46(7), pp. 89–115, p. 89.

32. Hirson, *Yours for the Union*, pp. 156–8.

33. Bonner and Segal, *Soweto*, p. 25; Stadler, 'Birds in the Cornfield', p. 97.

34. French, 'James Mpanza', p. 183.

35. Ibid., p. 350.

36. Hirson, *Yours for the Union*, p. 154.

37. The Communist Party of South Africa was later renamed the South African Communist Party.

38. French, 'James Mpanza', p. 350; Jonathan Grossman argues, in general, that: 'The political method of the Party promoted the isolation from the mass of workers … it was a political method and the substance of policies of the third period which did not connect, or provide the theoretical means of connecting, with the concrete situation'; J. Grossman (1985), 'Class Relations and the Policies of the Communist Party of South Africa 1921–1950', p. 195.

39. Hirson, *Yours for the Union*, p. 154.

40. French, 'James Mpanza', p. 60.

41. M.A. Lopez (2012), 'The Squatters' Movement in Europe: A Durable Struggle for Social Autonomy in Urban Politics', *Antipode*, 45(4), pp. 1–22, p. 6.

42. M. Foucault (1982), 'The Subject and Power', *Critical Inquiry*, 8(4), pp. 777–95, p. 780.

43. French, 'James Mpanza', p. 63.

44. Ibid., p. 60.

45. Ibid., p. 350.

46. C. Mampuru (April 1983 [1933]), 'Essay on James Sofasonke Mpanza', p. 1, quoted in French, 'James Mpanza', p. 314.

47. The sub-tenants who constituted the bulk of the squatter community could not vote in Advisory Board elections because to qualify, you had to be a regis-

tered household head of a Council house and be up to date with your rental to the last month preceding the election; French, 'James Mpanza', p. 262.

48. Hirson, *Yours for the Union*, p. 149.

49. L. Bank (2011), *Home Spaces, Street Styles: Contesting Power and Identity in a South African City*, London: Pluto Press; B. Bozzoli (1991), *Women of Phokeng: Consciousness, Life Strategy, and Migrancy in South Africa, 1900–1983*, London: James Currey; M. Ramphele (1993), *A Bed Called Home: Life in the Migrant Labour Hostels*, Cape Town, South Africa: David Philip.

50. A practice also found within the black community; see M.J. Maluleke (2011), 'Culture, Tradition, Custom, Law and Gender Equality', paper presented at the Conference of the South African Chapter of the International Association of Women Judges (SAC-IAWJ) in partnership with the North-West University, Potchefstroom, South Africa, 12–13 August 2011, p. 13, www.researchgate. net/publication/262621814_Culture_Tradition_Custom_Law_and_Gender_ Equality (accessed 4 April 2020).

51. T. Lodge (1983), *Black Politics in South Africa since 1945*, Johannesburg, South Africa: Ravan Press, p. 147.

52. Minister of Native Affairs Major Piet van Byl, quoted in French, 'James Mpanza', p. 95.

53. Ibid., p. 92; Stadler, 'Birds in the Cornfield', p. 105.

54. Bonner and Segal, *Soweto*, p. 2; Hirson, *Yours for the Union*, p. 149.

55. French, 'James Mpanza', p. 92; Bonner and Segal (*Soweto*, p. 23) note that: 'In an attempt to overcome the extreme material hardships faced by the squatters, the committee handed out coal, firewood and milk bought with the funds from the Sofasonke Party'.

56. Stadler, 'Birds in the Cornfield', p. 102.

57. Hirson, *Yours for the Union*, p. 149.

58. This is a quotation from a Johannesburg City Council Supplementary Memorandum submitted in August 1947 to the Moroka Commission that was set up to investigate a violent eruption in Moroka, a slum in the Soweto area; Stadler, 'Birds in the Cornfield', p. 105.

59. Quoted in French, 'James Mpanza', p. 176.

60. Quoted in ibid., p. 192.

61. Ibid., p. 142.

62. Legassick, *Towards Socialist Democracy*, p. 184.

63. Ibid., p. 185.

64. Ibid., p. 188.

65. P. Bond (2000), *Cities of Gold: Essays on South Africa's New Urban Crisis*, Trenton, NJ: Africa World Press, p. 6.

66. Legassick, *Towards Socialist Democracy*, p. 187.

67. P. Alexander (2000), *Workers, War and the Origins of Apartheid: Labour and Politics in South Africa, 1939–48*, London: James Currey, p. 119.

68. Quoted in French, 'James Mpanza', p. 22.

69. The Native Urban Areas Act of 1923 stipulated that only 'natives' who were employed could live in the city; ibid., pp. 164, 189.

70. Ibid., p. 71.

71. Stadler, 'Birds in the Cornfield', p. 123.

72. Hirson (*Yours for the Union*, p. 149) observes: 'The [Orlando] sub-tenants had no rights, being in the house and location on sufferance. Ultimately it was these rightless dwellers who took action.'

73. French, 'James Mpanza', p. 52; Stadler, 'Birds in the Cornfield', p. 109.

74. Bonner and Segal, *Soweto*, p. 19.

75. Bond, *Cities of Gold*, p. 37.

76. F.F. Piven and R. Cloward (1977), *Poor People's Movements: Why They Succeed, How They Fail*, New York: Pantheon Books.

77. French, 'James Mpanza', p. 108.

78. Ibid.

79. Alexander, *Workers, War and the Origins of Apartheid*.

80. The Office of Census and Statistics, for example, 'recorded 6,587 white strikers … in reality [there were] more than 15,000'; while the strike rate (i.e. the number of strikers per thousand workers per year) was recorded as 2.7 for black and white workers, for the whole decade it was 6.7 for black workers and 8.8 for white workers; ibid., p. 129.

81. Grossman, 'Class Relations'.

82. For two decades, Mpanza participated in Orlando local elections for seats on the Advisory Boards, mostly in the form of a joint slate with the African Democratic Party in what proved to be a winning alliance that consistently trumped the South African Communist Party's candidates; French, 'James Mpanza', pp. 117, 129.

83. Lopez, 'The Squatters' Movement in Europe', p. 5. See M. Castells (1983), *The City and the Grassroots: A Cross-cultural Theory of Urban Social Movements*, Berkeley, CA: University of California Press, p. 322.

84. On the politics of Abahlali baseMjondolo, see R. Pithouse (2008), A Politics of the Poor: Shack Dwellers' Struggles in Durban', *Journal of Asian and African Studies*, 43(1), pp. 63–94; R. Pithouse (2019), 'Abahlali baseMjondolo and the Popular Struggle for the Right to the City in Durban, South Africa', http://base.d-p-h.info/en/fiches/dph/fiche-dph-8418.html (accessed 3 May 2019).

85. Stadler, 'Birds in the Cornfield', p. 104.

86. Hirson, *Yours for the Union*, p. 154.

87. Stadler, 'Birds in the Cornfield', p. 104.

88. For an illuminating and critical account of the role of the black petty bourgeoisie in the struggles of the 1950s, see Grossman, 'Class Relations'.

89. Ibid., pp. 359–60, p. 375.

90. J. Lucas (2000), 'Civic Organization in Alexandra in the Early 1990s: An Ethnographic Approach', in G. Adler and J. Steinberg (Eds), *From Comrades to Citizens: The South African Civics Movement and the Transition to Democracy*,

London: Macmillan, pp. 145–74; A.W. Marx (1992), *Lessons of the Struggle: South African Internal Opposition, 1960–1990*, Cape Town, South Africa: Oxford University Press.

91. J. Cole (1987), *Crossroads: The Politics of Reform and Repression, 1976–1986*, Johannesburg, South Africa: Ravan Press, p. 40; I. van Kessel (2000), *'Beyond Our Wildest Dreams': The United Democratic Front and the Transformation of South Africa*, Charlottesville, VA: University Press of Virginia, p. 62.

92. N.L. Clark and W.H. Worger (2004), *South Africa: The Rise and Fall of Apartheid*, London: Longman; M.J. Murray (1994), *The Revolution Deferred*, London: Verso; J. Seekings (2000), *The UDF: A History of the United Democratic Front in South Africa 1983–1991*, Cape Town, South Africa: David Philip; Van Kessel, *'Beyond Our Wildest Dreams'*.

93. Ibid., p. 2.

94. Mostly, according to Seekings (*The UDF*, p. 121), the 'UDF was forever "trailing behind the masses", as Popo Molefe [UDF general secretary] put it'.

95. Ibid., p. 61; Van Kessel, *'Beyond Our Wildest Dreams'*, p. 4.

96. Ibid., pp. 67, 71.

97. Ibid., pp. 304–5.

98. Ibid., pp. 62–8.

99. Ibid., p. 305.

100. Ibid.

101. Ibid.

102. Lucas, 'Civic Organization in Alexandra in the Early 1990s', p. 160.

103. Ibid.

104. Ibid., p. 173.

105. Ibid., p. 174.

106. Lucas, 'Civic Organization in Alexandra in the Early 1990s'.

107. Van Kessel, *'Beyond Our Wildest Dreams'*, p. 62.

108. Ibid., p. 302.

109. Cole, *Crossroads*, p. 40.

110. Interview no. 26, people's committee member, Pietermaritzburg, 27 January 2013.

111. Cole, *Crossroads*.

112. Benson, 'A "Political War of Words and Bullets"', p. 372.

113. Ibid., p. 369.

114. Ibid., p. 385.

3   *AMAKOMITI* ARE EVERYWHERE

1. S. Zikode (2006), 'The Third Force', *Journal of Asian and African Studies*, 41(1/2), pp. 185–9, http://abahlali.org/node/17 (accessed 3 April 2020).

2. A. Bayat (1997), *Street Politics: Poor People's Movements in Iran*, New York: Columbia University Press, p. 63; M. Castells (1977), *The Urban Question: A*

Marxist Approach, Cambridge, MA: MIT Press, p. 57; J.E. Hardoy and D. Satterthwaite (1989), *Squatter Citizen: Life in the Urban Third World*, London:
Earthscan Publications, p. 17.

3. A. Harber (2011), *Diepsloot*, Johannesburg, South Africa: Jonathan Ball, p. 10;
   H. Sapire (1992), 'Politics and Protest in Shack Settlements of the Pretoria-
   Witwatersrand-Vereeniging Region, South Africa, 1980–1990', *Journal of
   Southern African Studies*, 18(3), pp. 670–97, p. 114.
4. M. Mayekiso (1996), *Township Politics: Civic Struggles for a New South Africa*,
   New York: Monthly Review Press, p. 131.
5. See L. Lippard (1997), *The Lure of the Local: Senses of Place in a Multicentred
   Society*, New York: The New Press, p. 7.
6. See Appendix 2 for a list of places and the corresponding interviews con-
   ducted.
7. Bayat, *Street Politics*, p. 27.
8. P. Alexander, C. Runciman and B. Maruping (2015), *South African Police
   Service Data on Crowd Incidents: A Preliminary Analysis*, Johannesburg,
   South Africa: Social Change Research Unit, University of Johannesburg; C.
   Runciman, T. Ngwane and P. Alexander (2012), 'A Protest Analysis of South
   Africa's Rebellion of the Poor: Some Initial Results', paper presented at the
   Society for the Advancement of Science in Africa conference, University of
   Cape Town, 1–4 July.
9. See Lippard, *The Lure of the Local*, p. 7.
10. Interview no. 29, people's committee member, Durban, 29 January 2013.
11. Interview no. 34, resident, Newcastle, 4 February 2013.
12. Council for Scientific and Industrial Research, 'Ventilated Improved Pit (VIP)
    Toilet: A Dry Sanitation Option', www.csir.co.za/Built_environment/santech-
    centre/docs/VIP_info_sheet.pdf (accessed 3 June 2019).
13. For a description of township civics, see Mayekiso, *Township Politics*, and M.J.
    Murray (1994), *The Revolution Deferred*, London: Verso, pp. 167–78.
14. C. Bundy (2000), 'Survival and Resistance: Township Organization and
    Non-violent Direct Action in Twentieth Century South Africa', in G. Adler
    and J. Steinberg (Eds), *From Comrades to Citizens: The South African Civics
    Movement and the Transition to Democracy*, London: Macmillan, p. 30.
15. A. Le Roux (2013), 'Contesting Space: A Ward Committee and a Social
    Movement Organisation in Thembelihle, Johannesburg', Master of Arts dis-
    sertation, Department of Sociology, University of Johannesburg, p. 85.
16. K. Rosenthal (2015), 'New Social Movements as Civil Society: The Case of Past
    and Present Soweto', in W. Beinart and M.C. Dawson (Eds), *Popular Politics
    and Resistance Movements in South Africa*, Johannesburg, South Africa: Wits
    University Press, p. 251.
17. Sinwell defines them as '"invited spaces" (those induced by the government)',
    as opposed to '"invented" (grassroots or autonomous movements)'; L. Sinwell
    (2009), 'Participation as Popular Agency: The Limitations and Possibili-

ties for Transforming Development in the Alexandra Renewal Project', PhD thesis, University of the Witwatersrand, pp. 82–3. See also A. Cornwall (2004), 'Spaces for Transformation? Reflections on Issues of Power and Difference in Participation in Development', in S. Hickey and G. Mohan (Eds), *Participation from Tyranny to Transformation: Exploring New Approaches to Participation in Development*, London: Zed Books, pp. 75–91, pp. 75 and 80.

18. RSA (Republic of South Africa) (2000), *Municipal Systems Act Number 32*, Pretoria, South Africa: Government Printers; RSA (2005), *Notice 965: Guidelines for the Establishment and Operation of Municipal Ward Committees*, Pretoria, South Africa: Government Printers.

19. RSA, *Municipal Systems Act Number 32*, Clause 2.3.3.

20. RSA, *Notice 965*, Clause 2.

21. Ibid., Clause 9.3.

22. Interview no. 53, ward committee member, East London, 24 February 2013.

23. RSA, *Notice 965*, Clause 16.1.

24. Ibid., Clause 11.4b.

25. Interview no. 54, ward councillor, East London, 25 February 2013; observation of office operations by the researcher, 25 February 2013.

26. Interview no. 53, ward committee member, East London, 24 February 2013; interview no. 31, ward committee member, Newcastle, 3 February 2013.

27. T. Smith (2008), *The Role of Ward Committees in Enhancing Participatory Local Governance and Development in South Africa: Evidence from Six Ward Committee Case Studies*, Cape Town, South Africa: University of the Western Cape, Community Law Centre, p. 53.

28. Interview no. 26, people's committee and ANC member, Pietermaritzburg, 27 January 2013; interview no. 21, people's committee and Democratic Alliance member, Brakpan, 23 January 2013.

29. Symphony Way Pavement Dwellers (2011), *No Land! No House! No Vote! Voices from Symphony Way*, Cape Town, South Africa: Pambazuka Press, p. xi.

30. Interview no. 60, group of residents, Mthatha, 27 February 2013.

31. Interview no 26, 2013.

32. Interview no. 33, CPF member, Newcastle, 4 February 2013.

33. Interview no. 25, CPF member, Pietermaritzburg, 27 January 2013.

34. Interview no. 33, 2013.

35. Interview no. 25, 2013.

36. Interview 33, 2013; interview no. 18, CPF member, Randfontein, 22 January 2013.

37. E. Pelser, J. Schnetler and A. Louw (2002), *Not Everybody's Business: Community Policing in the SAPS' Priority Areas*, ISS Monograph 71, Pretoria, South Africa: Institute of Security Studies, www.issafrica.org/pubs/Monographs/No71/Content.HTML (accessed 4 July 2020).

38. Interview 20, CDF member, Germiston, 23 January 2013.

39. The Reconstruction and Development Programme was the ANC's vision and policy framework for making the 'new South Africa' address the needs of the working class and the poor: those 'disadvantaged' during the apartheid era. It set specific targets for social development and was the ANC's election manifesto during the first democratic elections. See ANC (1994), *Reconstruction and Development Programme, a Policy Framework*, Johannesburg, South Africa: Umanyano.

40. D. Miller (1996), 'The Ambiguities of Popular Participation in Development: A South African Case Study', paper presented at the ACDESS Workshop *South African within Africa: Emerging Policy Frameworks*, Berea, Johannesburg.

41. RSA, *Municipal Systems Act Number 32*; RSA (2003), *Traditional Leadership and Governance Framework Amendment Act Number 31*, Pretoria, South Africa: Government Printers.

42. S. Khan, B. Lootvoet and S. Vawda (2006), 'Transcending Traditional Forms of Governance: Prospects for Co-operative Governance and Service Delivery in Durban's Tribal Authority Areas', *Transformation*, 62, pp. 84–117, p. 89.

43. M. Davis (2006), *Planet of Slums*, London: Verso, p. 46.

44. J. Beall (2006), *Exit, Voice and Tradition: Loyalty to Chieftainship and Democracy in Metropolitan Durban, South Africa*, London: London School of Economics, Crisis States Research Centre, January, pp. 8 and 17; Khan, Lootvoet and Vawda, 'Transcending Traditional Forms of Governance', p. 86.

45. L. Sinwell, J. Kirshner, K. Khumalo, O. Manda, P. Pfaffe, C. Phokela and C. Runciman (2009), *Service Delivery Protests: Findings from Quick Response Research on Four 'Hot-spots' – Piet Retief, Balfour, Thokoza, Diepsloot*, Johannesburg, South Africa: Centre for Sociological Research, University of Johannesburg.

46. B. Maruping, Z. Mncube and C. Runciman (2014), 'Rebellion of the Poor Quantitative Data Analysis Report', unpublished internal report of the Research Chair for Social Change Protest Monitoring Project, University of Johannesburg, p. 30.

47. Interview no. 6, ad hoc protest committee member, Vryburg, 6 December 2012.

48. Interview no. 8, people's committee member, Vryburg, 6 December 2012.

49. P. Alexander (2010), 'Rebellion of the Poor: South Africa's Service Delivery Protests – a Preliminary Analysis', *Review of African Political Economy*, 37(123), pp. 25–40, p. 31; P. Alexander and P. Pfaffe (2014), 'Social Relationships to the Means and Ends of Protest in South Africa's Ongoing Rebellion of the Poor: The Balfour Insurrections', *Social Movement Studies: Journal of Social, Cultural and Political Protest*, 13(2), pp. 204–21; H. Dawson (2014), 'Youth Politics: Waiting and Envy in a South African Informal Settlement', *Journal of Southern African Studies*, 40(4), pp. 861–82, p. 868.

50. Interview no. 3, ward committee member, Zeerust, 5 December 2012.

51. Interview no. 4, people's committee member, Zeerust, 5 December 2012.

52. Interview no. 35, group of residents, Newcastle, 4 February 2013.
53. Municipalities have the power to dissolve specific ward committees, for example Knysna Municipality (2012), 'Constitution for Ward Councillors of the Knysna Municipality', Clause 22, www.knysna.gov.za/wp-content/uploads/2012/12/Ward-Constituition.pdf (accessed 3 June 2019).
54. Interview no. 3, 5 December 2012.
55. Interview no. 60, group of residents, Mount Frere, 28 February 2013.
56. Khan, Lootvoet and Vawda, 'Transcending Traditional Forms of Governance', pp. 109–10.
57. Interview no. 26, people's committee member, Pietermaritzburg, 27 January 2013.
58. Miraftab elaborates: 'While the former grassroots actions [in "invited spaces"] are geared toward providing the poor with coping mechanisms and propositions to support survival of their informal membership, the grassroots activity of the latter [in "invented spaces"] challenges the status quo in the hope of larger societal change and resistance to the dominant power relations'; F. Miraftab (2004), 'Invited and Invented Spaces of Participation: Neoliberal Citizenship and Feminists' Expanded Notion of Politics', *Wagadu*, no. 1, pp. 1–7, p. 1.
59. Interview no. 22, people's committee member, Pretoria, 24 January 2013.
60. Interview no. 22, 24 January 2013; N. Pingo (2013), 'Institutionalisation of a Social Movement: The Case of Thembelihle, the Thembelihle Crisis Committee and the Operation Khanyisa Movement and the Use of the Brick, the Ballot and the Voice', Master of Science dissertation, Development Planning, University of the Witwatersrand, p. 57.
61. Interview no. 61, 27 February 2013.
62. Interview no. 43, people's committee member, Graaff-Reinet, 17 February 2013.
63. Interview no. 2, resident, Mahikeng, 4 December 2012.
64. Interview no. 31, ward committee member, Newcastle, 3 February 2013.
65. Miller, 'The Ambiguities of Popular Participation in Development'.
66. Interview no. 24, group of CDF members, Pretoria, 24 January 2013.
67. Alexander, 'Rebellion of the Poor'; Alexander, Runciman and Maruping, 'South African Police Service Data on Crowd Incidents'; Alexander and Pfaffe, 'Social Relationships'; S. Booysen (2011), 'Between Centralisation and Centralism – the Presidency of South Africa', in *The African National Congress and the Regeneration of Political Power*, Johannesburg, South Africa: Wits University Press, pp. 404–43; Runciman, Ngwane and Alexander, 'A Protest Analysis of South Africa's Rebellion of the Poor'; K. von Holdt, M. Langa, S. Molapo, N. Mogapi, K. Ngubeni, J. Dlamini and A. Kirsten (2011), *The Smoke that Calls: Insurgent Citizenship, Collective Violence, and the Struggle for a Place in the New South Africa*, Working Paper 1, Johannesburg, South Africa: Centre for the Study of Violence and Reconciliation, and Society Work and Develop-

ment Institute, https://2b912727-9f2a-44dd-9a10-190714b850bf.filesusr.com/ugd/4e496b_c7b9277c0db448979905a3ae75d99205.pdf (accessed 18 October 2020).

68. Statistics South Africa (2016), 'GHS Series Volume VII: Housing from a Human Settlement Perspective' (media release), April.

69. Alexander, 'Rebellion of the Poor', p. 37; R. Pithouse (2007), 'The University of Abahlali baseMjondolo', *Voices of Resistance from Occupied London*, no. 2, p. 1, http://abahlali.org/node/2814/ (accessed 3 July 2019).

70. H.Y. Cho, L. Surendra and E. Park (Eds) (2008), *States of Democracy: Oligarchic Democracies and Asian Democratization*, Mumbai, India: Earthworm Books, p. 7.

71. M. Burawoy (2005), 'For Public Sociology', *American Sociological Review*, 70, pp. 4–28; A. Gouldner (1970), *The Coming Crisis of Sociology*, New York: Basic Books; E.O. Wright (2010), *Envisioning Real Utopias*, London: Verso.

4 FATAL EMBRACE BY THE ANC IN DUNCAN VILLAGE

1. L. Bank (2011), *Home Spaces, Street Styles: Contesting Power and Identity in a South African City*, London: Pluto Press, p. 26.

2. StatsSA (Statistics South Africa) (2011), *Census 2011: Statistical Release. Pretoria: StatsSA*, www.statssa.gov.za/census/census_2011/census_products/Census_2011_Statistical%20release.pdf (accessed 3 July 2019).

3. D. Fryer and B. Hepburn (2010), *It's Jobs, Stupid! Social Exclusion, Education, and the Informal Sector in Grahamstown, Fort Beaufort and Duncan Village*, Working Paper Series 5, Grahamstown, South Africa: Institute of Social and Economic Research, Rhodes University, p. 11; UNESCO (United Nations Educational, Scientific and Cultural Organization) (2015), 'Duncan Village: Provision of Sustainable Electrical Reticulation South Africa', MOST Clearing House: Best Practices, www.unesco.org/most/africa12.htm (accessed 3 May 2019).

4. Bank, *Home Spaces, Street Styles*, p. 60; UNESCO, 'Duncan Village'.

5. Sophiatown was an area in Johannesburg renowned for its cultural vibrancy, nightlife and interracial living, and was demolished by the apartheid regime in 1955. See: T. Huddleston (1956), *Naught for Your Comfort*, New York: The Country Life Press; South African History Online (2015), 'Sophiatown Timeline 1899–1955', www.sahistory.org.za/topic/sophiatown-timeline-1899-1955 (accessed 3 March 2019).

6. C.S. White (2008), 'The Rule of Brigadier Oupa Gqozo in Ciskei: 4 March 1990 to 22 March 1994', Master of Arts thesis, Rhodes University, Grahamstown, p. 18.

7. S. Phalatse (2000), 'From Industrialization to De-industrialization in the Former Homelands: The Case of Mogwase, North-West', *Urban Forum*, 11, pp. 149–61, pp. 150–52.

8. J. Maree (1982), 'SAAWU in the East London Area 1979–81', *South African Labour Bulletin*, 4/5, pp. 34–49.

9. Bank, *Home Spaces, Street Styles*, pp. 89–90.

10. Ibid., p. 91.

11. J. Seekings (2000), 'The Development of Strategic Thought in South Africa's Civic Movements, 1977–1990', in G. Adler and J. Steinberg (Eds), *From Comrades to Citizens: The South African Civics Movement and the Transition to Democracy*, London: Macmillan, p. 70; Bank, *Home Spaces, Street Styles*, p. 93.

12. A. Mashinini (1986), 'Dual Power and the Creation of People's Committees', *Sechaba*, April, pp. 25–30.

13. I. van Kessel (2000), *'Beyond Our Wildest Dreams': The United Democratic Front and the Transformation of South Africa*, Charlottesville, VA: University Press of Virginia, p. 69.

14. Bank, *Home Spaces, Street Styles*, pp. 92–3.

15. C.M. Ngcaba (2014), *May I Have This Dance?*, Cape Town, South Africa: Cover2Cover Books, p. 52. Some Mdantsane people were renting shacks in Duncan Village, nearer job opportunities.

16. Banks, *Home Spaces, Street Styles*, p. 192.

17. Comments made by Greg Ruiters during Trevor Ngwane's presentation (2015), '"Amakomiti" – the Political Economy of Shantytown Organising', second panel on problems and prospects for anti-capitalist resistance, *World Conference of Political Economists*, Chris Hani Institute, COSATU House, Johannesburg, 19–21 June.

18. Interview no. 2DV, ward councillor and ex-DVRA committee member, Duncan Village, 4 October 2020.

19. L. Trotsky (2008), *History of the Russian Revolution*, Chicago, IL: Haymarket Books, p. 150. For an alternative view, see Van Kessel, *'Beyond Our Wildest Dreams'*, p. 34.

20. S. Ellis and T. Sechaba (1992), *Comrades against Apartheid: The ANC and the South African Communist Party in Exile*, London: James Currey, p. 197.

21. J. Saul (2014), 'The Transition: The Players Assemble, 1970–1990', in J. Saul, J. and P. Bond, *South Africa: The Present as History, from Mrs Ples to Mandela and Marikana*, Johannesburg, South Africa: Jacana, pp. 88–91; J. Seekings (2000), *The UDF – a History of the United Democratic Front in South Africa 1983–1991*, Cape Town, South Africa: David Philip, p. 207; E. Zuern (2006), 'Elusive Boundaries: SANCO, the ANC and the Post-apartheid South African State', in R. Ballard, A. Habib and I. Valodia (2006), *Voices of Protest: Social Movements in Post-apartheid South Africa*, Durban, South Africa: University of KwaZulu-Natal, pp. 185–7; M. Ndletyana (1998), 'Changing Role of Civic Organisations from the Apartheid to the Post-apartheid Era: A Case Study of the ACO', Master of Arts dissertation, University of the Witwatersrand.

22. M. Mayekiso (1996), *Township Politics: Civic Struggles for a New South Africa*, New York: Monthly Review Press, p. 142; M. Mayekiso (1992), 'Hands Off the Civics and Civil Society!', *Work in Progress*, February, p. 21; M. Mayekiso (1992), 'Working-class Civil Society: Why We Need It, and How We Get It', *African Communist*, 129, pp. 33–40; B. Nzimande and M. Sikhosana (1992), 'Civil Society and Democracy', *African Communist*, 128, pp. 37–51; B. Nzimande and M. Sikhosana (1992), 'Civil Society Does Not Equal Democracy', *Work in Progress*, September, pp. 26–7; B. Nzimande and M. Sikhosana (1991), 'Civics Are Part of the National Democratic Revolution', *Mayibuye*, June, pp. 37–9.

23. Interview no. 2DV, 4 October 2020.

24. For negotiations and deals made in the Johannesburg City Council, see Mayekiso, *Township Politics*, pp. 210 and 218.

25. Zuern, 'Elusive Boundaries', p. 183.

26. M.J. Murray (1994), *The Revolution Deferred*, London: Verso, p. 146; D. Pillay (1990), 'The Communist Party and the Trade Unions', *South African Labour Bulletin*, 15(3), pp. 19–27; Zuern, 'Elusive Boundaries', p. 183.

27. E. Maloka (2013), *The South African Communist Party: Exile and after Apartheid*, Johannesburg, South Africa: Jacana, p. 118; Murray, *The Revolution Deferred*, p. 146.

28. L. Callinicos (2004), *Oliver Tambo: Beyond the Engeli Mountains*, Cape Town, South Africa: David Philip, p. 415.

29. J. Grossman (1996), *'For Our Children Tomorrow': Workers in Struggle in South Africa 1973–1995*, Research Paper No. 1, Amsterdam, the Netherlands: Institute for Critical Research, pp. 2 and 6; Murray, *The Revolution Deferred*, p. 145.

30. The structures associated with community development workers were not covered in the research; however, they, like the other committees, were linked to the ANC committees which are covered here.

31. Interview no. 1DV, community member and ex-DVRA committee member, Duncan Village, 3 October 2013.

32. Interview no. 8DV, ward committee and area committee member, Duncan Village, 2 October 2013.

33. Seekings, 'The Development of Strategic Thought in South Africa's Civic Movements', p. 72.

34. Van Kessel, *'Beyond Our Wildest Dreams'*, p. 151.

35. Interview no. 1DV, 3 October 2013.

36. Interview no. 5DV, area committee member, Duncan Village, 6 October 2020.

37. Interview no. 1DV, 3 October 2013.

38. Interview no. 5DV, 6 October 2013.

39. Interview no. 2DV, 4 October 2013; interview no. 8DV, ANC ward councillor and ex-DVRA member, Duncan Village, 2 October 2013.

40. Interview no. 2DV, 4 October 2013.

41. Buffalo City (Metropolitan) Municipality (2015), 'List of Ward Councillors', www.buffalocitymetro.gov.za/Municipality/List-of-all-Ward-Councillors (accessed 3 May 2019).
42. Interview no. 2D, 4 October 2013.
43. Interview no. 3DV, ANC Branch Executive Committee member, ANC Women's League committee member and SANCO BEC member, Duncan Village, 5 October 2013.
44. Interview no. 6DV, ANC ward councillor, Duncan Village, 1 October 2013.
45. Republic of South Africa (2005), *Notice 965: Guidelines for the Establishment and Operation of Municipal Ward Committees*, Pretoria, South Africa: Government Printers.
46. Interview no. 6DV, ANC ward councillor, Duncan Village, 1 October 2013.
47. Interview no. 8DV, 2 October 2013.
48. Interview no. 1DV, 3 October 2013.
49. Interview no. 4DV, area committee member and ANC BEC member, Duncan Village, 5 October 2013.
50. Interview no. 3DV, ANC Branch Executive Committee member, ANC Women's League committee member, Duncan Village, 5 October 2013.
51. Interview no. 6DV, 1 October 2013; Interview no. 2DV, Duncan Village, 4 October 2013.
52. Interview no. 1DV, 3 October 2013.
53. Interview no. 9DV, ward committee member and ANC Youth League member, Duncan Village, 1 October 2013.
54. Interview no. 5DV, area committee member, Duncan Village, 6 October 2013. Legal shacks are those that are in the municipality's database, and illegal ones belong to people who set up shacks without authority of the state. A legal shack will have a number painted on its door.
55. Interview no. 2DV, 4 October 2013.
56. Interview no. 6DV, 1 October 2013.
57. Interview no. 5DV, 6 October 2013.
58. Interview no. 10DV, group of seven community members, Duncan Village, 25 February 2013; interview no. 2D, 4 October 2013.
59. B. Stanwix and C. van der Westhuizen (2012), *Predicted Poverty Impacts of Expanding the Community Work Programme in South Africa: An Analysis of Income Poverty and Inequality*, Cape Town, South Africa: Development Policy Research Unit, University of Cape Town, commissioned by the Trade and Industrial Policy Strategies, p. 4.
60. Interview no. 2DV, 4 October 2013.
61. Interview no. 10D, 25 February 2013.
62. Fryer and Hepburn, *It's Jobs, Stupid!*, pp. 8–9; P. Ndhlovu (2015), 'Understanding the Local State, Service Delivery and Protests in Post-apartheid South Africa: The Case of Duncan Village and Buffalo City Metropolitan Municipality, East London', Master of Arts in Industrial Sociology thesis, Soci-

ology Department, University of the Witwatersrand, p. 7; UNESCO, 'Duncan Village'.

63. Interview no. 8DV, 2 October 2013.
64. Interview no. 6DV, 1 October 2013.
65. Interview no. 1DV, 3 October 2013.
66. On protests in Duncan Village, see: Ndhlovu, 'Understanding the Local State, Service Delivery and Protests in Post-apartheid South Africa', p. 3; L. Bank (2015), 'Duncan Village Hyper-ghetto', *Despatch Live*, 2 July, www.dispatch-live.co.za/opinion/duncan-village-hyper-ghetto-2/ (accessed 3 August 2019).
67. Ibid.; Ndhlovu, 'Understanding the Local State, Service Delivery and Protests in Post-apartheid South Africa', p. 18.
68. Interview no. 4DV, 5 October 2013.
69. Interview no. 8DV, 2 October 2013.
70. Interview no. 5DV, 6 October 203.
71. Interview no. 6DV, 1 October 2013.
72. Ibid.
73. Ibid.
74. Interview no. 8DV, 2 October 2013.
75. Interview no. 6DV, 1 October 2013.
76. Ngcaba, *May I Have This Dance?*, p. 53.
77. A. Gramsci (1971 [1999]), *Selections from the Prison Notebooks*, Ed. Q. Hoare and G. Nowell-Smith, Chennai, India: Orient Longman, http://courses.justice.eku.edu/pls330_louis/docs/gramsci-prison-notebooks-vol1.pdf (accessed 2 May 2019).
78. G. Hart (2002), *Disabling Globalisation: Places of Power in Post-apartheid South Africa*. Pietermaritzburg, South Africa: University of Natal Press, p. 45.
79. R. Pithouse (2013), 'Conjunctural Remarks on the Political Significance of "the Local"', *Thesis Eleven*, 115(1), pp. 95–111, pp. 96–7.
80. Hart, *Disabling Globalisation*, p. 47.
81. J. Lucas (2000), 'Civic Organization in Alexandra in the Early 1990s: An Ethnographic Approach', in G. Adler and J. Steinberg (Eds), *From Comrades to Citizens: The South African Civics Movement and the Transition to Democracy*, London: Macmillan, p. 169; Ndhlovu, 'Understanding the Local State, Service Delivery and Protests in Post-apartheid South Africa', p. 18.
82. Hart, *Disabling Globalisation*, p. 45.
83. F. Miraftab (2004), 'Invited and Invented Spaces of Participation: Neoliberal Citizenship and Feminists' Expanded Notion of Politics', *Wagadu*, 1, pp. 1–7; L. Sinwell (2012), '"Transformative Left-wing Parties" and Grassroots Organizations: Unpacking the Politics of "Top-down" and "Bottom-up" Development', *Geoforum*, 43, pp. 190–98.
84. Ndhlovu ('Understanding the Local State, Service Delivery and Protests in Post-apartheid South Africa', p. 18) notes: 'Drawing from the fieldwork observation of protests in Duncan Village, it can be argued that protests have

become part of the culture in Duncan Village. Every time when electricity went off, children as young as five years were seen unconsciously [*sic*] gathering tyres and calling for protest action to bring back electricity.'

5   *IINKUNDLA* OF NKANENG:
THE RURAL IN THE URBAN DIALECTIC

1. Gavin Capps reports: 'South Africa is estimated to hold 87 [per cent] of the world's PGM [platinum group metals: platinum, palladium, rhodium, iridium, osmium and ruthenium] reserves and, in 2009, accounted for 76 [per cent] of world platinum production and 33 [per cent] of palladium'; G. Capps (2012), 'Victim of its Own Success? The Platinum Mining Industry and the Apartheid Mineral Property System in South Africa's Political Transition', *Review of African Political Economy*, 39(131), pp. 63–84, p. 66. See also K. Forrest (2014), 'Rustenburg's Fractured Recruitment Regime: Who Benefits?', *African Studies*, 73(2), pp. 149–68, p. 165; M. Kibet (2013), 'Migration into Rustenburg Local Municipality between 1996 and 2001', *Journal of Social Development in Africa*, 28(1), pp. 65–85, p. 69; B. Mosiane (2011), 'Livelihoods and the Transformative Potential of Cities: Challenges of Inclusive Development in Rustenburg, North West Province, South Africa', *Singapore Journal of Tropical Geography*, 32(1), pp. 38–52, pp. 41–2.
2. Benchmarks (2011), *Communities in the Platinum Minefields: Policy Gap 6. A Review of Platinum Mining in the Bojanala District of the North West Province: A Participatory Action Research Approach*, Johannesburg, South Africa: The Benchmarks Foundation, p. 35, www.bench-marks.org.za/research/rustenburg_review_policy_gap_final_aug_2012.pdf (accessed 3 August 2018).
3. Moodie and Ndatshe define a 'homeboy' as someone from one's own home district; D. Moodie with V. Ndatshe (1994), *Going for Gold: Men, Mines and Migration*, Johannesburg, South Africa: Ravan Press, p. 309.
4. K.R. Cox, D. Hemson and A. Todes (2004), 'Urbanisation in South Africa and the Changing Character of Migrant Labour', *South African Geographical Journal*, 86(1), pp. 7–16, p. 12.
5. Bokone Bophirima Province (North West Province) (2015), 'Bokone Bophirima Province', www.nwpg.gov.za/nwglance.htm (accessed 3 May 2019). L. Donnelly (2008), 'Caught in Platinum's Gleam', *Mail and Guardian*, 29 June, http://mg.co.za/article/2008-06-29-caught-in-platinums-gleam (accessed 3 May 2019).
6. GlobalSecurity.org, 'North West', www.globalsecurity.org/military/world/rsa/north-west.htm (accessed 25 October 2020).
7. Ibid.
8. Industrial Development Corporation (2015), 'North West Province', www.idc.co.za/home/north-west/north-west-regional-director.html (accessed 3 May 2019).

9. *Mining Prospectus* (2013), 'Pending Decision to Close Several Mine Shafts: Amplats Mine Closures to Create Devastating Consequences for SMEs', 4 February, www.miningprospectus.co.za/articles/pending-decision-to-close-several-mine-shafts-4386.html (accessed 3 May 2015).

10. Kibet, 'Migration into Rustenburg Local Municipality between 1996 and 2001', p. 77.

11. Rustenburg Local Municipality (2011), *Housing Sector Plan for the Rustenburg Local Municipality (Draft)*, Rustenburg, South Africa: UWP Consultants, November, p. 16.

12. Benchmarks, *Communities in the Platinum Minefields*, p. 35.

13. Rustenburg Local Municipality, *Housing Sector Plan for the Rustenburg Local Municipality (Draft)*, p. 18.

14. A. Bezuidenhout and S. Buhlungu (2011),'From Compounded to Fragmented Labour: Mineworkers and the Demise of Compounds in South Africa', *Antipode*, 43(2), pp. 237–63, p. 252; Forrest, 'Rustenburg's Fractured Recruitment Regime', p. 151; Mosiane, 'Livelihoods and the Transformative Potential of Cities', p. 42.

15. Forrest, 'Rustenburg's Fractured Recruitment Regime', p. 161.

16. Ibid., p. 165.

17. A. Bowman and G. Isaacs (2014), *Demanding the Impossible? Platinum Mining Profits and Wage Demands in Context*, Occasional Policy Paper No. 11, Johannesburg, South Africa: SWOP, University of the Witwatersrand, p. 165.

18. Interview no. 2NK, CPF committee member and ex-ward councillor, Nkaneng, 7 July 2013.

19. Rustenburg Local Municipality (2012), *Plan for the Upgrading of Informal Settlements Over the Period 2012/13–2014/15: Aligned to Outcome 8 and the Land Audit Findings*, Rustenburg, South Africa: Gudhluza Development Solutions, October, p. 14.

20. Interview no. 2NK, 7 July 2013.

21. Forrest, 'Rustenburg's Fractured Recruitment Regime', p. 165.

22. Cox, Hemson and Todes, 'Urbanisation in South Africa and the Changing Character of Migrant Labour', p. 12.

23. Ibid., p. 15.

24. Bowman and Isaacs, *Demanding the Impossible?*, p. 3. This coincided with the introduction of a 'living out allowance' paid to miners who left the compounds and hostels; this provided cover for the mine owners' failure to provide adequate shelter for miners, especially those wishing to lead family lives; see F. Cronje, J. Kane-Berman and L. Moloi (2014), *Digging for Development: The Mining Industry in South Africa and Its Role in Socio-economic Development*, report commissioned by the Embassy of Sweden, Johannesburg, South Africa: Institute of Race Relations, p. 8.

25. Interview no. 10NK, community member and founder member of community, Nkaneng, 4 July 2013.

26. Interview no. 3NK, group of community founder members, Nkaneng, 2 July 2013.

27. Ibid.

28. N. Mandela (1997), 'Address by President Nelson Mandela at Bleskop Stadium, Rustenburg', Mandela Speeches, South African Information Website, www.mandela.gov.za/mandela_speeches/1997/971018_rustenburg.htm (accessed 3 May 2019); South African History Online (2015), 'The Freedom Struggle in Rustenburg', www.sahistory.org.za/article/freedom-struggle-0 (accessed 3 March 2015).

29. Interview no. 3NK, 2 July 2013.

30. Ibid.

31. 'Five Madoda': in isiXhosa, *madoda* means 'men'; there is a history of self-organised workers' committee in the mines, often formed episodically and operating outside and against union structures during periods of heightened struggle, tensions or dissatisfaction.

32. L. Buur and S. Jensen (2004), 'Introduction: Vigilantism and the Policing of Everyday Life in South Africa', *African Studies*, 63(2), pp. 139–52, p. 144.

33. Interview no. 3NK, 2 July 2013.

34. For background on Mouthpiece, see D. Bruce (2001), *The Operation of the Criminal Justice System in Dealing with the Violence at Amplats*, research report, Johannesburg, South Africa: Centre for the Study of Violence and Reconciliation, p. 16.

35. Bezuidenhout and Buhlungu, 'From Compounded to Fragmented Labour', p. 239.

36. Some background to the 'nameless' committees, given names such as 'five men', which miners establish during periods of intolerable dissatisfaction with working conditions: it was from this organisational tradition that the committees which led the strike at Lonmin that culminated in the Marikana massacre emerged; see L. Sinwell, L. with S. Mbatha (2016), *'The Spirit of Marikana': The Rise of Insurgent Trade Unionism in South Africa*, Johannesburg, South Africa: Wits University Press; L. Sinwell (2015), 'AMCU by Day, Workers' Committee by Night: Insurgent Trade Unionism at Anglo Platinum (Amplats) Mine, 2012–2014', *Review of African Political Economy*, 42(146), pp. 591–605.

37. Interview no. 6NK, ANC committee member, Nkaneng, 23 June 2013.

38. Interview no. 5NK, ex-CPF committee member, ward committee member, also an ANC committee member, Nkaneng, 14 December 2012 and 2 July 2013; Interview Number 3NK, 2 July 2013.

39. Interview no. 2NK, 7 July 2013; Interview Number NK6, 23 July 2013.

40. Interview no. 1NK, Inkundla yaseLibode group interview, Nkaneng, 15 July 2013.

41. Interview no. 2NK, 7 July 2013.

42. Interview no. 3NK, 2 July 2013.

43. Interview no. 2NK, 7 July 2013.

44. Ibid.

45. Interview no. 7NK, personal assistant to ward councillor, also an ex-ANC Youth League committee member, Nkaneng, 25 June 2013.
46. South African Press Association (2013), 'Ex-mayor Loses Murder Appeal', *News24*, 30 July.
47. Interview no. 2NK, 7 July 2013.
48. Interview no. 4NK, spaza shop owner, a Mozambican national, Nkaneng, 4 July 2013.
49. Interview no. 1NK, 15 July 2013.
50. Interview no. 7NK, 25 June 2013.
51. Interview no. 1NK, 15 July 2013.
52. Interview no. 8NK, ANC committee member, Nkaneng, 16 July 2013.
53. Interview no. 2NK, 7 July 2013.
54. Interview no. 6NK, 23 June 2013.
55. Interview no. 1NK, 15 July 2013.
56. Ibid.
57. Republic of South Africa (2000), *Municipal Systems Act Number 32*, Pretoria, South Africa: Government Printers.
58. Interview no. 2NK, 7 July 2013.
59. K. Magubane (2013), 'Political Parties Talk Tough on Marikana, ANC Ahead of Elections', *Business Day Live*, 13 September, www.bdlive.co.za/national/politics/2013/09/13/political-parties-talk-tough-on-marikana-anc-ahead-of-elections (accessed 2 August 2014).
60. Interview no. 2NK, 7 July 2013.
61. Interview no. 6NK, 23 July 2013.
62. Interview no. 13NK, hostel committee member and AMCU shop steward, Nkaneng, 17 July 2013.
63. Interview no. 6NK, 23 July 2013.
64. S. Terblanche (2012), 'Municipal By-elections: Support Unchanged Except for Marikana',. *Leadership*, 20 November, www.leadershiponline.co.za/articles/municipal-by-elections-2012-3387.html (accessed 3 August 2019).
65. Interview no. 3NK, 2 July 2013; Interview no. 4NK, 4 July 2013.
66. L. Bank (2011), *Home Spaces, Street Styles: Contesting Power and Identity in a South African City*, London: Pluto Press, p. 140.
67. Ibid.

6 THEMBELIHLE SETTLEMENT: A VISION OF HOPE

1. M. Clark (2014), 'An Anatomy of Dissent and Repression: The Criminal Justice System and the 2011 Thembelihle Protest', Johannesburg, South Africa: Socio-Economic Rights Institute; M. Huchzermeyer (2009), 'The Struggle for In Situ Upgrading of Informal Settlements: A Reflection on Cases in Gauteng', *Development Southern Africa*, 26(1), pp. 59–73; A. Le Roux (2013), 'Contesting Space: A Ward Committee and a Social Movement Organisation in Them-

belihle, Johannesburg', Master of Arts dissertation, Department of Sociology, University of Johannesburg; N. Pingo (2013), 'Institutionalisation of a Social Movement: The Case of Thembelihle, the Thembelihle Crisis Committee and the Operation Khanyisa Movement and the Use of the Brick, the Ballot and the Voice', Master of Science dissertation, Development Planning, University of the Witwatersrand.

2. Le Roux ('Contesting Space', p. 144) has 'conceptualised [the TCC] as a SMO [social movement organisation] of a "special type". What is meant by this title is that it is more powerful (within the boundaries of its constituency), more ideologically socialist, and has more consistently, and over a long period of time, mobilised toward obtaining the goals of the community'; Pingo ('Institutionalisation of a Social Movement', p. 61) focuses on 'the Operation Khanyisa Movement and the blurry grey space it occupies as a social movement and electoral front'. The OKM is a sister organisation to the TCC, and is an electoral front that controlled one seat on the City of Johannesburg council from 2007 to 2016.

3. South African History Online (2015), 'Indian Community in Lenasia', p. 10, www.sahistory.org.za/indian-community-lenasia?page=10 (accessed 3 March 2019).

4. Clark ('An Anatomy of Dissent and Repression', p. 11) bases these figures on a study by Tselapedi and Dugard conducted between December 2010 and January 2011: T. Tselapedi and J. Dugard (2013), *Reclaiming Power: A Case Study of the Thembelihle Crisis Committee*, Cape Town, South Africa: Good Governance Learning Network, Active Citizenship Matters, p. 58. Estimates made by community leaders in May 2004 put the population at 27,000; CALS (Centre for Applied Legal Studies) (2006), *Access to Education for Learners in Thembelihle*, Johannesburg, South Africa: University of the Witwatersrand, p. 3.

5. I. Mafisa (2011), 'Hell Is Better than Living in Thembelihle, Say Residents', *The New Age*, www.thenewage.co.za/28482-22-53-Hell_is_better_than_living_in_ Thembelihle,_say_residents (accessed 4 June 2019).

6. Interview no. 6TL, resident and TCC committee member, 18 December 2013.

7. Interview no. 5TL, resident from the early days, Thembelihle, 22 December 2013.

8. Le Roux, 'Contesting Space', pp. 125–6.

9. South African Press Association (2014), 'Thembelihle Residents Protest over Electricity', 25 July, www.iol.co.za/news/thembelihle-residents-protest-over-electricity-1725504 (accessed 5 April 2020).

10. Personal communication with Siphiwe Mbatha, organiser of TCC and former personal assistant to the OKM councillor, 15 August 2014.

11. Interview no. 5TL, 22 December 2013.

12. Interview no. 6TL, 18 December 2013; Clark, 'An Anatomy of Dissent and Repression', p. 11.

13. Interview no. 5TL, 22 December 2013.
14. Interview no. 1TL, resident from the early days and ex-ANC committee member, Thembelihle, 19 December 2013.
15. CALS, *Access to Education for Learners in Thembelihle*, p. 8.
16. Ibid.; personal communications with Siphiwe Segodi, ex-chairperson of TCC, current spokesperson and labour rights activist in Thembelihle, on 8 May 2014 and 6 August 2015.
17. Interview no. 6TL, 18 December 2013.
18. CALS, *Access to Education for Learners in Thembelihle*, p. 8; personal communication with Siphiwe Segodi, 8 May 2014.
19. Interview no. 5TL, 22 December 2013.
20. S. Hall (1997), 'Old and New Identities, Old and New Ethnicities', in A.D. King (Ed.), *Culture, Globalisation and the World System: Contemporary Conditions for the Representation of Identity*, Minneapolis, MN: University of Minnesota Press, p. 44.
21. Interview no. 2TL, resident and member of early committees, Thembelihle, 18 December 2013.
22. Hall, 'Old and New Identities, Old and New Ethnicities', p. 44.
23. The Lehae housing development is a government project to provide free housing to working-class people. The houses are popularly called 'RDP houses' because of their association with the Reconstruction and Development Project.
24. Interview no. 2TL, 18 December 2013.
25. For a discussion of 'in situ' development versus 'greenfield' housing projects, see S. Masiteng (2013), 'In-situ Upgrading of Informal Settlements: A Case study of Barcelona 1 – Lamontville, Durban', Master of Arts dissertation, School of Built Environment and Development Studies, University of Kwa-Zulu-Natal, p. 5.
26. L. Wacquant (2008), *Urban Outcasts: A Comparative Sociology of Advanced Marginality*, Cambridge, UK: Polity Press, p. 73; see also L. Bank (2011), *Home Spaces, Street Styles: Contesting Power and Identity in a South African City*, London: Pluto Press, p. 215.
27. Interview no. 4TL, resident since the early days, Thembelihle, 21 December 2013.
28. Interview no. 5TL, 22 December 2013.
29. I was among the first group of 33 people arrested on 26 February 2015. We were charged with public violence. The state later withdrew charges against me for lack of evidence. See SocioEconomic Rights Institute (2015), 'Thembelihle Arrested Granted Bail after 5 Days in Jail', press statement, 3 March, www.seri-sa.org/index.php/more-news/329-press-statement-thembelihle-arrested-granted-bail-after-5-days-in-jail-3-march-2015 (accessed 2 April 2020).
30. South African Government Agency (2015), 'Police Raid Thembelihle Informal Settlement', *South African News*, 30 April, www.sanews.gov.za/south-

africa/police-raid-thembelihle-informal-settlement (accessed 3 April 2020); G. Nicolson (2015), 'SAHRC: Let's Talk about Xenophobia', *Daily Maverick*, 9 April, www.dailymaverick.co.za/article/2015-04-09-sahrc-lets-talk-about-xenophobia/#.VkRm8LcrLIU (accessed 3 July 2015).

31. RSA (Republic of South Africa) (2015), 'Gauteng Cooperative Governance Registers Thembelihle as Housing Project', South African Government media statement, 28 April, www.gov.za/speeches/media-statement-special-freedom-day-people-thembelihle-government-registers-thembelihle (accessed 30 April 2015).

32. Clark, 'An Anatomy of Dissent and Repression', p. 11; Huchzermeyer, 'The Struggle for In Situ Upgrading of Informal Settlements', p. 8.

33. See Clark, 'An Anatomy of Dissent and Repression', p. 11.

34. City Press (2011), 'Ten Years of Struggle', 10 September, www.citypress.co.za/columnists/thembelihle-ten-years-of-struggle-20110910/ (accessed 3 May 2019).

35. City of Johannesburg (2010), 'Peace Settling in Thembelihle', press release, 3 March, www.joburg.org.za/media_/MediaStatements/Pages/2010%20Press%20Realeases/2010-03-03-Peace-settling-in-Thembelihle.aspx (accessed 24 October 2020); personal communication with Siphiwe Segodi, 8 May 2014.

36. Interview no. 6TL, 18 December 2013.

37. M.J. Murray (1994), *The Revolution Deferred*, London: Verso, p. 101; T. Lodge and B. Nasson (1991), *All, Here, and Now: Black Politics in South Africa in the 1980s*, Cape Town, South Africa: David Philip, pp. 53 and 271.

38. CALS, *Access to Education for Learners in Thembelihle*, p. 3; Clark, 'An Anatomy of Dissent and Repression', p. 14; personal communication with Siphiwe Segodi, 8 May 2014; Tselapedi and Dugard, *Reclaiming Power*.

39. See Pingo, 'Institutionalisation of a Social Movement', p. 96.

40. *Umphakathi* in isiZulu means 'the community'.

41. Personal communication with urban studies sociologist Liela Groenwald, who was conducting research in the informal settlements around Thembelihle, 13 September 2014.

42. H. Sapire (1992), 'Politics and Protest in Shack Settlements of the Pretoria-Witwatersrand-Vereeniging Region, South Africa, 1980–1990', *Journal of Southern African Studies*, 18(3), pp. 670–97, p. 118.

43. H. Mashabela (1990), *Mekhukhu: Urban African Cities of the Future*, Johannesburg, South Africa: South African Institute of Race Relations.

44. Interview no. 5TL, 22 December 2013.

45. Interview no. 2TL, 18 December 2013.

46. Interview no. 4TL, 21 December 2013.

47. Interview no. 5TL, 22 December 2013.

48. Interview no. 2TL, 18 December 2013.

49. Interview no. 4TL, 21 December 2013.

50. Interview no. 2TL, 18 December 2013.

51. Ibid.
52. Interview no. 3TL, resident from the early days, Thembelihle, 18 December 2013.
53. Ibid.
54. Interview no. 4TL, 21 December 2013.
55. Interview no. 2TL, 18 December 2013.
56. Interview no. 5TL, 22 December 2013.
57. Interview no. 3TL, 18 December 2013.
58. Personal communication with Siphiwe Segodi, 8 May 2014.
59. Interview no. 3TL, 18 December 2013.
60. Interview no. 1TL, 19 December 2013.
61. Interview no. 5TL, 22 December 2013.
62. Ibid.
63. Interview no. 1TL, 19 December 2013; Interview no. 3TL, 18 December 2013.
64. Pingo, 'Institutionalisation of a Social Movement', p. 15.
65. Interview no. 4TL, 21 December 2013; Interview no. 5TL, 22 December 2013; Interview no. 1TL, 19 December 2013; City Press (2011), 'Ten Years of Struggle', 10 September. www.citypress.co.za/columnists/thembelihle-ten-years-of-struggle-20110910/ (accessed 3 May 2019).
66. Dolomite is a geological feature that can lead to sinkholes. This porous rock is found in various parts of South Africa; see J.E. Kaufman (2007), 'Sinkholes', US Department of the Interior, US Geological Survey, Fact Sheet 2007-3060, July, www.dnr.mo.gov/geology/geosrv/envgeo/sinkholes.htm (accessed 4 June 2019).
67. Interview no. 1TL, 19 December 2013.
68. The ANC government later changed its policy and agreed to build on dolomitic land in spite of the additional costs involved; see P. De Wet (2011), 'The Curious Case of the Apartheid Dolomite', www.dailymaverick.co.za/article/2011-09-16-the-curious-case-of-the-apartheid-dolomite/#.Ub3TxuenDtk (accessed 3 March 2019).
69. Interview no. 1TL, 19 December 2013.
70. Clark, 'An Anatomy of Dissent and Repression', p. 14; TCC (Thembelihle Crisis Committee) (2012), 'Chairperson's Report Prepared for the Annual General Meeting 14 July', informant's private archive.
71. Tselapedi and Dugard, *Reclaiming Power*, p. 62; TCC, 'Chairperson's Report Prepared for the Annual General Meeting 14 July', p. 1.
72. Personal communication with Siphiwe Segodi, 8 May 2014.
73. Interview no. 6TL, 18 December 2013.
74. Interview no. 4TL, 21 December 2013.
75. Ibid.
76. Ibid.

77. City of Johannesburg (2003) *The City of Johannesburg* vs *Occupiers of the Thembelihle Informal Settlement*, Case Number 03/10106, Founding Affidavit, Johannesburg High Court, p. 6.

78. This happened about a week after the great battle.

79. The APF and LPM were social movement-type organisations that acted as umbrella bodies for local community struggles around the provision of services, and land and housing respectively. For background to the APF, see S. Buhlungu (2006), 'Upstarts or Bearers of Tradition? The Anti-privatisation Forum of Gauteng', in R. Ballard, A. Habib and I. Valodia (Eds), *Voices of Protest: Social Movements in Post-apartheid South Africa*, Durban, South Africa: University of KwaZulu-Natal, pp. 67–87. For the LPM, see S. Greenberg (2006), 'The Landless People's Movement and the Failure of Post-apartheid Land Reform', in R. Ballard, A. Habib and I. Valodia (Eds), *Voices of Protest: Social Movements in Post-apartheid South Africa*, Durban, South Africa: University of KwaZulu-Natal, pp. 133–53.

80. TCC, 'Chairperson's Report Prepared for the Annual General Meeting 14 July', p. 2.

81. Interview no. 4TL, 21 December 2013.

82. Personal communication with Siphiwe Segodi, 8 May 2014.

83. Pingo, 'Institutionalisation of a Social Movement', p. 98.

84. Le Roux, 'Contesting Space', pp. 125–6; Pingo, 'Institutionalisation of a Social Movement', pp. 99–100.

85. See Le Roux, 'Contesting Space'.

86. Pingo, 'Institutionalisation of a Social Movement', p. 121; personal communication with Siphiwe Mbatha, 15 August 2014.

87. Interview no. 4TL, 21 December 2013.

88. Interview no. 1TL, 19 December 2013.

89. Interview no. 3TL, 19 December 2013.

90. Interview no. 3TL, resident since the early days.

91. R. Ballard, D. Bonnin, J. Robinson and T. Xaba (2007), 'Development and New Forms of Democracy in Durban', *Urban Forum*, 18(4), pp. 75–110; K. Barichievy, L. Piper and B. Parker (2005), 'Assessing "Participatory Governance" in Local Government: A Case-study of Two South African Cities', *Politeia*, 24(3), pp. 370–93; C. Bénit-Gbaffou (2008), 'Local Councillors: Scapegoats for a Dysfunctional Participatory Democratic System?', *Critical Dialogue: Public Participation in Review*, 4(1), pp. 26–33.

92. Interview no. 1TL, 19 December 2013.

93. See Le Roux, 'Contesting Space', p. 200.

94. Interview no. 1TL, 19 December 2013.

95. Interview no. 4TL, 21 December 2013.

96. Interview no. 6TL, 18 December 2013.

97. Personal communication with Siphiwe Segodi, 8 May 2014; TCC (2012), 'Minutes of the Annual General Meeting Held on 14 July 2012', informant's private archive.
98. Interview no. 6TL, 18 December 2013.
99. Interview no. 5TL, 22 December 2013.
100. Interview no. 3TL, 18 December 2013.
101. Interview no. 5TL, 22 December 2013.
102. Interview no. 3TL, 18 December 2013.
103. RSA, 'Gauteng Cooperative Governance Registers Thembelihle as Housing Project'.

7   *AMAKOMITI*: A VISION OF ALTERNATIVES

1. A. Bayat (1997), *Street Politics: Poor People's Movements in Iran*, New York: Columbia University Press, p. 61; C. Barker (2008), 'Some Thoughts on Marxism and Social Movements', unpublished paper, https://sites.google.com/site/colinbarkersite/ (accessed 12 July 2019).
2. Ibid., p. 1; S. Cohen (2011), 'The Red Mole: Workers' Councils as a Means of Revolutionary Transformation', in I. Ness and D. Azzellini (Eds), *Ours to Master and to Own: Workers' Control from the Commune to the Present*, Chicago, IL: Haymarket Books , p. 48.
3. L. Trotsky (2008), *History of the Russian Revolution*, Chicago, IL: Haymarket Books, p. 743.
4. See Bayat, *Street Politics*; A. Bayat (2010), *Life as Politics: How Ordinary People Change the Middle East*, Redwood City, CA: Stanford University Press; A. Bayat (2013), 'The Urban Subalterns and the Non-movements of the Arab Uprisings: An Interview with Asef Bayat', conducted by N. Ghandour-Demiri, 26 March, www.jadaliyya.com/Details/28301 (accessed 18 October 2020).
5. Bayat, *Street Politics*.
6. Ibid., p. 75.
7. Ibid., pp. 65–6.
8. Ibid., p. 51.
9. Ibid., p. 91.
10. Ibid., p. 95.
11. Ibid., p. 74.
12. I. van Kessel (2000) *'Beyond Our Wildest Dreams': The United Democratic Front and the Transformation of South Africa*, Charlottesville, VA: University Press of Virginia, pp. 304–5.
13. J. Seekings (2013), 'In Defence of the "Underclass": Social and Economic Disadvantage in South Africa', paper presented at the *Harvard African Studies Workshop*, Harvard University, 7 October; J. Seekings and N. Nattrass (2005), *Class, Race and Inequality in South Africa*, New Haven, CT: Yale University Press.

14. Bayat, *Street Politics*, p. 31.
15. Ibid., p. 60.
16. Van Kessel, *'Beyond Our Wildest Dreams'*, p. 230.
17. P. Alexander and P. Pfaffe (2013), 'Social Relationships to the Means and Ends of Protest in South Africa's Ongoing Rebellion of the Poor: The Balfour Insurrections', *Social Movement Studies: Journal of Social, Cultural and Political Protest*, 13(2), p. 4.
18. B. Hirson (1989), *Yours for the Union: Class and Community Struggle in South Africa*, London: Zed Books, p. 149.
19. A.W. Stadler (1979), 'Birds in the Cornfield: Squatter Movements in Johannesburg, 1944–1947', *Journal of Southern African Studies*, special issue on *Urban Social History*, 6(1), pp. 9–123, p. 123.
20. Alexander and Pfaffe, Social Relationships to the Means and Ends of Protest in South Africa's Ongoing Rebellion of the Poor', p. 4.
21. 'Black spots' were areas inhabited by black people wrongly resident in 'white areas'.
22. Stadler, 'Birds in the Cornfield', p. 106.
23. Ibid., p. 105.
24. Hirson, *Yours for the Union*, p. 155.
25. M. Castells (1977), *The Urban Question: A Marxist Approach*, Cambridge, MA: MIT Press, pp. 55–7.
26. Bayat, *Street Politics*, pp. 52, 62; J.E. Hardoy and D. Satterthwaite (1989), *Squatter Citizen: Life in the Urban Third World*, London: Earthscan Publications, p. 17.
27. A. Callinicos (1977), 'Soviet Power', *International Socialism*, 103, pp. 7–13, www.marxists.org/history/etol/writers/callinicos/1977/11/sovpower.htm (accessed 6 February 2020).
28. M. Friedman (2011), *A History of FOSATU: 'The Future Is in the Hands of the Workers'*, Houghton, South Africa: Mutloatse Arts Heritage Trust, p. 110.
29. Van Kessel, *'Beyond Our Wildest Dreams'*, p. 271. Manuel was a UDF leader in the Western Cape in the 1980s.
30. J. Cole (1987), *Crossroads: The Politics of Reform and Repression, 1976–1986*, Johannesburg, South Africa: Ravan Press.
31. Stadler, 'Birds in the Cornfield', p. 123.
32. T. Bell (1989), *Comrade Moss — a Political Journey* (political biography of Moses Mayekiso), Johannesburg, South Africa: Labour and Community Resources Project, Learn and Teach Publications.
33. Friedman, *A History of FOSATU*, pp. 46 and 110.
34. E. Webster (1985), *Cast in a Racial Mould: Labour Process and Trade Unionism in the Foundries*, Johannesburg, South Africa: Ravan Press, p. 279.
35. Ibid.

36. S. Buhlungu (2009), 'The Rise and Decline of the Democratic Organizational Culture in the South African Labor Movement, 1973 to 2000', *Labor Studies Journal*, 34(1), pp. 91–111, p. 99.

37. J. Grossman (1996), '*For Our Children Tomorrow': Workers in Struggle in South Africa 1973–1995*, Research Paper No. 1, Amsterdam, the Netherlands: Institute for Critical Research, p. 6.

38. Webster, *Cast in a Racial Mould*, p. 279.

39. Grossman, *'For Our Children Tomorrow'*, p. 6.

40. N. Alexander (2002), *An Ordinary Country: Issues in the Transition from Apartheid to Democracy in South Africa*, Pietermaritzburg, South Africa: University of Natal Press, pp. 41 and 43.

41. S. Huntington (1991), *The Third Wave: Democratization in the Twentieth Century*, Norman, OK: University of Oklahoma Press, pp. 112–15.

42. Alexander, *An Ordinary Country*, p. 48.

43. Ibid., p. 49.

44. Ibid.

45. Ibid., p. 57.

46. H. Marais (1998), *South Africa: Limits to Change – the Political Economy of Transformation*, London: Zed Books, p. 96. See also Alexander, *An Ordinary Country*, p. 57.

47. Buhlungu, 'The Rise and Decline of the Democratic Organizational Culture in the South African Labor Movement', pp. 101–2.

48. Ibid., p. 101.

49. R. Rees (1992), 'More Workers' Control Needed', *South African Labour Bulletin*, 16(7), pp. 56–7.

50. K. von Holdt (2000), 'From the Politics of Resistance to the Politics of Reconstruction: The Union and "Ungovernability" in the Workplace', in G. Adler and E. Webster (Eds), *Trade Unions and Democratization in South Africa, 1985–1997*, London: Macmillan, pp. 100–28.

51. Grossman, *'For Our Children Tomorrow'*, p. 2.

52. J. Cronin (1992), 'The Boat, the Tap and the Leipzig Way', *African Communist*, 130, pp. 41–54.

53. J. Saul (2014), 'The Transition: The Players Assemble, 1970–1990', in J. Saul and P. Bond, *South Africa: The Present as History, from Mrs Ples to Mandela and Marikana*, Johannesburg, South Africa: Jacana, p. 89; J. Seekings (2000), *The UDF – a History of the United Democratic Front in South Africa 1983–1991*, Cape Town, South Africa: David Philip, p. 280.

54. M. Mayekiso (1992), 'Hands Off the Civics and Civil Society!', *Work in Progress*, February, p. 21; B. Nzimande and M. Sikhosana (1992), 'Civil Society and Democracy', *African Communist*, 128, pp. 37–51.

55. Alexander, *An Ordinary Country*, p. 56.

56. Seekings, *The UDF*, p. 281.

57. Van Kessel, *'Beyond Our Wildest Dreams'*.

58. See V. Chibber (2013), *Postcolonial Theory and the Specter of Capital*, New York: Verso.

59. H. Sapire (1992), 'Politics and Protest in Shack Settlements of the Pretoria-Witwatersrand- Vereeniging Region, South Africa, 1980–1990', *Journal of Southern African Studies*, 18(3), pp. 670–97, p. 114.

60. L. Trotsky (1971), *1905*, Harmondsworth, UK: Penguin, p. 122, www.marxists. org/archive/trotsky/1907/1905/ch08.htm (accessed 5 April 2020).

61. D. Harvey (1985), *Consciousness and the Urban Experience: Studies in the History and Theory of Capitalist Urbanization*, Baltimore, MD: Johns Hopkins University Press, p. 48.

62. Ibid, p. 47.

63. Ibid., p. 48.

64. Buhlungu, 'The Rise and Decline of the Democratic Organizational Culture in the South African Labor Movement', p. 107.

65. Ibid., p. 102.

66. Bayat, *Street Politics*, p. 159.

67. S. Zikode (2006), 'The Third Force', *Journal of Asian and African Studies*, 41(1/2), pp. 185–9, http://abahlali.org/node/17 (accessed 3 April 2020); R. Pithouse (2008), 'A Politics of the Poor: Shack Dwellers' Struggles in Durban', *Journal of Asian and African Studies*, 43(1), pp. 63–94, pp. 79 and 90; R. Pithouse (2005), 'The Left in the Slum: The Rise of a Shack Dwellers' Movement in Durban, South Africa', paper presented at *History and African Studies Seminar*, University of KwaZulu-Natal, Durban, 23 November; F. Miraftab and S. Willis (2005), 'Insurgency and Spaces of Active Citizenship: The Story of Western Cape Anti-eviction Campaign in South Africa', *Journal of Planning Education and Research*, 25, pp. 200–217. Since Abahlali baseMjondolo, the shack dwellers' movements in South Africa, are indeed 'the left in the slum' (Pithouse, 'The Left in the Slum'), but some intricacy is necessary in identifying how they distinguish themselves from other left currents. They emphasise their organisational and political autonomy, including – importantly – their right to speak for themselves ('voice'), captured in the slogan 'Nothing About Us Without Us' (Zikode, 'The Third Force'). They espouse a 'politics of dignity', 'a living politics' and 'a politics of the poor – a homemade politics that everyone can understand and find a home in' (Zikode, quoted in Pithouse, 'A Politics of the Poor', p. 82). These slogans attest to their emphasis on self-activity of the masses, autonomy and independence *vis-à-vis* the bourgeois state and a left that seeks to bring from without and impose its ideas on the movement. Like their sister organisation, the Western Cape Anti-Eviction Campaign, they have an aversion to electoral politics and they have distrust for representative democracy. They are developing 'a new kind of liberative politics outside of the political parties' because 'no politician or political party can or will fight the struggle for you'; Western Cape Anti-Eviction Campaign (2009), 'Open Letter to US Activists Battling Evictions from the Western Cape Anti-Eviction

Campaign in South Africa', *The Nation*, 7 April, https://libcom.org/library/open-letter-us-activists-battling-evictions-western-cape-anti-eviction-campaign-south-af (accessed 5 April 2020). Sometimes this takes the form of a downplaying of 'ideology" in favour of a focus on the problems and issues vexing shack dwellers, for example: 'Poor people do not eat ideology, nor do they live in houses that are made of ideology. So for this decision, we have decided to suspend ideology for a clear goal: weaken the ANC, guarantee the security and protection of the shack dwellers'; S. Zikode (2014), 'Why Abahlali Endorsed the DA: S'bu Zikode speaks to GroundUp', http://groundup.org.za/content/why-abahlali-endorsed-da-sbu-zikode-speaks-groundup (accessed 5 April 2020). They open their meetings with a prayer and hymn, and close it by singing 'I am a socialist' (Pithouse, 'A Politics of the Poor', p. 79). Fanon, Marx, Biko and Badiou, among others, are employed by the movement's theoreticians to frame their public profile and inform political praxis; see N. Gibson (2003), *Frantz Fanon: The Postcolonial Imagination*, Cambridge, UK: Polity Press.

68. Zikode, 'The Third Force'.

69. A. Gramsci (1977), 'Unions and Councils, in *Selections from Political Writings 1910–1920*, London: Lawrence and Wishart, p. 100, www.marxists.org/archive/gramsci/1919/10/unions-councils.htm (accessed 4 April 2020). See also A. Callinicos (1977), 'Soviet Power', *International Socialism*, 1(103), pp. 7–13, www.marxists.org/history/etol/writers/callinicos/1977/11/sovpower.htm (accessed 4 April 2020).

70. R. Luxemburg (1970), *The Mass Strike*, New York: Pathfinder Press.

71. NUMSA (National Union of Metalworkers of South Africa) (2013), *NUMSA Special National Congress Declaration*, www.numsa.org.za/wp-content/uploads/2013/12/SNC-Declaration-final-copy.pdf (accessed 3 July 2019).

72. Ibid.

73. B. Maruping, Z. Mncube and C. Runciman (2014), 'Rebellion of the Poor Quantitative Data Analysis Report', unpublished internal report of the Research Chair for Social Change Protest Monitoring Project, University of Johannesburg.

74. P. Alexander, C. Runciman and T. Ngwane (2015), 'South Africa's Rebellion of the Poor', paper presented at the *3rd International Conference on Strikes and Social Conflicts*, Barcelona, 16–19 June, p. 10.

75. Republic of South Africa (2015), 'Gauteng Cooperative Governance Registers Thembelihle as Housing Project', South African Government media statement, April 28, www.gov.za/speeches/media-statement-special-freedom-day-people-thembelihle-government-registers-thembelihle (accessed 30 April 2020).

76. Abahlali baseMjondolo (2009), 'The ANC's Coup in Kennedy Road', press statement, 7 October, www.politicsweb.co.za/news-and-analysis/the-ancs-coup-in-kennedy-road (accessed 4 September 2019); N. Neocosmos (2009), 'South Africa: Attacks on Shackdwellers – a Failure of Citizenship?',

Pambazuka, 461, http://pambazuka.org/en/category/features/60925 (accessed 3 January 2020).

77. R. Pithouse (2010), 'Abahlali baseMjondolo and the Popular Struggle for the Right to the City in Durban, South Africa', http://base.d-p-h.info/en/fiches/dph/fiche-dph-8418.html (accessed 3 May 2019).

78. Interview no. 60, group of community members, Mthatha, 27 February 2013.

79. P. Alexander (2013), 'Marikana, Turning Point in South African History', *Review of African Political Economy*, 40(138), pp. 605–19, p. 605.

80. L. Sinwell (2015), 'AMCU by Day, Workers' Committee by Night: Insurgent Trade Unionism at Anglo Platinum (Amplats) Mine, 2012–2014', *Review of African Political Economy*, 42(146), pp. 591–605; L. Sinwell, L. with S. Mbatha (2016), '*The Spirit of Marikana': The Rise of Insurgent Trade Unionism in South Africa*, Johannesburg, South Africa: Wits University Press.

81. T. Ngwane (2012), 'Labour Strikes and Community Protests: Is There a Basis for Unity in Post-apartheid South Africa?', in M. Dawson and L. Sinwell (2012), *Contesting Transformation: Popular Resistance in 21st Century South Africa*, London: Pluto Press, pp. 125–42.

82. A. Nin (1932), 'The Soviets: Their Origin, Development and Functions', https://libcom.org/library/soviets-their-origin-development-functions-andreu-nin (accessed 3 May 2019).

83. Statistics South Africa (2016), 'GHS Series Volume VII: Housing from a Human Settlement Perspective', media release, 20 April, www.statssa.gov.za/?p=6429.

84. E.H. Carr (1950), *The Bolshevik Revolution: 1917–1923*, Harmondsworth, UK: Penguin, pp. 36–7.

85. NUMSA, *NUMSA Special National Congress Declaration*.

86. M. Davis (2006), *Planet of Slums*, London: Verso.

87. V.I. Lenin (1940), *'Left-wing Communism': An Infantile Disorder*, New York: International Publishers, p. 34.

88. S. Ashman (2012), 'Combined and Uneven Development', in B. Fine and A. Saad-Filho (Eds), *The Elgar Companion to Marxist Economics*, Cheltenham, UK: Edward Elgar, p. 65.

89. D. Gluckstein (1985), *The Western Soviets: Workers' Councils versus Parliament 1915–1920*, London: Bookmarks.

90. K. Marx and F. Engels (1993), *The Communist Manifesto*, http://www.gutenberg.org/ebooks/61 (accessed 25 October 2020).

91. C. Barker (2015), 'Beyond the Waves: Marxism, Social Movements and Revolution', paper presented at the *Alternatives Futures and Popular Protest* conference, Manchester, UK, 30 March–1 April, https://drive.google.com/file/d/1SvPQ8HSBwsImBnwcDQrqgMjtrbMDMCkn/view (accessed 5 April 2020). See also C. Barker, L. Cox, J. Krinsky and A.G. Nilsen (2013), *Marxism and Social Movements*, Leiden, the Netherlands: Brill.

92. G. Ruiters (2001), 'Environmental Racism and Justice in South Africa's Transition', *Politikon*, 28(1), pp. 95–103.

93. Grossman, *'For Our Children Tomorrow'*, p. 6.

94. P. Alexander, L. Sinwell, T. Lekgowa, B. Mmope and B. Xezwi (2012), *Marikana: A View from the Mountain and a Case to Answer*, London: Bookmarks, pp. 21 and 153.

95. Davis, *Planet of Slums*, p. 13.

96. A. Gramsci (1978), 'Once again on the Organic Capacities of the Working Class', in *Selections from Political Writings (1921–1926) with Additional Texts by Other Italian Communist Leaders*, Essay no. 73, http://marxism.halkcephesi. net/Antonio%20Gramsci/1926/10/organic_capabilities.htm (accessed 4 April 2020).

97. G. Hart (2002), *Disabling Globalisation: Places of Power in Post-apartheid South Africa*, Pietermaritzburg, South Africa: University of Natal Press, p. 45.

98. In his study of working-class militancy in the workplace in the twenty-first-century Global South (case studies: India, China and South Africa), Immanuel Ness concludes: 'Each case demonstrates that organizational representation is subordinate to the workers' movements themselves. To build on these struggles workers will need a disciplined and strong class-based organization... each of the struggles demonstrates that the time when workers can be taken for granted or ignored is over. Workers' movements are emerging, and will expand to contest the legitimacy of capital, the state, and existing unions'; I. Ness (2016), *Southern Insurgency: The Coming of the Global Working Class*, London: Pluto Press, p. 190.

99. A slogan from the 1980s labour movement that, in my recollection, referred to hope for a future where the working class will be free of all forms of oppression and exploitation.

POSTSCRIPT

1. Socialist Group (2020), 'Workers Are Scared: Together They Can Be Brave' (pamphlet issued in April, copy available from the author, email: tngwane@ uj.ac.za).

Index

Thanks to our Patreon Subscribers:

Abdul Alkalimat
Andrew Perry

Who have shown their generosity and comradeship in difficult times.

Check out the other perks you get by subscribing to our Patreon – visit patreon.com/plutopress.

Subscriptions start from £3 a month.

The Pluto Press Newsletter

Hello friend of Pluto!

Want to stay on top of the best radical books
we publish?

Then sign up to be the first to hear about our
new books, as well as special events,
podcasts and videos.

You'll also get 50% off your first order with us
when you sign up.

Come and join us!

Go to bit.ly/PlutoNewsletter